Born Jean-Baptiste Poquelin, **Molière** (1622–73) began his career as an actor before becoming a playwright who specialized in satirizing the institutions and morals of his day. In 1658, his theater company settled in Paris in the Théâter du Petit-Bourbon. The object of fierce attack because of such masterpieces as *Tartuffe* and *Don Juan*, Molière nonetheless won the favor of the public. In 1665, his company became the King's Troupe, and the following year saw the staging of *The Misanthrope*, as well as *The Doctor in Spite of Himself*. In 1668, he produced his bitterly comic *The Miser* and, in the remaining years before his death, created such plays as *The Would-Be Gentleman*, *The Mischievous Machinations of Scapin*, and *The Learned Women*. Molière collapsed onstage while performing his last play, *The Imaginary Invalid*, and died shortly thereafter.

Donald M. Frame was Moore Professor of French at Columbia University and an acclaimed scholar and translator of French literature. Among his notable works of translation are *The Complete Essays of Montaigne*, *The Complete Works of Rabelais*, and the Signet Classics *Tartuffe & Other Plays* and *Candide, Zadig, and Selected Stories*.

Virginia Scott is Professor Emerita in the Department of Theater of the University of Massachusetts at Amherst. She is the author of *Moliére: A Theatrical Life*, *The Commedia Dell'Arte in Paris*, and *Performance, Poetry and Politics on the Queen's Day: Catherine de Medici and Pierre de Ronsard at Fontainebleau* (with Sara Sturm-Maddox).

Since 1994, **Charles Newell** has been Artistic Director of Chicago's Court Theatre, where he has directed more than fifty productions. He has also directed at Goodman Theatre, Guthrie Theater, Arena Stage, the Acting Company, Glimmerglass Festival, Lyric Opera of Chicago, Opera Theatre of St. Louis, and Chicago Opera Theatre. Among his many honors are four Joseph Jefferson Director Awards and the 2012 Artistic Achievement Award given by the League of Chicago Theatres.

TARTUFFE
and Other Plays

Molière

TRANSLATED AND WITH AN INTRODUCTION BY
DONALD M. FRAME,
A FOREWORD BY
VIRGINIA SCOTT,
AND A NEW AFTERWORD BY
CHARLES NEWELL

SIGNET CLASSICS

SIGNET CLASSICS
Published by New American Library,
an imprint of Penguin Random House LLC
375 Hudson Street, New York, New York 10014

This book is a publication of New American Library. Previously published in a
New American Library edition.

First Signet Classics Printing, October 1967
First Signet Classics Printing (Newell Afterword), July 2015

For more information about Penguin Random House, visit penguinrandom-
house.com.

ISBN 978-0-451-47431-5

Printed in the United States of America

Penguin
Random
House

Contents

Contents

Introduction

Molière is probably the greatest and best-loved French author, and comic author, who ever lived. To the reader as well as the spectator, today as well as three centuries ago, the appeal of his plays is immediate and durable; they are both instantly accessible and inexhaustible. His rich resources make it hard to decide, much less to agree, on the secret of his greatness. After generations had seen him mainly as a moralist, many critics today have shifted the stress to the director and actor whose life was the comic stage; but all ages have rejoiced in three somewhat overlapping qualities of his: comic inventiveness, richness of fabric, and insight.

His inventiveness is extraordinary. An actor-manager-director-playwright all in one, he knew and loved the stage as few have done, and wrote with it and his playgoing public always in mind. In a medium in which sustained power is one of the rarest virtues, he drew on the widest imaginable range, from the broadest slapstick to the subtlest irony, to carry out the arduous and underrated task of keeping an audience amused for five whole acts. Working usually under great pressure of time, he took his materials where he found them, yet always made them his own.

The fabric of his plays is rich in many ways: in the intense life he infuses into his characters; in his constant preoccupation with the comic mask, which makes most of his protagonists themselves—consciously or unconsciously—play a part, and leads to rich comedy when their nature forces them to drop the mask; and in the weight of seriousness and even poignancy that he dares to include in his comic vision. Again and again he leads us from the enjoyable but shallow reaction of laughing at a fool to recognizing in that fool others whom we know, and ultimately ourselves; which is surely the truest and deepest comic catharsis.

Molière's insight makes his characters understandable and gives a memorable inevitability to his comic effects. He is seldom completely realistic, of course; his characters, for example, tend to give themselves away more generously and laughably than is customary in life; but it is their true selves they give away. It is an obvious trick, and not very realistic, to have Orgon in *Tartuffe* (Act I, scene 4) reply four times to the account of his wife's illness with the question "And Tartuffe?" and reply, again four times, to each report of Tartuffe's gross health and appetite, "Poor fellow!" But it shows us, rapidly and comically, that Orgon's obsession has closed his mind and his ears to anything but what he wants to see and hear. In the following scene, it may be unrealistic to have him in one speech (ll. 276–79) boast of learning from Tartuffe such detachment from worldly things that he could see his whole family die without concern, and in the very next speech (ll. 306–10) praise Tartuffe for the scrupulousness that led him to reproach himself for killing a flea in too much anger. But—again apart from the sheer comedy—it is a telling commentary on the distortion of values that can come from extreme points of view. One of Molière's favorite authors, Montaigne, had written about victims of moral *hubris:* "They want to get out of themselves and escape from the man. That is madness: instead of changing into angels, they change into beasts." Molière is presenting the same idea dramatically, as he does with even more power later (Act IV, scene 3, l. 1293), when Orgon's daughter has implored him not to force her to marry the repulsive Tartuffe, and he summons his will to resist her with these words:

Be firm, my heart! No human weakness now!

These moments of truth, these flashes of unconscious self-revelation that plunge us into the very center of an obsession, abound in Molière, adding to our insight even as they reveal his. And even as he caricatures aspects of himself in the reforming Alceste or in the jealous older lover in Arnolphe, so he imparts to his moments of truth not only the individuality of the particular obsession but also the universality of our common share in it.

*   *   *

Molière is one of those widely known public figures whose private life remains veiled. In his own time gossip was rife, but much of it comes from his enemies and is suspect. Our chief other source is his plays; but while these hint at his major concerns and lines of meditation, we must beware of reading them like avowals or his roles like disguised auto-biography.*

He was born Jean-Baptiste Poquelin in Paris early in 1622 and baptized on January 15, the first son of a well-to-do bourgeois dealer in tapestry and upholstery. In 1631 his father bought the position of *valet de chambre tapissier ordinaire du roi,* and six years later obtained the right to pass it on at his own death to his oldest son, who took the appropriate "oath of office" at the age of fifteen. Together with many sons of the best families, Jean-Baptiste received an excellent education from the Jesuit Fathers of the Collège de Clermont. He probably continued beyond the basic course in rhetoric to two years of philosophy and then law school, presumably at Orléans.

Suddenly, as it appears to us, just as he was reaching twenty-one, he resigned his survival rights to his father's court position, and with them the whole future that lay ahead of him; drew his share in the estate of his dead mother and a part of his own prospective inheritance; and six months later joined in forming, with and around Madeleine Béjart, a dramatic company, the Illustre-Théâtre. In September 1643 they rented a court-tennis court to perform in; in October they played in Rouen; in January 1644 they opened in Paris; in June young Poquelin was named head of the troupe, and signed himself, for the first time we know of, "de Molière."

Molière's was an extraordinary decision. Apart from the financial hazards, his new profession stood little above pimping or stealing in the public eye and automatically involved minor excommunication from the Church. To write for the theater, especially tragedy, carried no great onus; to be an actor, especially in comedy and farce, was a proof of

---

* To learn what is established fact we turn to scholars like Michaut and Mornet; for a rich and informed sense of probability, to Fernandez or—with caution—Dussane.

immorality. Though Richelieu's passion for the stage had improved its prestige somewhat, this meant only that a few voices were raised to maintain its possible innocence against the condemnation of the vast majority.

Obviously young Molière was in love with the theater, and had to act. He may also have been already in love with Madeleine Béjart; their contemporaries were probably right in thinking them lovers, though all we actually know is that they were stanch colleagues and business partners. Their loyalty was tested from the first. Although the Béjarts raised all the money they could, after a year and a half in Paris the company failed and had to break up; Molière was twice imprisoned in the Châtelet for debt; he and the Béjarts left Paris to try their luck in the provinces. For twelve years they were on the road, mainly in the south.

For the first five of these they joined the company, headed by Du Fresne, of the Duc d'Épernon in Guyenne. When d'Épernon dropped them, Molière became head of the troupe. From 1653 to 1657 they were in the service of a great prince of the blood, the Prince de Conti, until his conversion. Even with a noble patron, the life was nomadic and precarious, and engagements hard to get. However, the company gradually made a name for itself and prospered. Molière gained a rich firsthand knowledge of life on many levels. In the last few years of their wanderings he tried his hand as a playwright with such plays as *L'Étourdi* and *Le Dépit amoureux*.

At last in 1658 they obtained another chance to play in the capital. On October 24 they appeared before young Louis XIV, his brother, and the court, in the guard room of the old Louvre, in a performance of Corneille's tragedy *Nicomède*, which Molière followed with his own comedy *The Doctor in Love*. Soon they became the Troupe de Monsieur (the King's brother) and were installed by royal order in the Théâtre du Petit-Bourbon. Though they still performed tragedies, they succeeded more and more in comedy, in which Molière was on his way to recognition as the greatest actor of his time.

Within a year he made his mark also as a playwright with *The Ridiculous Précieuses* (November 18, 1659), which, though little more than a sketch, bore the stamp of his orig-

inality, keen observation, and rich comic inventiveness.*
Nearly thirty-eight, Molière was to have thirteen more years
to live, and was to live them as though he knew this was all.
To his responsibilities as director and actor he added a hectic
but glorious career as a very productive playwright, author
of thirty-two comedies that we know, of which a good third
are among the comic masterpieces of world literature. The
stress of his many roles, of deadlines, and of controversy is
well depicted in *The Versailles Impromptu.* Success led to
success—and often to more controversy—but never to re-
spite. He was to be carried off the stage to his deathbed. No
doubt he wanted it that way, or almost that way; for probably
no man has ever been more possessed by the theater.

On February 20, 1662, at the age of forty, he married the
twenty-year-old Armande Béjart, a daughter (according to
the mostly spiteful contemporaries) or sister (according to
the official documents) of Madeleine. Though what we know
of their domestic life is almost nothing, contemporary gossip, a friend's letter, and Molière's own preoccupation in
several plays with a jealous older man in love with a flighty
young charmer, combine to suggest an uneasy relationship.
They had two sons who died in infancy and a daughter who
survived. The King himself and his sister-in-law (Madame)
were godfather and godmother to the first boy—no doubt
to defend Molière against a charge, or rumor, that he had
married his own daughter.

When the Petit-Bourbon theater was torn down in October 1660 to make way for the new façade of the Louvre,
things looked bad; but the King granted the company the
use of Richelieu's great theater, the Palais-Royal, which remained Molière's until his death. An early success there was
his regular, elaborate verse comedy, *The School for Husbands.* Within a year of his marriage he wrote his first great
play and one of his most popular, *The School for Wives.* It
aroused much controversy; when Molière published it, he
dedicated it to Madame; the King gave him the support he

---

* Since the fourteen plays (seven in each volume) in the present translation will be discussed in the introductory note to each, I shall do little
more than mention them here.

sought in the form of a pension of one thousand francs for this "excellent comic poet." *The Critique of the School for Wives* and *The Versailles Impromptu* (June and October 1663) completed Molière's victory in the eyes of the public.

However, his attack on extreme piety and hypocrisy in *Tartuffe* showed him the strength of his enemies. The first three-act version, performed in May 1664, was promptly banned. For the next five years much of his time and energy went into the fight to get it played: petitions, private readings, revisions, private performances. In August 1667 a five-act version entitled *The Impostor* was allowed a second public performance—then also banned. Only in February 1669 was the version that we know put on, with enormous success; and this time it was on the program to stay.

Meanwhile Molière had hit back at his enemies in 1665 in *Don Juan,* which he soon withdrew. In August of that year his company became The King's Troupe, and his pension was raised to six thousand francs. A year later he completed his greatest and most complex play, *The Misanthrope,* which met only a modest success, and the light but brilliant farce that often served as a companion piece, *The Doctor in Spite of Himself.* In 1668 he displayed the bitter comic profundities of *The Miser;* and in the last four years of his life—still to mention only his finest plays—*The Would-Be Gentleman, The Mischievous Machinations of Scapin, The Learned Women,* and *The Imaginary Invalid.*

Molière's last seven years were dogged by pulmonary illness. A bad bout in early 1666 and another in 1667 led him to accept a milk diet and spend much of the next four years apart from his wife in his house in Auteuil. The year before his own death saw those of his old friend Madeleine Béjart and later of his second son. As his health grew worse, he composed—characteristically—his final gay comedy about a healthy hypochondriac. Before its fourth performance, on February 17, 1673, he felt very ill; his wife and one of his actors urged him not to play that evening; he replied that the whole company depended a lot on him and that it was a point of honor to go on. He got through his part, in spite of one violent fit of coughing. A few hours later he was dead. Since he had not been able, while dying, to get a priest to come and receive his formal renunciation of his profession, a regular religious burial was denied at first, and later grudgingly granted—at night, with no notice, ceremony, or service—only after his widow's plea to the King. He died and was buried as he had lived—as an actor.

Translations of Molière abound. Two of the most available, both complete, are by H. Baker and J. Miller (1739) and Henri Van Laun (1875-76). The former is satisfactory, but its eighteenth-century flavor is not always Molière's; the latter is dull. Better for the modern reader are the versions of selected plays by John Wood (1953 and 1959), George Graveley (1956), and especially three others.

Curtis Hidden Page has translated eight well-chosen plays (Putnam, 1908, 2 vols.) which include three verse comedies done into unrhymed verse. Though it sometimes lacks sparkle, his version is always intelligent and responsible.

Morris Bishop's recent translation of nine plays (one for Crofts Classics, 1950, eight for Modern Library, 1957) is much the best we have for all but two. His excellent selection includes six in prose (*Précieuses, Critique, Impromptu, Physician in Spite of Himself, Would-Be Gentleman, Would-Be Invalid*) and three done into unrhymed verse (*School for Wives, Tartuffe, Misanthrope*). His knowledge of Molière and talent for comic verse make his translation lively and racy, and his occasional liberties are usually well taken.

Richard Wilbur has translated Molière's two greatest verse plays, *The Misanthrope* and *Tartuffe*, into rhymed verse (Harcourt, Brace, & World, Inc., 1955 and 1963). They are the best Molière we have in English. My sense of their excellence is perhaps best stated personally. I have long wanted to try my hand at translating Molière. When the Wilbur *Misanthrope* appeared, I decided not to attempt it unless I thought I would do that play either better or at least quite differently. When I finally tried it, I was surprised to find how different I wanted to make it. Wilbur's end product is superb; but in his *Misanthrope* I sometimes miss the accents of Molière.* His *Tartuffe* seems to me clearly better, since it follows the original closely even in detail. Both are beautiful translations. Again and again my

---

*As, for one example, when Alceste's *"Non, elle est générale, et je hais tous les hommes"* (l. 118) becomes "No, I include all men in one dim view . . ."

quest for sense and for rhymes has led me to the same solution that Wilbur found earlier.

The question whether foreign rhyme should be translated into English rhyme has been often debated and seems to me infinitely debatable. I think a different answer may be appropriate for each poet, and perhaps for each translator. Page explains his rejection of rhyme as something unnatural to good English dramatic verse; but he also recognizes that he often found it harder to avoid rhyme than to use it, and that unrhymed verse is more difficult than rhymed to write well. I think this last point explains my disappointment at some of his and Bishop's lines. Against the point that rhymed dramatic verse is not natural in English, I would argue that it seems to me almost necessary for Molière. Wilbur has made the case brilliantly in his introduction to *The Misanthrope*, pointing to certain specific effects—mock tragedy, "musical" poetic relationships of words, even the redundancy and logic of the argument—which demand rhyme. In my opinion, rhyme affects what Molière says as well as the way he says it enough to make it worthwhile to use it in English, and the loss in precision need not be great.

Fidelity in meter, however, seems clearly to mean putting Molière's alexandrines into English iambic pentameter, and, although allowing some liberties with syllable-count as natural to English, holding rather closely to the precise count that the practice of Molière's day demanded. However, this reduction in length, while translating (which normally lengthens) even from French into English (which normally shortens), often forces the translator to choose between Molière's ever-recurring initial "and's" (and occasional "but's") and some key word in the same line. I have usually chosen to retain the key word; but at times I deliberately have not, for fear of losing too much of Molière's generally easy flow and making him too constipated and sententious.

Molière's characteristic language is plain, correct, functional, often argumentative, not slangy but conversational. Since in French—despite many savory archaisms—he does not generally strike the modern reader as at all archaic, he should not in English. For most of his writing, verse and prose, I have sought an English that is familiar and acceptable today but not obviously anachronistic.

However, there is much truth in Mornet's statement

that Molière is one of the few great writers who has no style, but rather all the styles of all his characters. The departures from the norm noted above are as common as the norm itself. The earthy talk of peasants and servants is in constant (and sometimes direct) contrast with the lofty affectation of bluestockings and *précieuses* and the pomposity of pedants; manner as well as matter distinguish a Don Juan from a Sganarelle, Lucile and Cléonte from Nicole and Covielle; Alceste's explosiveness colors his language and enhances his opposition to Philinte; Charlotte even speaks better French to Don Juan than to her peasant swain Pierrot. To render this infinite variety the translator must call to his aid all the resources of his language— anachronistic or not—that he can command.

A special problem is that of dialect, as in *Don Juan* and *The Doctor in Spite of Himself*. To the dialect of the Île de France that Molière uses, familiar to his audience, I see no satisfactory equivalent in English. Since part of the dialect humor rests on bad grammar ("j'avons" and the like) and rustic oaths, I have tried to suggest this by similar, mainly countrified, lapses and exclamations.

My aim, in short, has been to put Molière as faithfully as I could into modern English, hewing close to his exact meaning and keeping all I could of his form and his verve.

The edition I have mainly relied on for this translation is that of Molière's *Œuvres* by Eugène Despois and Paul Mesnard (Paris: Hachette, 1873–1900, 14 vols.). I have followed the standard stage directions and division of the play into scenes. The stage directions do not normally indicate entrances and exits as such, since in the French tradition these are shown in print by a change of scenes and signalized only in that way.

I should like to acknowledge three debts: to earlier translators, especially Page, Bishop, and Wilbur; to Sanford R. Kadet for his thorough reading of the *Tartuffe* and valuable suggestions; and, as always, to my wife, Katharine M. Frame, for her ready and critical ear and her unfailing encouragement.

—Donald M. Frame

Foreword

Molière is the most popular French playwright in the United States, the most frequently translated and produced. In fact, Molière's may be the only French plays many Americans will ever read or see performed onstage. Although written more than 325 years ago, his thirty-three farces, comedies, satires, and court entertainments include plays that are not only fresh and funny but marked by trenchant and still relevant observations about human nature and human foibles. His great subjects are the gender and marital wars, middle-class alienation, the gullibility of man faced with disease and death, and—often seen by theater producers as most applicable to us today—the malignancy of religious hypocrisy.

The playwright and actor who was to rename himself Sieur de Molière was baptized Jean-Baptiste Poquelin in Paris on January 15, 1622. Although his father, Jean Poquelin, was a middle-class merchant and member of the guild of upholsterers, Jean-Baptiste was given the education of a young gentleman. He attended the most prestigious school in Paris, the Collège de Clermont, a Jesuit institution on the Left Bank where noble and even royal children were sent to learn classical languages and the arts of speaking and writing. From there he may have gone to Orléans to study law—or his father may have bought him a degree. It would seem that the ambitious father wanted something more for his son than an apartment over a shop. Law was the way in which middle-class men prepared themselves for offices in the state bureaucracies, eventually becoming "nobles of the robe." So, Clermont, the law, and tomorrow the world.

Fate in the guise of a red-haired actress named Madeleine intervened. Madeleine Béjart was four years older than Jean-Baptiste Poquelin. She, too, came from a bourgeois background, but at the age of seventeen, Madeleine had herself "emancipated," that is, declared free of the control of her parents, and became the mistress of a nobleman, the count of Modène. The novelist Georges de Scudéry described her as an actress as "one of the best of the century who had the power to inspire in reality all the feigned passions that are seen on the stage." She certainly inspired passion in young Poquelin.

In June 1643, Jean-Baptiste along with Madeleine, her brother, and seven others signed a contract establishing themselves as the Illustrious Theater. According to their agreement, the heroes were to be played by Poquelin, Joseph Béjart, and one other, while Madeleine was to choose whatever roles she wanted. The theater opened on New Year's Day 1644 in a converted tennis court on the Left Bank. It was not a success. Joseph Béjart stuttered, while Poquelin, who wanted desperately to be a tragic actor, lacked, according to Angelique du Croisy, whose parents were members of the troupe, "those external gifts" required to play princes and heroes. He had a short neck and slightly bowed legs and was, as a later critic noted, categorically comic. Only Madeleine was truly suited to play the tragic repertory that was all that mattered in the 1640s.

After the end of the Wars of Religion in 1594, professional traveling troupes gave public performances in Paris, but the first permanent troupe was established there only in 1629, and theater was still in its early days when the Illustrious Theater tried to make a place for itself. In 1644, there were two "official" troupes approved by Louis XIII: the King's Actors at the Hôtel de Bourgogne and the Royal Troupe at the Théâtre du Marais. The Illustrious Théâtre had the protection of Gaston d'Orléans, Louis XIII's brother, although his patronage did not extend to the financial assistance that was so desperately needed.

The young actors hung on somehow, falling further and further behind, until July 1645, when Jean-Baptiste Poquelin—now calling himself Molière—found himself in debtors' prison. Once released, he left Paris with Madeleine and joined a provincial troupe led by Charles Dufresne. The long exile had begun.

Many biographers and critics have suggested that Molière changed his name in order to spare his family the embarrassment of being related to an actor. In fact, most actors adopted stage names, usually taken from nature or from a geographical location—du Parc, de la Grange, de Montfleury, de Brie—all of which allowed the actor or actress to use the particule, the "de" that indicates upper-class origin. No one was fooled by this obvious fiction, but actors, who were mostly from the artisan class or from theatrical families, liked to match their noble names to their noble roles. And perhaps this convention made it easier for them to accept their status as people whose profession meant exclusion from society and excommunication from the Church.

For thirteen years, Molière performed in the provinces of France. By 1653 the company was known as the troupe of Molière and Mlle. Béjart. In that same year, the prince de Conti, fifth in line for the French throne, became Molière's patron and friend. The stagestruck prince enjoyed strolling in his park at Pézenas with the actor, discussing plays and reading choice passages aloud.

Like most French theatergoers of his time, Molière was entranced by the antics of the Italian actors of the Commedia dell'Arte, whose improvised comic entertainments were seen both in Paris and throughout the country, and his first efforts as a playwright were French versions of several farces from the Italian repertory. In 1655 he wrote his first full-length play, *L'Étourdi* (*The Simpleton*). A year later he added *Le Dépit amoureux* (*The Vexation of Love*) to his repertory. Both are workmanlike farces based on Italian models with excellent roles for comic actors, especially for Molière himself, who had begun to specialize in playing a clever servant named Mascarille.

In this same year, the prince de Conti, suffering from the symptoms of syphilis, noisily reformed his life. He became zealously pious and dismissed the actors that "used to bear his name." From that time on, he was an implacable enemy of the theater, part of the devout party at court that would cause his former "friend" such extreme distress. However, the critic Chappeauzeau had written of the troupe that, although itinerant, it was "ordinarily just as good as that of the Hôtel [de Bourgogne]." If this were true, then perhaps it was time for Molière and his companions to test the waters in Paris. On October 24, 1658, a tryout was arranged by Louis XIV's younger brother, Philippe d'Orleans, known as Monsieur, and although the tragedy was not a success, a little farce by Molière called *Le Docteur amoureux* (*The Amorous Doctor*) saved the day.

The king awarded the Troupe of Monsieur the right to share with an Italian Commedia dell'Arte company a royal theater known as the Petit-Bourbon. The troupe of ten that began to play there on November 2, 1658, was celebrated for Molière, its farceur, and for its three beautiful actresses, Madeleine Béjart,

Catherine de Brie, and Marquise du Parc, but it lacked a young leading man to play lovers and heroes. Its initial repertory of tragedies by Corneille failed to please, but matters improved when Molière's two comic plays were introduced.

Paris was ready to laugh. In the late 1630s, farce had been largely driven from the stage by reformers led by Cardinal Richelieu. The most successful comic playwright of the 1640s and 1650s was Paul Scarron, who wrote primarily for an actor named Julian Bedeau, known as Jodelet. Molière announced a new direction for his troupe when he lured Jodelet away from the Marais. To welcome the old farceur, Molière wrote a new afterpiece, a short comic play to follow the main tragedy or comedy. Starring Molière as Mascarille and Bedeau as Jodelet, *The Ridiculous Précieuses* was accused of being nothing but a trifle, a miserable farce that was all Molière and his troupe were capable of staging. In one sense the attackers were right. *The Ridiculous Précieuses* is, according to seventeenth-century definitions, a farce in most ways. It is short and written in prose, it has middle-class provincials and servants for its characters, and it ends with indecency and violence. Like the farces performed on the same stage by the Italians, it features stock characters: one played in white face, the other in a black mask. On the other hand, it savagely mocks the language and manners of certain pretentious upper-class Parisian women and members of the complacent literary establishment. Its intention is not just to amuse but to condemn and correct, and its targets were only too aware that that "actor," that "farceur" had dared to declare himself a serious, satirical voice. It was a solid hit.

Another actor joined the troupe after Easter of 1659. He was a young leading man named Charles Varlet de la Grange, and his presence made it possible to offer comedies with romantic intrigues. Romantic intrigue was also in the offing for Molière. Although he and Madeleine had been together for many years, they had never married. Now Molière was involved with seventeen-year-old Armande Béjart, possibly Madeleine's younger sister, probably her daughter, whom he would marry in 1662.

La Grange's presence in the company, and Molière's own preoccupations, may have influenced the creation of a series of plays dealing with marriage, jealousy, and cuckoldry: *The Imaginary Cuckold* (1660), *Don Garcie of Navarre* (1661), *The School for Husbands* (1661), and *The School for Wives* (1662). The first was another afterpiece, the second a poetic failure. The third and especially the fourth introduced Molière's great character comedies. *The School for Wives* was an enormous success and the cause of a notorious literary quarrel.

Molière had marriage on his mind in the spring of 1661 when he was writing *The School for Husbands*. His role was Sganarelle, a rich, conservative Parisian bourgeois who is about to marry Isabelle, his much younger ward, whom he keeps in near seclusion. His brother, Ariste, has charge of Isabelle's sister, Léonor, but is far more liberal in his outlook. In his view, there is nothing wrong with dances and parties; "the school of the world teaches better than any book." Isabelle has caught the eye of a young neighbor Valère—the first of La Grange's seductive lovers—and gladly collaborates with him to betray Sganarelle. The two brothers are a study in contrasts: the one attuned to the new society of the young reign of Louis XIV, the other with a precarious hold on a world that is slipping away, where women are property whose value depends on their chastity. The women also differ. Léonor is straightforward and ready to engage in a reasonable marriage with her "good old man," while Isabelle is a practiced trickster who, seeing her choice narrowed to "Valère or despair," seizes on a strategy of deceit to escape Sganarelle's repressive ideal.

The School for Husbands is not a farce. It is in form a regular comedy, set on a Paris street following the Roman model. It is in three acts, not five, but it follows the unities of time and place, is written in verse, and is without any farce interludes or physical action. Its successor, *The School for Wives*, which opened in December 1662, is similar in form. The action takes place in less than twenty-four hours and is set on a street in a provincial city. It is in five acts and in verse, with farce interludes played by the servants. *The School for Wives* is, however, a far more complex and subtle play than its predecessor.

Between the two plays a number of important events happened. The company was put out of its theater at the Petit-Bourbon, but its members were granted use of another royal theater at the Palais-Royal. Molière wrote his first play on command, *Les Fâcheux*, commissioned by Superintendent of Finances Nicolas Fouquet for a festival meant to impress his magnificence on the young king. A disaster for Fouquet, whose career ended when Louis realized the extent of his probable misappropriation of state funds, the fête at Vaux-le-Vicomte put Molière on the road to royal favor. Finally, Molière married Armande Béjart on February 20, 1662, and she, now known as Mlle. Molière, joined the troupe. He was forty; she was about twenty.

The scandal of the marriage—had Molière married his own daughter, as some would claim?—magnified the scandal of the play *School for Wives*. Opening in time for the Christmas season of 1662 and the carnival of 1663, *The School for Wives* had thirty-one performances before the Easter break and another thirty-two after it was joined by its *Critique* on June 1. It was Molière's first enormous hit and has remained one of his most popular plays. The Comédie-Française, France's state theater, has played *The School for Wives* 1,593 times between its founding in 1680 and the turn of the millennium in 1999.

The play introduces Arnolphe, a rich provincial bourgeois, who has an obsessive fear of being betrayed sexually. In order to ensure his piece of mind, Arnolphe has bought a female child and has had her raised in extreme seclusion in a convent. He then brings the innocent Agnès to a second house he owns, away from his normal social activity, and prepares to marry her. Agnès is, of course, soon spotted on the balcony by Horace, an unpracticed seducer whose intentions are more or less honorable. In the end, the young lovers prevail over Arnolphe, whose final strangled "ouf" as he leaves the stage signals the defeat of his elaborate scheme to create for himself a marriage in which he has complete empire over his browbeaten bride.

Arnolphe is a far more complex character than Sganarelle, however. He is a little old-fashioned, to be sure, but he is friendly, generous, and socially ambitious. A bit of a libertine himself, he knows what young men want. And unlike Sganarelle, he makes the mistake of falling deeply in love with his charge, which sends him into a state of extreme sexual jealousy. Agnès is also more interesting than Isabelle. Bitterly aware of her lack of education and social savvy, she, too, learns quickly how to deceive her watchful guardian and, in the end, rejects his idea of marriage as "vexatious" and "painful" and opts for the pleasures offered by Horace, especially that little "je ne sais quoi" deep inside.

It was Molière himself who established the terms of what we call the quarrel of *The School for Wives* when he wrote an afterpiece, *The Critique of the School for Wives*. Opening on June 1, 1663, the *Critique* takes place in a Parisian drawing room where pedants, society women, and one reasonable fellow debate the merits of the play and argue about such lines as the servant Alain's famous declaration to his wife that "woman is the soup of man." The Marquis objects that the play cannot be good since the common people in the audience laughed at it, while the writer Lysidas argues that it sins against all the rules of art. It was this afterpiece—which doubled the run of the main piece—that actually prompted a flood of pamphlets and plays. Critics protested the play's sexual innuendos and irreverent religious references, although the true incentive to attack it may have been its success, which frightened the actors at the Hôtel de Bourgogne. Molière also included a rather obvious joke at the expense of Pierre Corneille's brother, Thomas, and the Corneilles unleashed their protégé Boursault whose personal attack on Molière, *The Portrait of the Painter*, was staged by the Hôtel.

Molière responded to the barrage with *The Impromptu at Versailles*, which joined the repertory on October 18. In this fascinating short play, Molière and the members of his troupe play themselves. He burlesques the king's actors, especially the obese Montfleury, who played kings and noble heroes, tries to rehearse his distracted company, and finally announces the end of the quarrel, responding firmly to the personal attacks mounted in Boursault's play and slyly suggesting that the real issue was that his play had made too much money.

Within months of the end of the commotion over *The School for Wives*, Molière was embroiled in another controversy, one that would change him and his work forever. In May 1664, as part of an elaborate festival at Versailles, Molière presented three acts of a new play entitled *The Hypocrite*, the first of several versions of *Tartuffe*. Further productions were immediately forbidden by the king. It would be nearly five years before the completed play would become Molière's most successful and profitable comedy.

The battle for *Tartuffe* was not fought with pamphlets and plays but with trips to court and petitions to the king. On the one side, Molière insisted that his targets were not the Church and the truly pious but only the hypocrites who used religion to their own advantage; on the other, socially conservative fundamentalists known as *les dévots* used all their influence to keep the play off the stage. Retitled *The Imposter* and with the central character, now called Panulphe, recostumed as a fashionable Parisian, the play opened in Paris in August 1667, and was closed by the president of the Parlement after one performance. In addition, the archbishop of Paris promised to excommunicate anyone who saw it or even read it. Why the king finally permitted it to be performed in February 1669 is not clear, but after five years of scandal, all Paris rushed to see it.

In the meantime Molière wrote a second attack on hypocrisy: *Don Juan, or The Stone Feast* (widely translated as *The Stone Guest.*) The most baroque of his plays and a modern favorite, *Don Juan* was allowed to run for fifteen performances between Mardi Gras and the Lenten closing in 1565, although it was censored after the first night and the actors were forced to donate part of their profits to the Capuchin friars. After the Easter break, the play did not reopen. It was not published until the complete works of Molière appeared in 1682, and then it was further censored. Its next appearance on the Paris stage was in 1841.

One would think that Don Juan, who believes only that two and two are four and who chooses hypocrisy as the way to thrive in a noble world of codes and masks, would have been found more offensive than the wily seducer Tartuffe. Perhaps he was, but because *Don Juan* was done only in Paris and the king never saw it, it was less noticed at court; or perhaps because it was so clearly meant as an indictment of Molière's former patron, Conti, it found admirers in those who universally disliked the prince and disputed the sincerity of his conversion. In the long run, *Don Juan* suffered a more extreme fate than *Tartuffe*, but Molière was apparently less committed to it.

Molière played neither Tartuffe nor Don Juan. In *Tartuffe* his role was Orgon, the rich bourgeois dupe with the beautiful young wife lusted after by the hypocrite. In *Don Juan* he played Sganarelle, whose only connection to the Sganarelle of *The School for Husbands* is the costume. Here he is the valet of the hero, who tries with limited skills and from a worldview distorted by superstition to persuade his master to mend his ways. Sganarelle is a burlesque version of the private directors of conscience many noblemen, including Conti, employed to put them on the high road to salvation.

Molière was, of course, accused of being himself an atheist or, more reasonably, a "libertine," a free thinker and a free liver. He probably was. His life was irregular, he was deeply sexual, and he had some questionable friends. And his constant protest that he was not targeting the Church is disingenuous. The fundamentalist wing of the Roman Catholic Church represented a danger to the rational and secular state that was developing in France in the early years of the personal reign of Louis XIV. Molière, educated by the more liberal Jesuits, had every reason to fear the power of the *dévots* and every reason to believe that the king did as well. He was right, eventually, but the struggle cost him. His almost personal relationship with the king was over, as perhaps was his sense of his own power to influence change. He became a cynical survivor.

After 1666 he was ill with the tuberculosis that would kill him. His marriage was troubled; his son was dead. He continued to write entertainments for the court and comedies for the Paris audience. In February 1673, during the fourth performance of his new play, *The Imaginary Invalid,* Molière had a hemorrhage onstage and died in his apartment on the rue de Richelieu a few hours later. His enemies almost had the last word when the local parish priest refused him Christian burial because he was an actor. The king intervened and Molière was escorted to his grave at night, silently, with torches and a crowd of hundreds. For them it was, as a friend wrote, a "farewell to laughter."

—Virginia Scott

The Ridiculous Précieuses

THE RIDICULOUS PRÉCIEUSES

A prose comedy in seventeen scenes, first performed November 18, 1659, following Corneille's tragedy *Cinna*, at the Théâtre du Petit-Bourbon, by Molière's company, then under the patronage of the King's brother and known as the Troupe de Monsieur. Molière played Mascarille. In the farce tradition, the characters had either stock names (Mascarille, Gorgibus), or the stage names of the actors who played them (La Grange, Du Croisy, the pale-faced Jodelet), or nicknames—Cathos (pronounced *Cat-o*) for Catherine de Brie, Magdelon (the *g* is silent) for Madeleine Béjart, Marotte for Marie Ragueneau. Molière's success in the role almost led him to adopt "Mascarille" as a new stage name. Although some wounded *précieuses* succeeded in having the play momentarily banned, the second performance, only two weeks after the first, was triumphant.

This was Molière's first big success as a writer. He was almost thirty-eight and had made the theater his life for over sixteen years: first in Paris (where he failed), then for over twelve years of growing success in the provinces, then in Paris again. At first mainly director-manager-actor, in the last several years he had written at least four plays. Now for the first time, without abandoning the stock resources of French farce and Italian *commedia dell' arte*, he dared to rely mainly on his own gifts of observation, dialogue, and mimicry. The result is still essentially and frankly farce, but also shrewd and delightful caricature. There is a reality to these characters that is new, not only to Molière but to the French comic stage. Preciosity is Protean and timeless: Cathos and Magdelon, their cos-

3

tumes and mannerisms brought up to date, are as alive today as they were three centuries ago.

The preciosity of the time was a natural exaggeration of France's seventeenth-century quest of elegance and refinement. It is marked already early in the century in Honoré d'Urfé's best-selling pastoral novel, *Astrée,* later in the salon of Catherine, marquise de Rambouillet ("the incomparable Arthénice"), and more recently in the bluestocking salon and novels *(Le Grand Cyrus, Clélie)* of Madeleine de Scudéry. Many sober heads attacked it. Though Molière touches Mlle. de Scudéry in passing, he chooses a surer target, not the great *précieuses* themselves but two of their silly latter-day provincial imitators. Though there are touches of preciosity here and there in his own work, it was a natural target for his hatred of pretense, his earthiness, his robust love of life. Nothing could kill preciosity; Molière did much to make it a laughingstock.

THE RIDICULOUS PRÉCIEUSES

CHARACTERS

LA GRANGE ⎫ *rebuffed suitors*
DU CROISY ⎭

GORGIBUS, *a member of a good bourgeois family*
MAGDELON, *daughter of Gorgibus, a ridiculous* précieuse
CATHOS, *niece of Gorgibus, a ridiculous* précieuse
MAROTTE, *maid of the ridiculous* précieuses
ALMANZOR, *lackey of the ridiculous* précieuses
THE MARQUIS DE MASCARILLE, *valet of La Grange*
THE VISCOUNT DE JODELET, *valet of Du Croisy*
TWO CHAIR-CARRIERS
NEIGHBORS
FIDDLERS

Scene 1. LA GRANGE, DU CROISY

DU CROISY. Seigneur La Grange . . .

LA GRANGE. What?

DU CROISY. Look at me for one moment without laughing.

LA GRANGE. Well?

DU CROISY. What do you think of our visit? Are you quite happy about it?

5

LA GRANGE. In your opinion, has either of us reason to be?

DU CROISY. Not completely, to tell the truth.

LA GRANGE. For my part, I admit I am thoroughly shocked. Tell me, did anyone ever see two cornfed country wenches put on more exaggerated airs than those two, or two men treated with more disdain than we were? They could hardly prevail upon themselves to have chairs brought for us. I have never seen so much whispering in one another's ears as they put on, so much yawning, so much rubbing of their eyes, so much asking: "What time is it?" Did they answer any more than yes or no to anything we could say to them? And in short, won't you admit that even if we had been the lowest people on earth, we couldn't have been treated worse than we were?

DU CROISY. It seems to me you're taking the matter much to heart.

LA GRANGE. Indeed I am, and so much so that I mean to take revenge on this impertinence. I know the thing that made them despise us. Preciosity has not merely infected Paris, it has also spread in the provinces, and these ridiculous snobs of ours have inhaled a good dose of it. In short, they are a strange concoction of *précieuse* and coquette. I see what you have to be in order for them to receive you well; and if you will follow my suggestion, we'll put on a show for the two of them that will make them see their folly, and may teach them to know their way around a little better.

DU CROISY. And how do we do that?

LA GRANGE. I have a certain valet named Mascarille, who passes in many people's opinion for a kind of wit; for there's nothing cheaper than wit nowadays. He's a real character, who has taken it into his head to insist on playing the man of quality. He has confirmed pretensions to gallantry and to writing poetry, and disdains the other valets to the point of calling them brutes.

DU CROISY. Well, what do you mean to do with him?

LA GRANGE. What do I mean to do? We must . . . But first let's get out of here.

Scene 2. GORGIBUS, DU CROISY, LA GRANGE

GORGIBUS. Well! You've seen my niece and my daughter; how are things coming along? What's the result of your visit?

LA GRANGE. That is something you can learn from them better than from us. All we can tell you is that we give you thanks for the favor you have done us, and remain your very humble servants.

GORGIBUS. Well, now! They seem to be leaving very dissatisfied. What can be the reason for their discontent? I must get some idea of what's going on. Hey there!

Scene 3. MAROTTE, GORGIBUS

MAROTTE. What do you wish, sir?

GORGIBUS. Where are your mistresses?

MAROTTE. In their boudoir.

GORGIBUS. What are they doing?

MAROTTE. Making lip cream.

GORGIBUS. That's too much creamery. Tell them to come down. (*Exit* MAROTTE.) Those hussies, with their lip cream, I think they want to ruin me. All I see around is whites of eggs, virgin's milk, and a thousand other kinds of junk that I don't know anything about. Since we've been here they've used up the fat of a dozen pigs, at least, and four valets could live every day on the sheep's trotters they consume.

Scene 4.   MAGDELON, CATHOS, GORGIBUS

GORGIBUS. That certainly is a necessary expense, all you put out to grease your snouts! Now you just tell me what you did to those gentlemen, for me to see them leaving so coldly. Didn't I order you to receive them as persons I wanted to give you as husbands?

MAGDELON. And what esteem, Father, do you expect us to have for the irregular procedure of those individuals?

CATHOS. How in the world, Uncle, could a girl with the slightest sense put up with their persons?

GORGIBUS. And what do you find wrong with them?

MAGDELON. Theirs is fine gallantry indeed! What! Start right out with marriage!

GORGIBUS. And what do you want them to start with? Concubinage? Isn't their procedure one that you have reason to be gratified with, as well as I? Could anything be more obliging than that? And the holy bond that they seek, isn't that evidence of their honorable intentions?

MAGDELON. Oh, Father, that kind of talk is utterly bourgeois. It makes me ashamed to hear you speak that way, and you should learn a little about how things are done with an elegant air.

GORGIBUS. I have no use for airs or songs. I tell you that marriage is a simple and a holy thing, and that it is acting honorably to begin with it.

MAGDELON. Good heavens, if everyone were like you, how soon a romance would be ended! A fine thing it would be if Cyrus married Mandane at the start, and if Aronce were wedded to Clélie without any difficulty!*

GORGIBUS (to CATHOS). What's this one telling me?

MAGDELON. Father, my cousin here will tell you just as well as I that marriage must never come until after the other adventures. A lover, to be agreeable, must know how to utter fine sentiments, breathe from his heart things sweet, tender, and passionate; and his suit must follow the rules. First he must see, in church, or on a walk, or at some public ceremony, the person with whom he falls in love; or else be fatally taken to her house by a relative or friend, and leave there dreamy and melancholy. For a time he hides his passion from the beloved object, and meanwhile pays her several visits, in which some question of gallantry never fails to be brought up to exercise the wits of the company. Comes the day of the declaration, which should ordinarily be made in some garden walk, while the company has moved on a bit; and this declaration is followed by instant wrath, which shows in our blushes, and which, for a time, banishes the lover from our presence. Then he finds a way to appease us, to accustom us imperceptibly to his talk about his passion, and to draw from us that admission that pains us so. After that come the adventures, the rivals that cross an established inclination, the persecutions of fathers, the jealousies conceived over false appearances, the laments, the despairs, the abductions, and what follows. That is how things are done

*All these persons are characters in Mlle. de Scudéry's long and immensely popular novels *Artamène ou Le Grand Cyrus* (1648–53, 10 vols.) and *Clélie* (1654–61, 10 vols.), two source books for preciosity.

with elegance; and those are the rules that cannot be dispensed with in proper gallantry. But to come point-blank to the conjugal union, to make love only by making the marriage contract, and to take the romance precisely by the tail! I repeat, Father, nothing could be more mercantile than such a procedure; and just the picture it gives me makes me nauseated.

GORGIBUS. What the devil is this jargon I hear? That's the grand style all right!

CATHOS. Indeed, Uncle, my cousin hits the truth of the matter. How can one receive people well who are completely incongruous in matters of gallantry? I'll wager they have never seen the map of Tenderland,* and that Sweet-Notes, Small-Attentions, Gallant-Notes, and Pretty-Verses are unknown lands to them. Don't you see that their whole person shows this, and that they do not have that air that makes a good first impression? To come to pay their court with an unadorned leg, a hat disarmed of feathers, an uncurled head of hair, and a coat that suffers from an indigence of ribbons . . . ! Good heavens, what kind of lovers are these! What frugality in attire and what aridity in conversation! One can't endure it, one can't abide it. I also noted that their neckcloths are not of the right make, and that their breeches are a good half a foot short of being wide enough.

GORGIBUS (aside). I think they're both crazy, and I can't understand a word of this gibberish. (Aloud) Cathos, and you, Magdelon . . .

MAGDELON. Oh! I beg you, Father, divest yourself of those strange names, and address us otherwise.

GORGIBUS. How's that? Those strange names? Aren't they the names you were christened with?

MAGDELON. Good heavens, how vulgar you are! For my part, one thing that astounds me is that you could have

---

*La Carte de Tendre, a map of the land of love published by Mlle. de Scudéry in Clélie.

a daughter as clever as I. Did anyone, in the grand style, ever speak of Cathos or Magdelon? And won't you admit that one of those names would be enough to discredit the finest romance in the world?

CATHOS. It is true, Uncle, that even a slightly delicate ear suffers frantically on hearing those words pronounced; and the names Polyxène, which my cousin has chosen, and that of Aminte,* which I have adopted, have a grace that you must acknowledge.

GORGIBUS. Listen: just one word will do it. I don't intend that you shall have any other names than those that were given you by your godfathers and godmothers. And as for the gentlemen in question, I know their families and their possessions, and it is my firm will that you make ready to receive them as husbands. I'm getting tired of having you on my hands, and taking care of two girls is a little too heavy a load for a man of my age.

CATHOS. As for me, Uncle, all I can tell you is that I consider marriage a very shocking thing. How can one endure the thought of sleeping beside a man who is actually naked?

MAGDELON. Allow us to catch our breath a bit amid the high society of Paris, where we have only just arrived. Let us weave the web of our romance at leisure, and do not push the conclusion so hard.

GORGIBUS (aside). There's no doubt about it, they're completely daft. (Aloud) Once more, I don't understand a thing about all this twaddle; I intend to be absolute master; and, to cut short every kind of talk, either you will both be married before very long, or, my word, you shall be nuns! This I swear to you.

---

*It was normal practice for the précieuses to choose new names for themselves.

Scene 5.   CATHOS, MAGDELON

CATHOS. Good heavens, my dear, how sunk your father's spiritual form is in matter! How thick is his intelligence, and how dark it is in his soul!

MAGDELON. What can you expect, my dear? I am dismayed for him. I can hardly convince myself that I can really be his daughter, and I think some day some adventure will come and unfold for me a more illustrious birth.

CATHOS. I could well believe it; yes, there is all the likelihood in the world. And as for me, too, when I look at myself . . .

Scene 6.   MAROTTE, CATHOS, MAGDELON

MAROTTE. Here is a lackey asking if you're at home. He says his master wants to come in and see you.

MAGDELON. Stupid girl, learn to pronounce yourself less vulgarly. Say: "Here is a necessity who asks if you might find it commodious to be visible."

MAROTTE. Mercy me! I don't know no Latin, and I haven't learned philophosy like you in *The Great Sire*.*

MAGDELON. Such impertinence! How can one bear it? And who is this lackey's master?

MAROTTE. He said his name is the Marquis de Mascarille.

*The Great Cyrus (Le Grand Cyrus), the novel by Mlle. de Scudéry commented on earlier.

MAGDELON. Ah, my dear, a marquis! *(To* MAROTTE*)* Yes, go and say that he may see us. *(To* CATHOS*)* No doubt he is some wit who has heard about us.

CATHOS. Assuredly, my dear.

MAGDELON. We must receive him in this downstairs room rather than in our bedroom. Let's at least arrange our hair a bit and live up to our reputation. *(To* MAROTTE*)* Quick, come in here and tender us the counselor of the graces.

MAROTTE. My word, I don't know what sort of animal that is. You've got to talk Christian if you want me to understand you.

CATHOS. Bring us the mirror, you ignoramus, and take good care not to sully the glass by the communication of your image.

Scene 7.   MASCARILLE, TWO CARRIERS

MASCARILLE. Hey there, porters, hey! There, there, there, there, there, there! I think these rascals mean to break me in pieces by crashing against the walls and the pavements.

FIRST CARRIER. Well! That's because the door is narrow. And you had to have us come all the way in here.

MASCARILLE. I should think so. You louts, would you have me expose the portliness of my plumes to the inclemencies of the pluvious season, and imprint my shoes in mud? Come, get your chair out of here.

SECOND CARRIER. Then pay us, please, sir.

MASCARILLE. Huh?

SECOND CARRIER. I say, sir, for you to give us our money, please.

MASCARILLE *(giving him a slap)*. What, rascal, ask money of a person of my quality?

SECOND CARRIER. Is that the way you pay poor folk? And your quality—can we eat it for dinner?

MASCARILLE. Aha! Aha! I'll teach you to know your place! These oafs dare to stand up to me!

FIRST CARRIER *(picking up one of the poles of his chair)*. All right! Pay us real quick.

MASCARILLE. What?

FIRST CARRIER. I say I want to have some money right away.

MASCARILLE. He is reasonable.

FIRST CARRIER. Make it quick.

MASCARILLE. Yes, of course. Now *you* speak properly; but the other fellow is a knave who doesn't know what he is saying. Here: are you satisfied?

FIRST CARRIER. No, I'm not satisfied: you slapped my partner's face, and . . . *(raising the pole again)*

MASCARILLE. Gently now. Here, this is for the slap. People get anything they want from me when they go about it in the right way. All right, come back and get me in a while to take me to the Louvre for the King's *petit coucher.**

---

*As opposed to the more accessible *grand coucher*, this was the King's most intimate reception, when he was going to bed.

Scene 8.   MAROTTE, MASCARILLE

MAROTTE. Sir, my mistresses will be down right away.

MASCARILLE. Tell them not to hurry; I'm comfortably established here to wait.

MAROTTE. Here they are.

Scene 9.   MAGDELON, CATHOS, MASCARILLE, ALMANZOR

MASCARILLE *(after bowing)*. Ladies, you will no doubt be surprised at the audacity of my visit; but your reputation makes you suffer this misadventure, and merit has such potent charms for me that I pursue it everywhere.

MAGDELON. If you pursue merit, it is not on our lands that you should hunt.

CATHOS. If you see merit here with us, you must have brought it here yourself.

MASCARILLE. Ah! Your statement I categorically deny. Renown testifies truly in reporting your worth; and you will score pique, repique, and capot* over all the gallant society of Paris.

MAGDELON. Your complaisance carries the liberality of its praises a little too far; and my cousin and I shall take good care not to let our seriousness fall into the sweet trap of your flattery.

*A grand coup in piquet, something like a grand slam redoubled in bridge.

CATHOS. My dear, we should have chairs brought.

MAGDELON. Ho there, Almanzor!

ALMANZOR. Madame?

MAGDELON. Quick, carriage us hither the commodities of conversation.

MASCARILLE. But is there at least any security here for me?

CATHOS. What do you fear?

MASCARILLE. Some theft of my heart, some assassination of my freedom. Here I see eyes that look like very dangerous lads, fit for a surprise attack on a person's liberty and for treating a soul as a Turk treats a Moorish slave. What the devil is this? As soon as one approaches them, they are simply murderously on guard! Ah! Faith, I mistrust them, and I'm getting out of here, or else I want a solid safeconduct to insure that they will do me no harm.

MAGDELON. My dear, he's the sprightly type.

CATHOS. I see, he's a regular Amilcar.*

MAGDELON. Have no fear: our eyes have no evil designs, and your heart may sleep assured of their probity.

CATHOS. But have mercy, sir, do not be inexorable toward this chair which has been holding out its arms to you for a quarter of an hour; give some satisfaction to its desire to embrace you.

MASCARILLE (after combing his wig and adjusting his knee ruffles). Well, ladies, what do you say about Paris?

MAGDELON. Alas! What could we say? One must be the antipodes of reason not to confess that Paris is the great

*A gay lover in Mlle. de Scudéry's Clélie.

bureau of marvels, the center of good taste, wit, and gallantry.

MASCARILLE. For my part, I maintain that outside Paris there is no salvation for people of breeding.

CATHOS. That is an incontestable truth.

MASCARILLE. It *is* a bit muddy; but we have the sedan chair.

MAGDELON. True, the sedan chair is a marvelous entrenchment against the assaults of mud and bad weather.

MASCARILLE. You receive many visits: what great wit belongs to your circle?

MAGDELON. Alas! We are not yet known; but we are on our way to be, and we have a special friend who has promised to bring with her all the writers for the *Collection of Choice Miscellanies.**

CATHOS. And certain other men too whose names we have heard as those of the sovereign arbiters of elegance.

MASCARILLE. I'm the man who will arrange that for you better than anyone. They all come to see me, and I may say that I never rise in the morning without a half-dozen wits in waiting.

MAGDELON. Oh! Heavens! We'll be obliged to you, but with the utmost obligation, if you will do us that kindness. For after all, one must be acquainted with all those gentlemen if one wants to belong to elegant society. They are the ones who make reputations in Paris, and you know that there is one of them such that mere association with him gives you a name for being in the know, even without any other reason. But for my part, what I particularly consider is that by means of these intellectual visits one keeps informed about a hundred things

*The *Recueil des pièces choisies* (1653), a handbook of preciosity.

that one absolutely must know and which are of the essence of wit. Thus one learns every day the gossip of gallantry, the pretty exchanges of prose and verse. One finds out at the right time: "So-and-So has composed the prettiest play in the world on such-and-such a subject; this lady has written words to that tune; this man has done a madrigal about favors enjoyed; that one has composed stanzas about an infidelity; Mr. So-and-So wrote a sextain yesterday evening to Miss Such-and-Such, to which she sent him her answer this morning around eight o'clock; a given author has formed a given project; this one is on the third part of his novel; that other is putting his works through the press." This is what makes you shine in company; and if you don't know these things, I wouldn't give a pin for all the wit you may have.

CATHOS. Indeed, I think it is really *too* ridiculous for a person to have pretensions to wit and not know every least little quatrain that is composed every day; and for my part, I would fairly die of shame if it came to the point where someone asked me if I had seen something new and I had not seen it.

MASCARILLE. It is shameful, indeed, not to have the first look at everything that is done; but don't be worried; I mean to establish in your house an Academy of Wits, and I promise you that there won't be a scrap of verse written in Paris that you will not know by heart before anyone else. I myself, even as you see me, make a bit of a stab at it when I'm in the mood; and in the finest circles in Paris you will find current two hundred songs of my making, as many sonnets, four hundred epigrams, and more than a thousand madrigals, without counting the riddles and the portraits.

MAGDELON. I confess to you I'm frantically fond of portraits; I think nothing is as gallant as that.

MASCARILLE. Portraits are difficult, and require a deep mind. You'll see some of mine that will not displease you.

CATHOS. For my part, I'm terrifyingly in love with riddles.

MASCARILLE. They exercise the mind, and I made up four just this morning which I'll give you to guess.

MAGDELON. Madrigals are charming when they're neatly turned.

MASCARILLE. That is my special talent, and I'm working on putting all Roman history into madrigals.

MAGDELON. Ah! Assuredly, that will be the ultimate in beauty. I reserve at least one copy, if you have it printed.

MASCARILLE. I promise you each one, and in the best binding. It's beneath my rank, but I do it only to earn money for the booksellers, who simply persecute me.

MAGDELON. I imagine it's a great pleasure to see oneself in print.

MASCARILLE. To be sure. But by the way, I must tell you an impromptu that I made up yesterday while I was visiting a duchess friend of mine; for I'm devilishly good at impromptus.

CATHOS. Impromptus are the genuine touchstone of wit.

MASCARILLE. Then listen.

MAGDELON. We are all ears.

MASCARILLE.
> Oh! Oh! I was caught unaware:
> While I was gazing at you, free from care,
> Your eye, so sly, did take my heart in fief.
> Stop thief, stop thief, stop thief, stop thief, stop thief!

CATHOS. Ah! Heavens above! That is carried to the limits of gallantry.

MASCARILLE. Everything I do seems cavalier; it doesn't smell of the pedant.

MAGDELON. It's more than two thousand leagues removed from it.

MASCARILLE. Did you notice that beginning: "Oh! Oh!"? Here's something extraordinary: "Oh! Oh!" Like a man who suddenly takes note of something: "Oh! Oh!" Surprise: "Oh! Oh!"

MAGDELON. Yes; I think that "Oh! Oh!" is admirable.

MASCARILLE. It seems like nothing at all.

CATHOS. Oh, good Lord! What are you saying? That's the kind of thing that's beyond price.

MAGDELON. Beyond a doubt; and I would rather have written that "Oh! Oh!" than an epic poem.

MASCARILLE. Egad! You have good taste.

MAGDELON. Well, it's not completely bad.

MASCARILLE. But don't you also admire "I was caught unaware"? "I was caught unaware": I was not noticing—a natural way of speaking—"I was caught unaware." "While . . . free from care": while innocently, without malice, like a poor sheep. "I was gazing at you," that is to say, I took pleasure considering you, I was observing you, I was contemplating you. "Your eye, so sly" . . . What do you think of that expression "so sly"? Is it not well chosen?

CATHOS. Well indeed.

MASCARILLE. "Sly," surreptitious. It seems like a cat that has just caught a mouse: "sly."

MAGDELON. Nothing could be better.

MASCARILLE. "Did take my heart in fief," snatched it
away from me, tore it from me. "Stop thief, stop thief,
stop thief, stop thief, stop thief!" Wouldn't you say it
was a man shouting and running after a thief to have
him arrested? "Stop thief, stop thief, stop thief, stop
thief, stop thief!"

MAGDELON. One must admit that it has a witty and gallant turn.

MASCARILLE. I want to tell you the tune I've composed
for it.

CATHOS. You have learned music?

MASCARILLE. I? Not at all.

CATHOS. Then how can this be?

MASCARILLE. People of quality know everything without
ever having learned anything.

MAGDELON (to CATHOS). Obviously, my dear.

MASCARILLE. Listen and see if you find the tune to your
taste. Ahem, ahem! La, la, la, la, la. The brutality of
the season has furiously outraged the delicacy of my
voice; but no matter, this is still casual and cavalier
style. (He sings.)
          Oh! Oh! I was caught . . .

CATHOS. Ah! Now that's a passionate tune! Couldn't you
die listening to it?

MAGDELON. There's chromatics in it.

MASCARILLE. Don't you find the thought well expressed
by the song? "Stop thief! . . ." And then, like someone
shouting really loud: "stop, stop, stop, stop, stop, stop
thief!" And suddenly, like a person out of breath:
"stop thief!"

MAGDELON. There you see knowledge of the sublety of things, the height of sublety, the sublety of subleties. It is all marvelous, I assure you; I am ecstatic over the tune and the words.

CATHOS. I have never yet seen anything of such power.

MASCARILLE. Everything I do comes to me naturally, without study.

MAGDELON. Nature has treated you as a truly impassioned mother, and you are her spoiled child.

MASCARILLE. Now, how do you spend your time?

CATHOS. On nothing at all.

MAGDELON. Up to now, we have been frightfully starved for amusements.

MASCARILLE. I am at your disposal to take you to the theater one of these days, if you like; as a matter of fact they are due to put on a new play that I would very much like for us to see together.

MAGDELON. That cannot be refused.

MASCARILLE. But I ask you to applaud in the right way when we're there; for I've pledged myself to play up the show, and the author came to ask me just this morning. It's the custom here for authors to come and read their new plays to us people of quality, so as to pledge us to think they are excellent and give them a reputation; and I leave you to imagine whether, when we say anything, the pit dares to contradict us. For my part, I am very scrupulous about it; and when I have given my promise to some poet, I always shout "That is beautiful!" before the candles are lit.

MAGDELON. You don't need to tell *me:* Paris is a wonderful place. A hundred things happen here every day that you don't know in the provinces, however clever you may be.

CATHOS. Enough: now that we are informed, we will make it our duty to cry out properly at everything that is said.

MASCARILLE. I may be mistaken, but you certainly look like a person who has written a comedy.

MAGDELON. Well, there might be something in what you say.

MASCARILLE. Ah! My word, we shall have to see it. Between ourselves, I have completed one which I want to have performed.

CATHOS. Oh! What troupe will you give it to?

MASCARILLE. A fine question! To the Grands Comédiens.* They are the only ones who know how to bring things out. The others are ignoramuses who recite the way people speak; they don't know how to make the verses boom out, and to stop at the fine passage; and how is one to know which is the fine line if the actor doesn't pause and thus inform you that it's time to make a racket?

CATHOS. Indeed, there is a way of making the audience feel the beauties of a work; and things have no value but that which is given them in performance.

MASCARILLE. How do you like my trimmings? Do you find them congruent with the coat?

CATHOS. Completely.

MASCARILLE. The ribbon is well chosen.

*The official royal troupe of the Hôtel de Bourgogne, Molière's chief rivals.

MAGDELON. Frantically well. It's pure Perdrigeon.*

MASCARILLE. What do you say of my knee ruffles?

MAGDELON. They are in exactly the right style.

MASCARILLE. I can at least boast that they are a good quarter-ell wider than any that are made.

MAGDELON. I must admit I have never seen elegance of attire carried to such a height.

MASCARILLE. Just apply a moment to these gloves the operation of your olfactory sense.

MAGDELON. They smell terrifyingly good.

CATHOS. I have never breathed an aroma of loftier quality.

MASCARILLE (offering his powdered wig). And this?

MAGDELON. It is utterly uppercrust; the sublimity of the brain is deliciously touched by it.

MASCARILLE. You say nothing of my plumes. How do you like them?

CATHOS. Frightfully handsome.

MASCARILLE. Do you know that each feather costs me a louis d'or? For my part, I have a mania for wanting to go in for all the most beautiful things.

MAGDELON. I assure you that you and I are in sympathy: I have a frenzied delicacy about everything I wear; and even to my stockings, I cannot abide anything that is not of the best make.

MASCARILLE (crying out suddenly). Ouch, ouch, ouch, gently! Damme, ladies, you are treating me very badly;

*The most stylish Parisian men's furnisher of the time.

I have cause to complain of your conduct; it is not honorable.

CATHOS. Why, what is it? What's the matter?

MASCARILLE. What? Both of you against my heart at the same time? Attack me right and left! Ah! It's against the law of nations; the match is unfair; and I'm going to cry "Murder."

CATHOS. One must admit he says things in a very special way.

MAGDELON. He has an admirable turn of wit.

CATHOS. You are more afraid than hurt, and your heart cries out before it's skinned.

MASCARILLE. The devil you say! It's skinned from head to foot.

Scene 10.   MAROTTE, MASCARILLE, CATHOS, MAGDELON

MAROTTE. Madame, someone is asking to see you.

MAGDELON. Who?

MAROTTE. The Viscount de Jodelet.

MASCARILLE. The Viscount de Jodelet?

MAROTTE. Yes, sir.

CATHOS. Do you know him?

MASCARILLE. He's my best friend.

MAGDELON. Show him right in.

MASCARILLE. We haven't seen each other for some time, and I am delighted at this encounter.

CATHOS. Here he is.

Scene 11. JODELET, MASCARILLE, CATHOS, MAGDELON, MAROTTE

MASCARILLE. Ah! Viscount!

(They embrace.)

JODELET. Ah! Marquis!

MASCARILLE. How happy I am to meet you!

JODELET. What a joy for me to see you here!

MASCARILLE. Kiss me a bit more, please.

MAGDELON *(to* CATHOS*)*. My dear, we are beginning to be known; see, high society is finding its way to our door.

MASCARILLE. Ladies, allow me to present this gentleman. Upon my word, he is worthy of your acquaintance.

JODELET. It is only just that I should come and render unto you your due; your attractions assert their seigniorial rights over every sort of person.

MAGDELON. This is carrying your civilities to the uttermost confines of flattery.

CATHOS. This day must be marked in our calendar as a most happy one.

MAGDELON *(to* ALMANZOR*)*. Come, boy, must I always tell

you things twice? Don't you see we need the increment of one chair?

MASCARILLE. Don't be surprised to see the Viscount look as he does. He's just getting over an illness that has left his face as pale as you see.*

JODELET. This is the fruit of vigils at court and the fatigues of war.

MASCARILLE. Do you know, ladies, that you see in the Viscount one of the most valiant men of our century? He's a dyed-in-the-wool hero.

JODELET. You're not a bit behind me, Marquis; and we know what you're capable of too.

MASCARILLE. It is true that we have seen each other in the thick of it.

JODELET. And in some pretty hot spots.

MASCARILLE *(looking at both girls)*. Yes, but not as hot as it is here. Ha, ha, ha!

JODELET. Our acquaintance began in the army; and the first time we saw each other, he was in command of a cavalry regiment in the Maltese galleys.

MASCARILLE. That is true; but still you were in service before I was, and I remember that I was only a minor officer when you were in command of two thousand horses.

JODELET. War is a fine thing; but, my word, the court today rewards very badly men like us who have seen service.

----

*The actor Jodelet always played his part in white-face. He may have been quite ill (though not for military reasons) when this play was first produced; he died only a few months later.

MASCARILLE. That's what makes me want to hang up my sword.

CATHOS. As for me, I have a frantic weakness for men of the sword.

MAGDELON. I love them too, but I want to have wit season their courage.

MASCARILLE. Viscount, do you remember that half-moon fortification that we took from the enemy at the siege of Arras?

JODELET. What do you mean, half-moon? That was a full moon, no less.

MASCARILLE. I think you're right.

JODELET. I certainly should remember, my word! I was wounded there in the left leg by a grenade, and I still bear the scars. *(To CATHOS)* Just feel a bit there, I beg you, you'll feel something, it was there.

CATHOS. It's true, it's a big scar.

MASCARILLE *(to MAGDELON)*. Give me your hand a moment and feel this one, here, right at the back of my head; have you got it?

MAGDELON. Yes, I feel something.

MASCARILLE. That's a musket shot I got in my last campaign.

JODELET *(baring his chest)*. Here's a wound that pierced me through and through in the attack on Gravelines.

MASCARILLE *(starting to unbutton his breeches)*. I'm going to show you a fierce wound.

MAGDELON. That's not necessary; we believe it without looking.

MASCARILLE. These are honorable marks that show what we're made of.

CATHOS. We have no doubt about what you're made of.

MASCARILLE. Viscount, do you have your carriage here?

JODELET. Why?

MASCARILLE. We could take these ladies for a drive outside the gates and offer them a little entertainment.

MAGDELON. We can't go out today.

MASCARILLE. Then let's have some fiddlers in and dance.

JODELET. My word, that's a good idea.

MAGDELON. To that we consent; but then we need some increase in company.

MASCARILLE. Hey there! Champagne, Picard, Bourguignon, Casquaret, Basque, La Verdure, Lorrain, Provençal, La Violette! The devil take all lackeys! I don't think there's a gentleman in France worse served than I am. Those louts are always leaving me all alone.

MAGDELON. Almanzor, tell the gentleman's servants to go fetch some fiddlers, and bring in the ladies and gentlemen from next door to populate the solitude of our dance.

MASCARILLE. Viscount, what do you say about those eyes?

JODELET. Well, Marquis, what do you think of them yourself?

MASCARILLE. As for me, I say that our freedom will be hard put to it to get out of here with clean breeches. At least for my part I am all shaken up, and my heart is dangling only by a thread.

MAGDELON. How natural is everything he says! He puts things the most charmingly possible.

CATHOS. It is true that he makes a frantic expenditure of wit.

MASCARILLE. To show you that I am sincere, I mean to make an impromptu about it. *(He meditates.)*

CATHOS. Oh! I entreat you to with all my heart's devotion: let us have something that was composed for us.

JODELET. I would like to do as much, but I find myself a little depleted in the poetic vein from the quantity of bleedings I have given it these past few days.

MASCARILLE. What the devil is the matter? I always do the first line well, but I have trouble doing the others. My word, this is a bit too much under pressure; I'll make you an impromptu at leisure, and you'll find it the finest in the world.

JODELET. He has a devilish wit.

MAGDELON. And gallant, and well turned.

MASCARILLE. Viscount, tell me now, is it long since you've seen the Countess?

JODELET. It's more than three weeks since I paid her a visit.

MASCARILLE. Do you know, the Duke came to see me this morning and wanted to take me to the country to hunt a stag with him?

MAGDELON. Here come our friends.

Scene 12.   JODELET, MASCARILLE, CATHOS, MAGDELON,
           MAROTTE, LUCILE *(a neighbor)*, FIDDLERS

MAGDELON. Gracious, my dears, we do ask your pardon.
These gentlemen had a fancy to give a soul to our feet,
and we sent for you to fill the voids in our assembly.

LUCILE. We are certainly obliged to you.

MASCARILLE. This is just an improvised dance; but one of
these days we will offer you one in due form. Have the
fiddlers come?

ALMANZOR. Yes, sir, they are here.

CATHOS. Then come, my dears, take your places.

MASCARILLE *(dancing alone by way of prelude)*. La, la, la,
la, la, la, la, la.

MAGDELON. He has a perfectly elegant figure.

CATHOS. And looks to dance most properly.

MASCARILLE *(taking MAGDELON as partner)*. My freedom
will risk dancing the courante as well as my feet. Keep
time, fiddlers, keep time. Oh! What ignoramuses!
There's no way of dancing to them. The devil take you!
Can't you keep time? La, la, la, la, la, la, la, la. Steady,
O ye village fiddlers!

JODELET *(dancing next)*. Hey there, don't hurry the beat
so fast; I'm just out of a sickbed.

Scene 13.   DU CROISY, LA GRANGE, CATHOS, MAGDE-
LON, LUCILE, JODELET, MASCARILLE, MAROTTE,
FIDDLERS

LA GRANGE *(with a stick)*. Aha! You rascals, what are you
doing here? We've been looking for you for three
hours.

MASCARILLE *(feeling the blows)*. Ouch! Ouch! Ouch! You
didn't tell us there would be blows.

JODELET. Ouch! Ouch! Ouch!

LA GRANGE. Aren't you the one, you wretch, to try to play
the man of consequence?

DU CROISY. That'll teach you to know your place.

(Exeunt.)

Scene 14.   MASCARILLE, JODELET, CATHOS, MAGDELON,
MAROTTE, LUCILE, FIDDLERS

MAGDELON. Why, what is the meaning of this?

JODELET. It's a wager.

CATHOS. What! Let yourself be beaten in that way!

MASCARILLE. Good Lord! I didn't want to pay any attention to it; for I'm a violent man, and I would have been
carried away.

MAGDELON. Endure an affront like that in our presence!

MASCARILLE. It's nothing; let's finish the dance anyway. We've known them a long time; and among friends, you don't take offense over such a trifle.

Scene 15.   DU CROISY, LA GRANGE, MASCARILLE, JODE-
LET, MAGDELON, CATHOS, MAROTTE, LUCILE,
FIDDLERS

LA GRANGE. My word, you rogues, you won't have the laugh on us, I promise you. Come in, you.

(Enter three or four ruffians.)

MAGDELON. What effrontery is this, to come and molest us so in our own house?

DU CROISY. What, ladies, shall we endure our own lackeys being better received than ourselves, and coming to make love to you at our expense, and offering you a dance?

MAGDELON. Your lackeys?

LA GRANGE. Yes, our lackeys; and it is neither fair nor honorable for you to spoil them for us as you are doing.

MAGDELON. Oh heavens! What insolence!

LA GRANGE. But they shall not have the advantage of using our clothes to catch your eyes with; and if you *will* love them, my word, it shall be for themselves alone. Quick, let them be stripped at once.

JODELET. Farewell to our finery.

MASCARILLE. Down go the Marquisate and the Viscountcy!

DU CROISY. Aha! You rascals, you have the audacity to poach on our preserves! You'll have to go somewhere else and seek the means to make yourselves agreeable in the eyes of your beauties, I assure you.

LA GRANGE. It's really too much to supplant us, and supplant us with our own clothes.

MASCARILLE. O Fortune, how great is thy inconstancy!

DU CROISY. Quick, have every least thing stripped off them.*

LA GRANGE. Take away all those togs, hurry up. Now, ladies, in the state they are in, you may continue your amours with them as much as you please; we leave you every sort of freedom for that, and we protest to you, this gentleman and I, that we shall not be the least bit jealous.

CATHOS. Oh! What a humiliation!

MAGDELON. I'm bursting with spite.

FIDDLER (to the MARQUIS). What's all this now! Who's going to pay us?

MASCARILLE. Ask my lord the Viscount.

FIDDLER (to the VISCOUNT). Who's going to give us our money?

JODELET. Ask my lord the Marquis.

---

*This stripping, traditionally slow and laborious, left Mascarille in a lackey's livery, Jodelet in a cook's white cap and apron.

Scene 16.   GORGIBUS, MASCARILLE, JODELET, MAGDE-
LON, CATHOS, FIDDLERS

GORGIBUS. Ah, you hussies, you've got us in a fine mess,
so I see! And it's a fine business indeed that I've just
learned from those gentlemen who are on their way
out!

MAGDELON. Oh, Father, it's a cruel trick they've played
on us!

GORGIBUS. Yes, it's a cruel trick, but it's a result of your
impertinence, you wretches! They resented the treatment you gave them; and now I, for my sins, must swallow the affront.

MAGDELON. Oh, I swear that we shall be revenged, or I'll
die in torment. And you, you rogues, do you dare stay
here after your insolence?

MASCARILLE. Treat a marquis like that! That's society for
you! The slightest fall from favor makes us despised by
those who cherished us. Come on, comrade, let's seek
our fortune elsewhere; I see very well that only vain
appearances are loved here, and that there's no consideration for naked virtue.

(Exeunt.)

Scene 17.   GORGIBUS, MAGDELON, CATHOS, FIDDLERS

FIDDLER. Sir, we mean for you to give us our due, since
they have failed to, for our playing here.

GORGIBUS *(beating them)*. Yes, yes, I'll give you your due,
and here is the coin I mean to pay you with. And you

two hussies, I don't know what keeps me from doing the same to you. We're going to be the talk and the laughingstock of everybody, and that's what you've brought on yourselves by your idiocies. Go away and hide, you baggages; go away and hide forever. And you who are the cause of their folly, you crack-brained absurdities, pernicious pastimes of idle minds, novels, verses, songs, sonnets, and moonets, may the devil take you all!

The School for

Husbands

THE SCHOOL FOR HUSBANDS

A verse comedy in three acts, first performed June 24, 1661, at the Théâtre du Palais-Royal, by Molière's company, the Troupe de Monsieur. Molière played Sganarelle; Ariste was probably Jodelet's brother De l'Espy; Valère, La Grange; Isabelle, Catherine de Brie.

The School for Husbands is overshadowed more than it deserves to be by Molière's second treatment of the same theme a year and a half later in *The School for Wives*. Though it lacks the richness of his greatest work, *The School for Husbands* is his first demonstration of complete mastery of his craft, and a delightful piece in its own right. Drawing still (as he always will) on the resources of farce to sustain the comic tone, he chooses the "higher" form (three acts, in verse) of the comedy of intrigue, peoples it with living characters, and uses it to propound a lesson on how older men should treat young women: that it is better to be loved than feared.

As usual, he takes his material where he finds it. His theme is reminiscent of Terence, Larivey, and Lope de Vega; certain devices, of Boccaccio, Lope, and others; his moral is generous but familiar. What is new, as usual, is the life that Molière breathes into his play. In part this reflects his own concern with the central problem; for in eight months, at the age of forty, he was to marry the twenty-year-old Armande Béjart, and, one gathers, to be torn by love and jealousy of her for the rest of his life. She was the sister (or possibly the daughter) of his old love and devoted partner Madeleine Béjart; he himself had helped to bring her up.

The play clearly shows that an older man who is young

39

in heart may be an excellent mate for his young ward
Molière must have wished to be seen in the good brother
Ariste; but it is typical of him to have written for himself
as actor, the role of the grouchy and grotesque Sganarelle

THE SCHOOL FOR HUSBANDS

SGANARELLE } *brothers*
ARISTE

ISABELLE } *sisters*
LÉONOR

LISETTE, *waiting maid to Léonor*
VALÈRE, *suitor of Isabelle*
ERGASTE, *valet to Valère*
CONSTABLE
NOTARY

The scene is in Paris.

ACT I

Scene 1.   SGANARELLE, ARISTE

SGANARELLE. Brother, let's end this talk, at my
    request,
And each one live his life as he thinks best.
Although I have to yield to you in age,
And though you're old enough to be a sage,
Yet let me tell you I have no intention
Of being guided by your reprehension;
My own advice is what I choose to heed;
My way of life suits me quite well indeed.

ARISTE. But everyone condemns it.

41

SGANARELLE.   Oh yes, cranks
  Like you, brother.

10 ARISTE.   A kind remark; much thanks.

SGANARELLE. Since I must hear you out, I'd like to
  know
  What these fine critics find to censure so.

ARISTE. That surly humor, whose severity
  Shuns all the pleasures of society,
  Gives all your actions an eccentric air,
  And lends uncouthness even to what you wear.

SGANARELLE. Of course, I must be fashion's slave,
  Oh yes!
  And not content myself in how I dress!
  Wouldn't you like to see, for all your chat,
20 My *elder* brother, sir (for you are that,
  Thank God, by twenty years, to speak straight out,
  But that is hardly worth talking about),
  Wouldn't you like to see me ape the ways
  Of your young fashionable popinjays,
  Wear one of their ridiculous *chapeaux*
  That bare weak brains to every breeze that blows,
  And a blond wig that takes up so much space
  As quite to obfuscate the human face?
  A tiny doublet, like to disappear,
30 And a great collar reaching down to here?
  Those sleeves, at dinner sampling every food,
  Those petticoats, as breeches misconstrued?
  Those ribbons on the shoes, which look as sweet
  As feathers look upon a pigeon's feet?
  And those great canions, reaching from the knees
  Which rob the legs of freedom and of ease,
  And give our gallant fops a straddling gait
  As though on shuttlecocks they ambulate?
  This is the way you'd like to see me dressed:
40 Wearing this trash, like you and all the rest.

ARISTE. Always we must accept the general ways,
  And never draw on us the public gaze.

In clothes as well as speech, the man of sense
Will shun all these extremes that give offense,
Dress unaffectedly, and, without haste,
Follow the changes in the current taste.
I have no wish to set men on the road
Of those who always overdo the mode
And, loving its extremes, would feel distress
If anyone outdid them in excess.   *50*
But I maintain no reason makes it right
To shun accepted ways from stubborn spite;
And we may better join the foolish crowd
Than cling to wisdom, lonely though unbowed.

SGANARELLE. This speech betrays your age, and that
    white hair
You hide beneath the black peruke you wear.

ARISTE. I never fail to note with some surprise
The importance that my age has in your eyes,
And that you always seem to be on fire
To blame my joyfulness and my attire,   *60*
As if old age, debarred from all affection,
Must bend on death alone its whole reflection;
As if it had not ugliness enough
Without becoming slovenly and gruff.

SGANARELLE. Say what you will, I mean nevertheless
To make no changes in the way I dress.
I want a hat, no matter what is said,
That gives comfortable shelter to my head;
A long closed doublet whose appropriate form
Helps me digest and keeps my stomach warm;   *70*
A pair of breeches made to fit my thighs,
And shoes in which my feet won't agonize.
Our fathers wore these, wisely, in their day;
And any fop can look the other way.

Scene 2.   LÉONOR, ISABELLE, LISETTE, ARISTE,
                          SGANARELLE

LÉONOR *(to* ISABELLE*)*. In case he scolds you, leave it
    all to me.

LISETTE *(to* ISABELLE*)*. Still in his room avoiding
    company?

ISABELLE. He's built that way.

LÉONOR.   But, sister, that's not good.

LISETTE. Be glad his brother does not share his mood,
    Madame; thank fate for its benevolence
80 That it assigned you to the one with sense.

ISABELLE. Today's a miracle, beyond a doubt:
    He neither locked me in nor took me out.

LISETTE. Him and his ruff, I'd see him in hell-fire . . .

SGANARELLE. Where are you going, *if* I may inquire?

LÉONOR. We don't know yet. I asked my sister pray
    To take the air with me this lovely day;
    But . . .

SGANARELLE *(to* LÉONOR *and* LISETTE*)*. You two, go
    wherever you see fit.
    Go on, both of you, make the most of it.
              (To ISABELLE*)*
    But you, ma'am, if you please, I tell you no.

90 ARISTE. Oh, come, brother, why not let all three go?

SGANARELLE. Brother, your servant.

ARISTE.   When has youth
    been sage?

SGANARELLE. Youth is a fool, and so sometimes is age.

ARISTE. You think it's bad for her and Léonor . . . ?

SGANARELLE. For her to be with me—I like that more.

ARISTE. But . . .

SGANARELLE. But on me her actions must depend,
And I shall do my duty toward our friend.

ARISTE. You think I care about her sister less?

SGANARELLE. Lord! We each do as we see fit, I
    guess.
They have no kin; their father, late our friend,
Consigned them to us as he neared his end,   *100*
Charging us each to take one for our bride,
Or, should we not, another mate provide;
Gave us a father's and a husband's power
By contract over them from that sad hour.
For one you took responsibility;
That of the other thus devolved on me.
You govern yours according to your will;
So please let me direct the other still.

ARISTE. To me . . .

SGANARELLE.   To me it seems, to speak straight
    out,
I talk as one who knows what he's about.   *110*
You let yours run around free, well arrayed:
All right; give her a lackey and a maid:
I don't mind; she can chase about and loaf,
Freely sniffed at by every foppish oaf:
Do as you will. But I intend that mine
Live not by hers, sir, but by my design,
Dress in a decent woolen serge or baize,
And wear black only on the proper days;
That closeted, as girls should be, indoors,
She put her mind all on her household chores,   *120*
Mending my clothes when other work is done,

Or knitting me some stockings just for fun;
And that, completely deaf to all sweet talk,
She never go unchaperoned to walk.
In short, I know what's what; the flesh is weak;
Horns are an ornament I do not seek;
And since her lot calls her to marry me,
I mean to answer for her personally.

ISABELLE. You've no cause . . .

SGANARELLE.   Silence. Nothing to discuss.
130   I'll teach you how to go out without us.

LÉONOR. How's that, sir . . . ?

SGANARELLE.   The fact is, to be concise,
I'm not talking to you; you're much too nice.

LÉONOR. You don't approve our seeing Isabelle?

SGANARELLE. I don't. Frankly, you spoil her,
    Mademoiselle.
Your visits here I can at best deplore;
Oblige me by not making any more.

LÉONOR. Then listen while I speak out frankly too.
On all of this I do not know her view;
But I know what distrust would do to me;
140   And, born of the same parents though we be,
We hardly can be sisters if, in fact,
She comes to love you for the way you act.

LISETTE. Indeed, I am appalled at all these quirks.
Imprison women? Are we among Turks?
I hear they treat them there like slaves, or worse,
And that is why God marks them with his curse.
You must think us quite ready to discard
Our honor, that you put it under guard.
Come, do you really think all these precautions
150   Are any obstacle to our intentions,
And that, when we've a mind, we can't prevail,
And make a fool out of the smartest male?

You act like madmen when you spy on us;
The surest thing is to rely on us.
The greatest danger is for you to hector:
Our honor wants to be its own protector.
You almost give us a desire to sin
When you take such great care to hem us in;
And if a husband used constraint on me,
I just might let him see what he should see.   160

SGANARELLE. There is your education for you, master;
   Hearing this does not make your heart beat faster?

ARISTE. Brother, her talk should only make us laugh.
   There's much in what she says on her behalf:
   Their sex enjoys a little liberty;
   There's no great point in such austerity;
   Suspicions, locks, and bars are all misplaced,
   And will not keep our girls and women chaste.
   'Tis honor that must hold them to their duty,
   Not our severe confinement of their beauty.   170
   It must be a strange woman, I confess,
   Who owes her virtue solely to duress.
   We hope to rule their every step in vain;
   I say the heart is what we have to gain;
   My honor I would think in jeopardy,
   For all my worry, in the custody
   Of one who, if temptation should assail,
   Would lack only a ready chance to fail.

SGANARELLE. Nonsense.

ARISTE.   Perhaps; but I maintain, in truth,
   That with a smile we should instruct our youth,   180
   Be very gentle when we have to blame,
   And not put them in fear of virtue's name.
   Thus I've raised Léonor up to this time:
   Her freedom I have never seen as crime.
   Her youthful wishes met with my consent;
   Nor have I had, thank God, cause to repent.
   I've let her mingle in society,
   See dances, entertainments, comedy:
   Things I have thought to be of such a kind

190   As serve to fashion a young person's mind.
       Better to have her make the world her school
       In how to live, than any book or rule.
       She likes to spend on linen, bows, and dress:
       What then? My wish is for her happiness;
       And those are pleasures that can be allowed
       To girls in families suitably endowed.
       Her father's order makes her marry me,
       But I have no desire for tyranny.
       I know our ages set us far apart;
200   I leave the choice to her unhampered heart.
       Four thousand crowns a year on which to live
       And all the care a tender heart can give:
       If these, in her opinion, compensate
       For her so early marrying me late,
       She's welcome to my hand; if not, she's free.
       She would do better elsewhere, I agree.
       I'd rather that another had her hand,
       Than have her marry me at my command.

SGANARELLE. How sweet he is! Sugar and honey yet!

210 ARISTE. At least thank God I am no martinet.
       I'd hate to practice those forbidding ways
       That force children to count their fathers' days.

SGANARELLE. But when their youth is spent in liberty
       You cannot curb them very easily;
       And you will not avoid your share of strife
       When the time comes to change her way of life.

ARISTE. Well, then, why change it?

SGANARELLE.   Why?

ARISTE.   Yes.

SGANARELLE.   I don't
       know.

ARISTE. Is honor wounded when I treat her so?

SGANARELLE. What? If you marry her, she'll be as free
220   As now, when just a girl, she seems to be?

ARISTE. Why not?

SGANARELLE.   You will look kindly, will you not,
  On every ribbon, every beauty spot?

ARISTE. No doubt.

SGANARELLE.   When the whim strikes her, off
    she'll prance
  To every gathering and every dance?

ARISTE. Yes, really.

SGANARELLE.   And the fops will find their way?

ARISTE. What then?

SGANARELLE.   With all their presents and their
    play?

ARISTE. Indeed.

SGANARELLE.   Your wife may listen to their line?

ARISTE. All right.

SGANARELLE.   You'll watch all this without a sign
  Of how these gallant calls give you a pain?

ARISTE. Of course I will.

SGANARELLE.   You're old, and you're insane. 230
              (To ISABELLE)
  Go in; such wicked talk should not be heard.

ARISTE. I mean to trust my wife in deed and word
  And always live my life as I have done.

SGANARELLE. You'll make a fine cuckold; that will
    be fun.

ARISTE. Of course I do not know my destiny;

But I do know that if *you* fail to be
Just that, you will not have yourself to blame,
For that is where all your precautions aim.

SGANARELLE. Go on, laugh all you like—and while
          you can:
240   Practically sixty, and a funny man!

LÉONOR. I'll guarantee him not to meet that fate
If I should be selected as his mate:
He's sure of that; but were I matched with you,
I wouldn't answer for what I might do.

LISETTE. We hate to cheat someone who treats us
          right.
But someone like you—'twould be sheer delight.

SGANARELLE. You, hold your tongue, and hang your
          head for shame.

ARISTE. For her remarks you have yourself to blame.
Farewell. But, brother, take this thought to heart:
250   To lock your wife up is not very smart.
Your servant.   *(Exit.)*

SGANARELLE.   I'm not yours. Oh, what a match!
For each, the other is a perfect catch.
A lovely family! An insane antique
Who plays the rake with a forlorn physique;
A bossy girl who's an accomplished flirt;
Pert servants; no, Wisdom could not convert
This household, and might even go insane,
Counseling sense and reason all in vain.
Such company might easily dispel
260   The seeds of honor lodged in Isabelle;
And so I mean to take the girl away
Into the country for a little stay.

Scene 3. ERGASTE, VALÈRE, SGANARELLE

VALÈRE *(to* ERGASTE, *from backstage).* Ergaste, there
  goes the Argus I abhor,
Strict tutor of the girl that I adore.

SGANARELLE. Sometimes I feel something akin to rage
  At the corrupted morals of this age!

VALÈRE. I must go up to him and say hello.
  He is a man whom I intend to know.

SGANARELLE. You never see the old austerity
  That was the essence of civility;
  Young people hereabouts, unbridled, now   *270*
  Just want . . .

VALÈRE.   He hasn't even seen my bow.

ERGASTE. That's his bad eye, or so it would appear;
  Let's try this side.

SGANARELLE.   I must get out of here.
  From staying in the city there can come
  Only . . .

VALÈRE.   I must gain access to his home.

SGANARELLE. Eh? . . . I thought someone spoke.
  The countryside
Offers few follies that I can't abide.

ERGASTE. Go on.

SGANARELLE.   How's that? . . . I'm hearing things,
  I swear.
There are restraints to girls' amusements there . . . *280*
Is that for me?

ERGASTE.   Go nearer.

SGANARELLE.   There, no fop
  Comes . . . What the . . . ! Still? He bows, and will
    not stop!

VALÈRE. Sir, by saluting you do I intrude?

SGANARELLE. That may be.

VALÈRE.   At the risk of being rude.
  I so desire the honor of knowing you,
  I could not keep from saying how do you do.

SGANARELLE. All right.

VALÈRE.   And adding, in all honesty,
  That I am at your service. Count on me.

SGANARELLE. That's nice.

VALÈRE.   That we are neighbors, as we are,
290   Sir, I attribute to my lucky star.

SGANARELLE. Well, good for you.

VALÈRE.   But come, sir, have you heard
  What circulates at court as the latest word?

SGANARELLE. What do I care?

VALÈRE.   But curiosity
  Is naturally piqued by novelty.
  No doubt you'll see that wonderful affair
  Greeting the birthday of a princely heir?

SGANARELLE. If I wish.

VALÈRE.   Paris really is unique;
  Its pleasures elsewhere you may vainly seek;
  Country people and pastimes are so few. . . .
  How do you spend your time?

SGANARELLE.   I've things to do.   *300*

VALÈRE. Our minds need relaxation, and give way
  Unless we mix with work a little play.
  What do you do before you go to bed?

SGANARELLE. Just as I please.

VALÈRE.   No doubt; that is well
  said;
  And your good sense is fully manifest
  In that you do only what suits you best.
  But that I fear you have too much to do,
  I'd spend an evening now and then with you.

SGANARELLE. Your servant.

Scene 4.   VALÈRE, ERGASTE

VALÈRE.   What do you think about
  this clown?

ERGASTE. He has a brusque retort, a werewolf frown.   *310*

VALÈRE. It drives me mad!

ERGASTE.   What?

VALÈRE.   What? It drives me mad
  To see my love ruled by this cloddish cad,
  This watchful dragon, whose severity
  Will not allow her any liberty.

ERGASTE. That helps your cause, and you have
  grounds for hope
  In that he gives your love so little rope.
  Be steadfast in the course you have begun:

A woman that is watched is halfway won.
A father's or a husband's gloomy wrath
320 Has always smoothed a hopeful lover's path.
I am no flirt; I fear I lack the talent;
And I do not profess to be a gallant;
But I have served these predatory men,
Who always said their greatest joy was when
They found one of these husbands full of spleen,
Who never come back home without a scene,
These arrant brutes who, without rhyme or reason
Check on their wives in every hour and season,
And harshly, arrogantly criticize
330 Their actions right before the suitors' eyes.
"We know," these hunters say, "that here's our
    chance,
And we can ask no better circumstance
Than feminine resentment at these slurs,
In which the witness readily concurs."
In short, few things could augur quite so well
As this severity toward Isabelle.

VALÈRE. But in four months in which my love has
    grown
I haven't got a word with her alone.

ERGASTE. Love lends inventiveness—but not to you;
And if I had been . . .

340 VALÈRE.   But what could you do
When she is never seen without that churl,
And there is not one servant, man or girl,
Who might be tempted by the hope of gain
To give assistance to a luckless swain?

ERGASTE. She hasn't learned yet that you love her so?

VALÈRE. To tell the truth, I simply do not know.
Where'er she goes, escorted by that bear,
Just like her shadow, she has found me there;
Each day my eyes have tried to tell her of
350 The extraordinary power of my love.
My eyes have spoken loud; but who can tell
Whether their speech is known to Isabelle?

ERGASTE. Their language may go by as if unheard
  Without the written or the spoken word.

VALÈRE. How can I put an end to my dejection
  And learn whether she knows of my affection?
  Tell me some way.

ERGASTE.   That is what we must find.
  Let's come into your house and search our mind.

ACT II

Scene 1. ISABELLE, SGANARELLE

SGANARELLE. All right, I know the house, the person too,
360   From the account of him I've had from you.
ISABELLE *(aside)*. Heaven! Be propitious, and do
not condemn
An innocently loving stratagem. .

SGANARELLE. Didn't you say you hear his name's
Valère?

ISABELLE. Yes.

SGANARELLE. Then rest easy, I'll go on from there;
I'll tell this pert young man a thing or two.

ISABELLE *(aside)*. I know, this seems a brazen thing
to do;
But to a proper judge, my harsh abuse
Should be a full and adequate excuse.

Scene 2. SGANARELLE, ERGASTE, VALÈRE

SGANARELLE. Let's waste no time. Here we are.
(Knocks.) What? I say,
Who goes there? . . . Oh, I'm dreaming. . . . Hey
370   there! Hey!
I'm not surprised, knowing what I know now,
That he should greet me so, and scrape and bow;
But this mad hope of his, with all due speed,
I . . .

56

(ERGASTE *comes out of the door abruptly.*)

      Damn the clumsy ox, who pays no heed,
And nearly makes me fall, and blocks the door!

VALÈRE. Sir, I regret . . .

SGANARELLE.   It's you I'm looking for.

VALÈRE. I, sir?

SGANARELLE.   Yes, you. Isn't your name
  Valère?

VALÈRE. Yes.

SGANARELLE. Pray, one word, if you've the time to
  spare.

VALÈRE. There's nothing I would not be glad to do.

SGANARELLE. No, no. I've come to do something for
  you,   *380*
And that is what brings me to see you here.

VALÈRE. Here, sir?

SGANARELLE.   Yes. How astounded you appear!

VALÈRE. I have good reason, and this honor still
  Delights . . .

SGANARELLE.   Forget the honor, if you will.

VALÈRE. Will you not come inside?

SGANARELLE.   There is no need.

VALÈRE. I beg you, sir.

SGANARELLE.   No further; no, indeed.

VALÈRE. Out here I cannot hear a word you say.

SGANARELLE. I will not budge.

VALÈRE.   All right! I must give way.
                              (To ERGASTE)
      Quick, since the gentleman prefers the street,
      Bring a chair here.

390 SGANARELLE.   I will talk on my feet.

VALÈRE. Should I allow you . . . ?

SGANARELLE.   What I must endure!

VALÈRE. I could not bear to treat you like a boor.

SGANARELLE. It is no better to refuse your ear.
      I come to speak to you; you will not hear.

VALÈRE. So, I obey you.

SGANARELLE.   That's the way to be;
      I have no use for such formality.
      Now will you listen?

VALÈRE.   Yes, I gladly do.

SGANARELLE. Then tell me, do you know I'm tutor to
      A young and rather pretty demoiselle
400 Living near by, whose name is Isabelle?

VALÈRE. Yes.

SGANARELLE. Then I fear I do not tell you much.
      But do you know, you whom her beauties touch,
      That I regard her not as just my ward,
      But destine her to share my bed and board?

VALÈRE. No.

SGANARELLE. Well, you know it now. Therefore
    pray cease
Your pointless suit, and leave the girl in peace.

VALÈRE. Who, I, sir?

SGANARELLE.   You. Let's put pretense aside.

VALÈRE. Who says I yearn for your intended bride?

SGANARELLE. Some persons whom I trust to be
    precise.

VALÈRE. But who?

SGANARELLE.   Herself.

VALÈRE.   Herself?

SGANARELLE.   Does that suffice?   *410*
She's loved me from a child, and, as is fit,
Has given me a full account of it;
And furthermore has told me to declare
That since you dog her footsteps everywhere,
Her heart, which your persistence mortifies,
Knows all too well the language of your eyes,
That your secret desires are all too plain,
And that it is superfluous and vain
To labor further to express a plea
Offensive to the love she feels for me.   *420*

VALÈRE. You say it's she herself that sends you here
    To . . .

SGANARELLE. Yes, to give this message, frank and
    clear,
And say that having seen how much you yearn,
She would have let you know her mind in turn
Much sooner, if her heart, so strongly stirred,
Had had someone by whom to send you word;
But that the pains of an extreme constraint
Led her to wish to use me to acquaint

You with the fact that, as by now you see,
430 Her heart is not for anyone but me,
That all your ogling will not help a bit,
And that if you possess your share of wit,
You will make other plans. For now, farewell.
I've told you everything I came to tell.

VALÈRE. Tell me, Ergaste, what do you make of this?

SGANARELLE *(aside).* He surely is surprised!

ERGASTE.   Unless I miss
My guess, you have no reason for dismay;
This hides some subtle mystery, I'd say;
And this is not the message she would send
440 To put a suitor's passion to an end.

SGANARELLE *(aside).* This really hit him hard.

VALÈRE.   You think it strange . . .

ERGASTE. Yes . . . But he's watching; let's get out of
    range.

SGANARELLE. How his confusion shows upon his face!
He cannot take this message with good grace.
Let's talk to Isabelle. In her we find
The effect of education on the mind:
Virtue she loves; her heart is so much in it
That a man's glance offends her in a minute.

Scene 3.   ISABELLE, SGANARELLE

ISABELLE *(alone).* I fear this suitor, on his passion
    bent,
450 May not have grasped my message's intent;
So from these fetters, from this prison here,
I'll send one more to make my meaning clear.

SGANARELLE. Here I am back.

ISABELLE.   Well then?

SGANARELLE.   Your words have had
　A plentiful effect; your man is sad.
　He first attempted to deny his flame;
　But when he learned from whom my message
　　came,
　The news straightway left him abashed and mute,
　And I believe he's through with his pursuit.

ISABELLE. I fear we will not be so fortunate
　And that he still may be importunate.   *460*

SGANARELLE. And on what do you base this fear of
　yours?

ISABELLE. Just now, no sooner had you gone outdoors
　Than, at the window for a breath of air,
　I saw a young man, at the corner there,
　Who first, and in a most audacious way,
　Bade me, from that young malapert, good day,
　And then, right into my own chamber, threw
　A box containing a sealed billet-doux.
　I would have tossed it right back at his feet,
　But he had vanished quickly down the street,   *470*
　And my heart swells with anger at this trick.

SGANARELLE. This is a clever rascal, really slick!

ISABELLE. Duty demands I send right back again
　Letter and box to this accursed swain.
　But for that service, on whom could I call?
　I would not dare to ask you . . .

SGANARELLE.   Not at all.
　You'd show your love and faith; it's all I ask;
　And joyfully my heart accepts this task.
　You obligate me in the strongest way.

ISABELLE. Then here.

SGANARELLE.   That's fine. Let's see. What does
480   he say?

ISABELLE. Heavens! Do not open it.

SGANARELLE.   But I don't see . . .

ISABELLE. He's sure to think that this was done by me.
  A decent girl must never even scan
  A letter sent to her by any man:
  The curiosity she then displays
  Reveals a secret pleasure in his praise;
  And so this letter must, to be genteel,
  Be taken back unopened, under seal,
  To make him recognize today at last
490 That my disdain for him is unsurpassed,
  To lead him to admit he loves in vain,
  And not give way to silliness again.

SGANARELLE. How right she is in everything she says!
  Your virtue charms me, and your prudent ways.
  I see that you have learned my lessons well
  And proved worthy to be my Isabelle.

ISABELLE. Yet I would never tell *you* what to do:
  Open it if you wish; it's up to you.

SGANARELLE. No, not at all; your reasons are too
      good;
500 And I shall do your errand as I should,
  Go on to get a few things off my chest,
  And then return and set your mind at rest.

Scene 4.   SGANARELLE, ERGASTE

SGANARELLE. My heart floats in a beatific whirl
  When I observe the soundness of that girl.
  What a fine sense of honor! What a jewel!
  To treat as treachery a swain's pursual,

To see his note as proof of impudence,
And have me take it back to show offense!
Seeing all this, I'd really like to know
Whether my brother's ward would answer so.   510
Faith! Girls are what we bring them up to be.
Hey!

ERGASTE. What?

SGANARELLE.   Here. Tell your master this from me:
That henceforth he is not to make so bold
As to send letters in a box of gold;
That Isabelle's annoyance is outspoken.
You see, even the seal has not been broken.
He'll gather what she feels about his love
And what success he may be hopeful of.

Scene 5.   VALÈRE, ERGASTE

VALÈRE. What did he just give you, that surly ox?

ERGASTE. Why, sir, this letter, which, inside this box,   520
    Isabelle, I am told, received from you,
    And which, he says, angered her through and
        through;
    So that she sends it promptly back unread.
    Hurry up, read it. What can she have said?

LETTER (VALÈRE *reads.*)
"This letter will no doubt surprise you; and I may
be considered very bold for both the plan of writing
it to you and my way of getting it to you; but I find
myself in a plight that makes me overstep the bounds.
My justified horror at a marriage with which I am
threatened in six days makes me risk anything; and in
my resolve to free myself from that by any means
whatever, I thought I should choose you rather than
despair. Do not think, however, that you are indebted

for everything to my evil destiny: it is not the constraint I am under that has engendered the feelings I have for you; but that is what makes me hurry so to reveal them, and pass over those formalities which feminine decorum demands. It will depend on you alone that I should soon be yours, and I wait only until you signify to me your love's intentions in order to let you know the resolution I have come to; but above all, bear in mind that time is pressing, and that two hearts in love must understand each other's unspoken thoughts."

ERGASTE. Well, sir! How's that for ingenuity?
　　Not bad for a young girl, if you ask me!
　　Would anybody think her capable
　　Of lovers' ruses?

VALÈRE.　　　　　She's adorable!
　　This master stroke of hers on my behalf
530　Augments my love for her again by half,
　　And, added to her beauty's potent sway . . .

ERGASTE. Here comes your dupe; think what you have to say.

Scene 6. SGANARELLE, VALÈRE, ERGASTE

SGANARELLE. Oh! Thrice, four times that edict* do I bless
　　That interdicts all luxury in dress!
　　Husbands may have less worry for their nests,
　　And wives, a limit set to their requests.
　　How I do thank the King for these decrees!
　　And how I wish, for the same husbands' ease,

---

*Of November 27, 1660; one of many given by Louis XIV against luxury in dress.

That the same ban applied to coquetry
As does to lace and to embroidery!   540
I bought a copy, and if all goes well
I shall read it aloud to Isabelle;
And shortly, when her day's affairs are done,
We'll have this for our after-supper fun.
                    (*Seeing* VALÈRE)
Ah! Will you still, you with the yellow locks,
Send tender love-notes in a golden box?
You thought you'd find some silly young coquette,
Keen for intrigue and for an amourette?
You see how she received your proposition:
Believe me, you're just wasting ammunition.   550
She's a good girl; she loves me; you're *de trop:*
Cast your eyes elsewhere, and pack up and go.

VALÈRE. Yes, yes, your merit, everyone agrees,
    Is far too great, and overcomes my pleas;
    And I am mad, although my love is true,
    To vie for Isabelle with such as you.

SGANARELLE. That's right, you're mad.

VALÈRE.   My folly was extreme
    To let her charms foster this silly dream;
    I could not know that my insane ambition
    Would meet such formidable competition.   560

SGANARELLE. You're right.

VALÈRE.   My hope is vanished now indeed;
    Without a murmur, sir, I do concede.

SGANARELLE. And you do well.

VALÈRE.   Alas! It's only right;
    And I see all your virtues shine so bright,
    That, much as I regret, I must defer
    To the fond feelings you arouse in her.

SGANARELLE. Of course.

VALÈRE.   I leave you master of the
    field.
    But this I beg you (on this only yield
    To the request, sir, of a wretched swain;
570   Since you alone cause his excessive pain):
    I conjure you to say to Isabelle
    That if for her I've spent three months in hell,
    My love is spotless, and without a thought
    Toward her of anything but what it ought.

SGANARELLE. Yes.

VALÈRE.   That had it been for me to decide,
    I would have fondly sought her for my bride,
    If destiny, in giving you her heart,
    Had not opposed my ardor from the start.

SGANARELLE. Good, good.

VALÈRE.   That she must not think,
    come what may,
580   My memory of her could fade away;
    That I am destined, till the day I die,
    To love her only, to my final sigh;
    And that if anything can end my suit,
    It is my just respect for your repute.

SGANARELLE. You're speaking wisely; and I'll give
    the sense
    To her of this, which offers no offense.
    But take my word, and strive with might and main
    To drive this passion clean out of your brain.
    Farewell.

ERGASTE (to VALÈRE). A goodly dupe.

SGANARELLE.   It is a shame,
590   This poor wight overpowered by his flame;
    But he himself brought on his misery,
    Trying to seize a fortress held by me.

Scene 7.   SGANARELLE, ISABELLE

SGANARELLE. I've never seen a lover's woe revealed
  Like his, on getting back his note still sealed:
  Losing all hope at last, he now gives way.
  But tenderly he conjured me to say
  That in his love for you he had no thought
  At which your honor might have been distraught,
  And that, had it been for him to decide,
  He would have fondly sought you for his bride,   600
  If destiny, in giving me your heart,
  Had not opposed his ardor from the start;
  That you must not imagine, come what may,
  His memory of you could fade away;
  That he is destined, till the day he die,
  To love you only, to his final sigh;
  And that if anything can end his suit,
  It is his just respect for my repute.
  These are his words: a worthy man, whose flame
  Deserves our pity rather than our blame.   610

ISABELLE *(aside)*. His love does not betray my own
    intent;
  His eyes always declared it innocent.

SGANARELLE. How's that?

ISABELLE.   I find you too compassionate
  To someone whom like death itself I hate;
  And if you loved me quite as you pretended,
  You'd see why I have grounds to be offended.

SGANARELLE. But he knew nothing of your in-
    clinations;
  And judging by his honest declarations,
  His love deserves . . .

ISABELLE.   Tell me, is this a proof,
  His aim to snatch me from beneath your roof?   620

And would a man of honor have recourse
To violence, and marry me by force?
As if I were a girl who would abase
Myself to live on, after such disgrace.

SGANARELLE. How's that?

ISABELLE.   Oh yes! Beyond all miscon-
    struction,
I've learned this traitor plans on an abduction;
I do not know what underhand technique
So soon informed him that within a week
You purpose to confer on me your hand,
630   As only yesterday you said you planned;
But he will try to interfere, they say,
And thus anticipate our wedding day.

SGANARELLE. Indeed that is not good.

ISABELLE.   Pardon me, please.
A worthy man, whose fault is just that he's . . .

SGANARELLE. He's wrong, and this has gone beyond
    a jest.

ISABELLE. Your mildness feeds this folly in his breast.
If you had spoken with asperity,
He'd fear your wrath and my severity;
For it is since he's seen his note rejected
640   That he declares his plan shall be effected;
And, so I've learned, his faith is resolute
That I look fondly on his brazen suit,
That I oppose our marriage as does he,
And would rejoice if I could be set free.

SGANARELLE. He's mad.

ISABELLE.   The role he plays for you is shrewd
And artfully intended to delude.
His own fine words reveal the traitor best.
I am, I must admit it, much distressed

That when a decent life is all I crave,
And to rebuff a lady-killing knave,   *650*
I'm subject to the deep humiliation
That he could harbor such an expectation!

SGANARELLE. There, never fear.

ISABELLE.   I tell you, as for me,
Unless you chasten his effrontery
And find some way in which to rid me soon
Of the attentions of this shameless loon,
I give it up, and will no longer stand
For the affronts I suffer at his hand.

SGANARELLE. Come, don't be so upset. There, little
    wife,
I'll go give him the lecture of his life.   *660*

ISABELLE. But tell him that denial is in vain,
That I know what I know; his aim is plain;
That now, whatever be his enterprise,
I challenge him to take me by surprise;
That if there's anything he plans to do,
He must know what my feelings are toward you,
And that he, to avert catastrophe,
Must not oblige me to repeat my plea.

SGANARELLE. I'll say what's needed.

ISABELLE.   But in such a way
As shows my heart means everything I say.   *670*

SGANARELLE. I'll not forget a thing, I do assure you.

ISABELLE. Impatiently I shall be waiting for you.
So hurry back as quickly as you can;
When you're away, I'm lost without my man.

SGANARELLE. I'll be right back, my child, just as I
    should.
                    (Alone)
How can she be so virtuous and good?
Happy am I! How great is my elation

To find a wife who meets my expectation!
Yes indeed, this is how a wife should be,
680   And not like some who, fond of coquetry,
Listen to all the men, and everywhere
Expose good husbands to the general stare.
Oho! Our enterprising young Don Juan!

Scene 8.   VALÈRE, SGANARELLE, ERGASTE

VALÈRE. What brings you back here, sir?

SGANARELLE.   Your carryings-on.

VALÈRE. What?

SGANARELLE.
                You know very well what's on my mind.
Really, I did not think you were so blind.
You try to gull me with your badinage,
Yet secretly you cling to your mirage.
I've tried to treat you gently from the start,
690   But you force me to say what's in my heart.
Aren't you ashamed that, being what you are,
You carry your effrontery so far,
Aim to abduct an honorable miss,
And threaten her main hope of married bliss?

VALÈRE. Who gave you, sir, this bizarre information?

SGANARELLE. Isabelle did; enough dissimulation.
Through me she bids you note, once and for all,
Her signs of where her preferences fall;
She says your project gives her much offense,
700   That death is better than such insolence,
And that there's going to be a real explosion
Unless you bring this thing to a conclusion.

VALÈRE. If what you tell me now is what she said,
I must admit my loving hope is dead:

All's ended, I can see; her words are clear,
And her decision one I must revere.

SGANARELLE. If? Do you doubt it, and suspect a feint
In my report of her annoyed complaint?
Must she herself then make her meaning plain?
All right, just so you learn your dreams are vain,   *710*
Come in, since you still hope to catch me out:
You'll see her heart is not in any doubt.

Scene 9.   ISABELLE, SGANARELLE, VALÈRE

ISABELLE. What? You could bring him here? What is
     your plan?
Will you take sides against me with this man?
Must I admire his merit, hold him dear,
And patiently endure his visits here?

SGANARELLE. No, I love you too well, my dear, for
     that.
But he treats all my words as idle chat,
Thinks I misrepresent your heart to be
Brimming with hate for him, with love for me.   *720*
And so I hoped that you would cure him of
An error that encourages his love.

ISABELLE. What? Has my soul then not yet spoken
     out
And made my wishes clear beyond all doubt?

VALÈRE. Yes, Madame; all this gentleman has said,
For you, has left confusion in my head:
I doubted, I confess; and your decree,
Determining my passion's destiny,
Concerns me so, I hope you will allow
That once again I hear it from you now.   *730*

ISABELLE. No, you should feel no shock at my
 decision;
 It simply states my feelings with precision;
 And these are based on equity, I find,
 Enough to make me wish to speak my mind.
 I want it to be known to both of you
 That chance offers two objects to my view
 Which, pulling me in different directions,
 Excite my heart with opposite affections.
 For one, whom I devotedly admire,
740 Esteem and tenderness alike conspire;
 The other one, for all his adoration,
 Has my antipathy and execration;
 To me the presence of the one brings joy,
 Giving me happiness without alloy,
 Whereas the other, by his very sight,
 Fills me with hatred and with secret spite.
 The one of them I would most gladly wed;
 The other—I would much rather be dead.
 But I have shown my sentiments too long,
750 The torment that I suffer is too strong;
 The one I love must act with speed and care,
 Reduce his hated rival to despair,
 And by a happy marriage set me free
 From torment worse than death can ever be.

SGANARELLE. Yes, yes, darling, your wish is my
 intent.

ISABELLE. Thus only shall I ever be content.

SGANARELLE. You shall be soon.

ISABELLE.   A girl may be unwise
 To speak so candidly, I realize.

SGANARELLE. No, not at all.

ISABELLE.   But in my present plight
760 I think a certain freedom is my right;
 And surely without shame I can speak straight
 To him whom I consider as my mate.

SGANARELLE. Yes, my poor itty-bitty turtledove.

ISABELLE. For heaven's sake, then, let him prove his
  love.

SGANARELLE. There, kiss my hand.

ISABELLE.   Let him with all dispatch
  Arrange an eagerly awaited match,
  And here accept in all sincerity
  My vow never to hear another's plea.
  (She pretends to kiss SGANARELLE, *and instead
          gives* VALÈRE *her hand to kiss.)*

SGANARELLE. Oh! little honeybear, poor little pet,
  You needn't languish long; now don't you fret: 770
  Hush, now.
              (To VALÈRE*)*
          You see, her love for me is true;
  She's not just saying what I tell her to.

VALÈRE. Well, Madame! You are candid, anyhow:
  I see from this just what I must do now,
  And soon I'll free you from the insolence
  Of one whose presence gives you such offense.

ISABELLE. No greater pleasure could you offer me,
  For this is a repellent sight to see,
  Odious, hateful; better to be blind . . .

SGANARELLE. Oh!

ISABELLE.   Do I hurt you when I speak my
  mind?   780
  Do I . . . ?

SGANARELLE. Good Lord, no, that's not what I mean;
  But when I look at his pathetic mien,
  I think you are too lavish with your spite.

ISABELLE. I cannot show too much in such a plight.

VALÈRE. Yes, you shall be content: three days, no
  more,
Shall rid you of the person you abhor.

ISABELLE. So be it. Farewell.

SGANARELLE.   I'm sorry for your lot,
  But . . .

VALÈRE.   I have no complaint, sir, indeed not:
  Madame is surely fair to both us two,
790 And I shall strive to make her wish come true.
  Farewell.

SGANARELLE.   Poor lad, he's overcome
  with woe.
            (To VALÈRE)
  Embrace me. You are both alike, you know.

Scene 10.   ISABELLE, SGANARELLE

SGANARELLE. He's to be pitied.

ISABELLE.   Not if you ask me.

SGANARELLE. Your love touches me to the last
  degree,
My sweet, and its reward must be unique:
Why make you be impatient for a week?
I'll marry you tomorrow, and invite . . .

ISABELLE. Tomorrow?

SGANARELLE.   Bashfulness hides your delight;
  You're overjoyed; I know how you react,
800 And that you wish it were an accomplished fact.

ISABELLE. But . . .

SGANARELLE.   For this marriage let us now prepare.

ISABELLE. Oh Heaven, give me help in my despair!

ACT III

Scene 1. ISABELLE

ISABELLE. A hundred times I'd rather lose my life
    Than let myself be made my guardian's wife;
    And since I seek just to escape this fate,
    I hope my censors will commiserate.
    It's dark, time flies; come on, I now must dare
    Entrust my fortunes to my dear Valère.

Scene 2. SGANARELLE, ISABELLE

SGANARELLE. I'm back. Tomorrow they will
    expedite . . .

ISABELLE. Heaven!

SGANARELLE.   You, darling? At this time of
810   night?
    Where are you going? When I left, you said
    That you were tired and going up to bed,
    And asked, finding yourself weary and worn,
    To sleep on undisturbed until the morn.

ISABELLE. That's true; but . . .

SGANARELLE.   What?

ISABELLE.   It's awkward to
    explain,
    And I'm afraid you'll think me quite insane.

76

SGANARELLE. What is this all about?

ISABELLE.   A mystery.
You see, my sister first moved in with me,
Then by her pleas effected my removal,
Although her reasons met my disapproval.   *820*

SGANARELLE. What?

ISABELLE.   Just imagine, she is smitten badly
With our young banished swain.

SGANARELLE.   Valère?

ISABELLE.   But madly.
Unparalleled is her infatuation,
And you can judge of its immoderation:
Since all alone, and at this hour, she came
To tell me all about her fretful flame,
Saying that, she will certainly expire
Unless she can obtain her heart's desire,
That they had lived for upwards of a year
Bound by a passion secret but sincere,   *830*
And that they'd even sworn by heaven above
That marriage soon should consecrate their love.

SGANARELLE. That wicked girl!

ISABELLE.   That learning the despair
To which my coldness has reduced Valère,
She came to ask me if she might console
Him for a blow that must distress his soul;
If from my window, speaking in my name,
She might hold conversation with her flame,
Recall to him, while mimicking my voice,
Sweet sentiments at which he may rejoice,   *840*
And in short make herself the addressee
Of the affection that he feels for me.

SGANARELLE. And what do you think . . . ?

ISABELLE.   I'm fit to be tied.

"What," said I, "sister, have you lost all pride?
Aren't you ashamed to be under the sway
Of such a man, who changes every day?
Can you forget your sex, and be untrue
To one whom Heaven has ordained for you?"

SGANARELLE. It serves him right, and I am overjoyed.

850 ISABELLE. I thought of reasons—I was so annoyed—
To reprehend her baseness, as is right,
And put off her requests at least tonight;
But she expressed such burning hopes and fears,
Uttered such sighs, and shed so many tears,
Harped so on what would be her desperation
If I obstructed her infatuation,
That finally I could not but give in;
And mindful that it might be thought a sin
To sponsor such a tryst as this would be,
860 I meant to ask Lucrèce to stay with me,
Whose virtues you extol so every day;
But you came back as I was on my way.

SGANARELLE. No, I'll not have this, in my house, at
      night.
If just my brother were concerned, all right;
But someone might observe you from below;
And she on whom my person I bestow
Must not just have a modest disposition
But be beyond all possible suspicion.
Let's turn the hussy out; as for her passion . . .

870 ISABELLE. No, no, we must not do it in this fashion;
And she would have good reason to complain
Of counting on my secrecy in vain.
Since go she must, and that without delay,
At least wait while *I* send her on her way.

SGANARELLE. Do that.

ISABELLE.   But you must not be seen or heard.
Just deign to watch her leave without a word.

SGANARELLE. Yes, I'll restrain my glee for love of
    you;
    But from the time you've bid her fond adieu,
    I shall be off; I'm itching to declare
    To poor Ariste this whole sordid affair.   880

ISABELLE. I conjure you, my name must not be
    known.
    Good night; right now I'm going up alone.

SGANARELLE. Until tomorrow.—I can hardly wait
    To tell my brother of this twist of fate!
    He's got a bellyful, poor simpleton;
    For twenty crowns I wouldn't miss this fun.

ISABELLE (inside the house). Yes, sister, to your grief
    I'm not insensible;
    But what you ask of me is reprehensible:
    My honor's dear to me, and it's at stake.
    Farewell: be on your way, for goodness' sake.   890

SGANARELLE. My, she is angry! I need hear no more.
    For fear she may come back, I'll lock the door.

ISABELLE (on her way out, veiled). O Heaven, be
    gracious!
    Aid my faltering wit!

SGANARELLE. Where is she bound? I'll follow along
    a bit.

ISABELLE. In my distress, darkness is on my side.

SGANARELLE. Right to her lover's house! Has she
    no pride?

Scene 3.   VALÈRE, SGANARELLE, ISABELLE

VALÈRE *(coming out hastily)*. Yes, yes, tonight some-
    how I mean to try
  To speak . . . Who's there?

ISABELLE.   Quiet, Valère, it's I;
  I got ahead of you; it's Isabelle.

900 SGANARELLE. It is not, and you lie, you Jezebel:
  She lives in honor while you live in shame,
  And falsely you've assumed her voice and name.

ISABELLE. But unless you have marriage as your
    goal . . .

VALÈRE. That's the one aspiration of my soul;
  And here I swear that if you'll have it so,
  Where'er you'll marry me, there will I go.

SGANARELLE. Poor self-deluded blockhead!

VALÈRE.   Never fear:
  Your guardian's power I defy, my dear;
  And long before he could rob me of you,
  A thousand times I'd pierce him through and
910   through.

SGANARELLE. Ah! I assure you that I do not crave
  To take from you this wretch, this passion's slave;
  Your plighted troth gives me no jealousy,
  And you *shall* wed her, if it's up to me.
  Yes, let's break up their little tête-à-tête:
  I so revere her father's memory yet,
  And labor so her sister to protect,
  That I must try to save her self-respect.
        (Knocks on the CONSTABLE'S *door.)*
  Hello!

Scene 4.   SGANARELLE, CONSTABLE, NOTARY,
ATTENDANT

CONSTABLE.   Who's there?

SGANARELLE.   Constable, how do you do.
Here, in your robe, sir, I have need of you: *920*
Please bring along your light and follow me.

CONSTABLE. We were just . . .

SGANARELLE.   This is an emergency.

CONSTABLE. What?

SGANARELLE.
                    See that house? We must sur-
    prise inside
Two persons who must soon be man and bride:
A girl of ours, misled, lured to his house
By one Valère, who vowed to be her spouse.
She is both virtuously and nobly born,
But . . .

CONSTABLE. In that case, sir, you've no cause to
    mourn,
Since here we have a notary.

SGANARELLE.   You do?

NOTARY. Notary royal.

CONSTABLE.   Honorable too.   *930*

SGANARELLE. Of course. Now, quiet, be on the *qui
    vive;*
Go in this door; allow no one to leave.
Your trouble shall be lavishly repaid;
But do not let *them* grease your palm instead.

CONSTABLE. What? Do you think a man of my
    profession . . . ?

SGANARELLE. I meant no harm. Don't get the wrong
    impression.
I'll get my brother here immediately.
Just bring the torch and light the way for me.
That mild and wrathless man, I'll cheer him up.
            (Knocks at ARISTE'S door.)
Hello!

Scene 5.   ARISTE, SGANARELLE

940 ARISTE. Who's knocking? You, brother? What's up?

SGANARELLE. Come on, wise guardian, supersenile
    knight,
I want to have you see a pretty sight.

ARISTE. How's that?

SGANARELLE.   I've news you were not waiting
    for.

ARISTE. What?

SGANARELLE.   May I ask, where is your Léonor?

ARISTE. Why ask me that? Gone dancing, I believe,
At a friend's house.

SGANARELLE.   Yes. Of course. By your
    leave,
I'll take you to your dancing demoiselle.

ARISTE. What are you getting at?

SGANARELLE.   You've trained her well:

"We should not be too strict and too severe;
Better rely on gentleness and cheer;   950
Suspicions, locks, and bars are all misplaced,
And will not keep our girls and women chaste;
We egg them on by such austerity;
Their sex demands a little liberty."
Your minx has taken all she wants, that's plain;
Her virtue's grown exceedingly humane.

ARISTE. What in the world is all this leading to?

SGANARELLE. My elder brother, this is made for you;
And fifty crowns would be a modest price
To see you thus repaid for being nice.   960
It's plain which sister had the better tutor:
One flees, the other chases, this same suitor.

ARISTE. You love to talk in riddles, I declare.

SGANARELLE. Oh, she went dancing—with Monsieur
   Valère;
I saw her go into his house tonight,
And in his arms she now takes her delight.

ARISTE. Who?

SGANARELLE.   Léonor.

ARISTE.   Come, no more joking, please.

SGANARELLE. Joking? . . . You think I'm talking
   pleasantries?
Poor soul, I'm telling you this one time more
That young Valère has got your Léonor,   970
And that he was engaged to this same belle
Before he started chasing Isabelle.

ARISTE. This makes so little sense you cannot mean it.

SGANARELLE. He won't believe it even when he's
   seen it.
It makes me mad. My word, age does no good
When this (pointing to his forehead) is lacking.

ARISTE.   What,
  brother, you would . . . ?

SGANARELLE. I would have nothing. Only follow me:
  Your mind shall be contented presently;
  You'll see whether I'm fooling; soon you'll know
980   That they became engaged a year ago.

ARISTE. I can't believe that she would thus consent
  To marry, and not tell me her intent,
  I, who, since she was but a little child,
  Have always been considerate and mild,
  And who have always, without reservation,
  Let her follow her every inclination.

SGANARELLE. Well, well, your eyes shall judge of
    the affair.
  The constable and notary are there:
  Her honor, which is what we're anxious for,
990   Is something that this marriage can restore;
  For you are not so doting, I believe,
  As still to want to wed your tarnished Eve,
  Unless you have some more fine theories
  To guard against the gossips' pleasantries.

ARISTE. I never will accept the weakling's part
  Of wanting to possess a loveless heart.
  But still I can't believe . . .

SGANARELLE.   You talk on so,
  We never shall be done; come on, let's go.

        Scene 6.   CONSTABLE, NOTARY, SGANARELLE,
                          ARISTE

CONSTABLE. There is no reason for compulsion here,
1000   Gentlemen; calm your passions, have no fear;
  If all you seek is marriage for these two,

You'll find them both impatient for it too;
Already young Valère has certified,
In writing, that he'll take her as his bride.

ARISTE. The girl . . .

CONSTABLE.   Locked in, and won't come out,
    she swears,
Unless your wishes coincide with theirs.

Scene 7.   CONSTABLE, VALÈRE, NOTARY,
SGANARELLE, ARISTE

VALÈRE *(at the window)*. No, gentlemen; indeed, until
    I hear
That you agree, no one shall enter here.
You know me; I have signed the document
On which you may see proof of my intent.   *1010*
If you consent that she shall marry me,
Sign it yourself, to show that you agree;
If not, believe me, you must take my life
Before you take away my darling wife.

SGANARELLE. No, we don't want to part you from
    your belle.

                (Aside)
He still believes that she is Isabelle.
Let's keep it so.

ARISTE.   But is it Léonor?

SGANARELLE. Shut up.

ARISTE.   But . . .

SGANARELLE.   Hush.

ARISTE.   I want to know . . .

SGANARELLE.   What for?
I tell you, please be quiet.

VALÈRE.   Come what may,
1020 Isabelle is my lawful fiancée;
And I am not, in fact, so bad a choice
That you can only blame, and not rejoice.

ARISTE. But what he says is not . . .

SGANARELLE.   Be quiet, you.
I will explain. Yes, without more ado,
We both consent that you take as your bride
The girl that we shall find with you inside.

CONSTABLE. Those are the terms the deed is drawn in, sir;
The name is blank, since we have not seen her.
The girl can sign it later. Now, you sign.

VALÈRE. All right with me.

1030 SGANARELLE.   And I insist. That's fine.
Oh, what a laugh! This will make history.
Brother, sign first . . .

ARISTE.   But all this mystery . . .

SGANARELLE. Damn it, you poor dunce, sign. I'll hear no more.

ARISTE. He says it's Isabelle; you, Léonor.

SGANARELLE. Suppose it is, brother, don't you agree
That each should make her choice completely free?

ARISTE. I do indeed.

SGANARELLE.   Then sign; for so do I.

ARISTE. Yes; but I don't see . . .

SGANARELLE.   You will by and by.

CONSTABLE. We shall be back.

SGANARELLE.   Now then, let me
   explain
What's happening.

Scene 8.   LÉONOR, LISETTE, SGANARELLE, ARISTE

LÉONOR.   Oh, what an utter pain!   1040
   How deadly dull I find these young gallants!
   It's on account of them I fled the dance.

LISETTE. Each one tries hard to please your eye, I'm
   sure.

LÉONOR. And that is just what I cannot endure.
   I'd rather hear good plain talk any day
   Than all the silly empty things they say.
   To them their blond wig is a smashing hit;
   And they assume they are the soul of wit
   When they come up with some ironic jest
   To the effect that older men love best.   1050
   And *I* prefer an older man's true zeal
   To all the love these youngsters claim they feel.
   But do my eyes deceive me . . . ?

SGANARELLE *(to ARISTE).*   Yes, that's true.
   Ah! Now I see her, and her servant too.

ARISTE. Léonor, I have reason for complaint:
   You know I've never used you with constraint;
   You have heard me a hundred times insist
   That you are free to love whome'er you list;
   And yet your heart, without concern for me,
   Has plighted faith and love in secrecy.   1060
   I am not sorry for my gentleness,

But your behavior gives me real distress;
And this was not a kindly thing to do
To one who cares so tenderly for you.

LÉONOR. I do not know what makes you speak this
way;
But as I was before, I am today;
Nothing can ever change my high esteem
For you alone; another bond would seem
A crime; and were my wishes satisfied,
1070 Tomorrow I would gladly be your bride.

ARISTE. Then, brother, what's this talk of strange
affairs?

SGANARELLE *(to* LÉONOR*)*. You mean you're not just
coming from Valère's?
You've not been pining for him, Mademoiselle,
And just today confessed to Isabelle?

LÉONOR. Such a portrayal is a real surprise.
Who can have fabricated all these lies?

Scene 9.   ISABELLE, VALÈRE, CONSTABLE, NOTARY,
ERGASTE, LISETTE, LÉONOR, SGANARELLE,
ARISTE

ISABELLE. Sister, I beg you to be slow to blame
If by my liberties I've smirched your name.
A sudden and appalling situation
1080 Inspired me to this shameful fabrication:
Though your example censures such a passion,
Fate has not treated us in the same fashion.
(To SGANARELLE*)*
To you, sir, I make no apology:
My action favors you as well as me.
We were not meant to share a common life:
Let's say I don't deserve to be your wife;

An honor such as that would be too great,
And I preferred to seek another mate.

VALÈRE. Sir, beyond words I glory and rejoice
To accept from you the lady of my choice.   *1090*

ARISTE. You'll have to swallow this with grace and
tact,
Brother: your training brought about this act.
I'm sorry for your lot, for I predict
You won't be pitied, though you have been tricked.

LISETTE. I'm grateful to him for this whole affair,
Which shows the outcome of his kind of care.

LÉONOR. I guess this action merits no acclaim,
But I cannot view it with any blame.

ERGASTE. The stars have made of him a cuckold born;
He's lucky to get off without a horn.   *1100*

SGANARELLE. I can't get over it; I am astounded;
Such treachery leaves all my wits confounded;
And I do not believe even the devil
Can match this wench's aptitude for evil.
For her I would have put my hand in fire:
Who can trust womankind, since she's a liar?
The best of them excels at machination;
Their sex was born to be the world's damnation.
To that deceitful sex I say farewell,
And heartily consign them all to hell.   *1110*

ERGASTE. Good.

ARISTE.   Come with me. Valère, we shall
assuage,
Tomorrow, if we can, my brother's rage.

LISETTE *(to the audience).* If any husband is a churl-
ish fool,
This is the place to send him—to our school.

The School for Wives

THE SCHOOL FOR WIVES

A verse comedy in five acts, first performed December 26, 1662, at the Théâtre du Palais-Royal by Molière's company, the Troupe de Monsieur. Arnolphe was played by Molière, Agnès by Catherine de Brie, and probably Horace by La Grange, Georgette by Mlle. de La Grange, Alain by Brécourt.

This is Molière's first great comedy and one of his best-loved. He had been married for ten months to young Armande Béjart; in age and presumably in passion he was an Arnolphe to her Agnès. Returning to the theme of *The School for Husbands,* he eliminates the benign older man (who in a sense survives in Chrysalde) and his ward, and concentrates on the domineering guardian and his ward. Sganarelle and Léonor are metamorphosed into two of the most fascinating characters in comic literature, Arnolphe and Agnès. Arnolphe is no mere grouch like Sganarelle, but the epitome of comic *hubris,* relishing and recording other men's marital misadventures, sneering at cuckolds, eager to hear of Horace's amorous fortunes, manipulating people, knowing all the answers. He knows how to avoid cuckoldry, and has taken elaborate measures to keep Agnès dependent and stupid. Nor is he merely comic; he is also polite, affable, generous, and in the end poignant, when caught in his own trap and hopelessly in love with his ward, who has no love for him. Agnès is one of the finest portraits ever drawn of a young girl who is just becoming a woman. Naïve at the outset, as Arnolphe has made her, she unfolds, with experience and love, like a flower—or like some other wild thing, with a single-track dedication to her aims and rights that leaves little room for pity. We are on her side, for she has

93

been a victim and remains one during most of the play; but once Arnolphe fails in love with her, her natural lack of concern for him is a little frightening. From then on it is hard not to see Armande in her and Molière in Arnolphe.

Few of Molière's plays are more structured, and more curiously so. The whole plot hangs on the nobiliary vanity that makes Arnolphe insist on being called Monsieur de la Souche (in this translation, Monsieur de La Forêt), so that Horace confides everything to his rival, and yet wins out. There is almost no action in the usual sense, but simply a series of recitals by Horace to Arnolphe of his love for Agnès, his plans to further it, and the results of Monsieur de La Forêt's counter-stratagems. The recital was a common device in the theater of Molière's day, but normally used only when decorum or plausibility ruled out onstage action. Molière, though usually rather indifferent to French neoclassical conventions, uses this one avidly in this play. His main reason, sketched in the *Critique,* is typical of his values and those of his time: the recital technique, by which the ever-successful young underdog not only confounds the apparently omnipotent older guardian but also, unaware of his double identity, tells him all about it, is a superbly exploited source of comic irony and focuses our attention not on the action itself but, much more interestingly, on the reaction to it of the increasingly pathetic know-it-all, Arnolphe.

The great and instant success of the play led to such a storm of criticism that Molière's next two plays, *The Critique of the School for Wives* and *The Versailles Impromptu,* were dramatic replies to his critics.

THE SCHOOL FOR WIVES

CHARACTERS

ARNOLPHE, *also known as Monsieur de La Forêt*
AGNÈS, *an innocent girl, brought up by Arnolphe*
HORACE, *in love with Agnès*
ALAIN, *a peasant, servant to Arnolphe*
GEORGETTE, *a peasant woman, servant to Arnolphe*
CHRYSALDE, *a friend of Arnolphe*
ENRIQUE, *brother-in-law of Chrysalde*
ORONTE, *Horace's father, a great friend of Arnolphe*
NOTARY

The scene is a house and garden in a small square in a town.

ACT I

Scene 1.   CHRYSALDE, ARNOLPHE

CHRYSALDE. You've come, you say, to offer her
    your hand?

ARNOLPHE. Yes, I'll complete tomorrow what I've
    planned.

CHRYSALDE. We're here alone, unheard: I think we
    may
  Therefore say freely what we have to say.

95

May I open my heart and not dissemble?
On your behalf your project makes me tremble.
In short, no matter how you view the fact,
To take a wife, for you, is a rash act.

ARNOLPHE. True, my fine friend. Perhaps at home
        you see
10   Cause to fear that disaster threatens me;
      The horns that on your brow I think you've got
      You take for marriage's predestined lot.

CHRYSALDE. Against these blows of chance there's
        no defense;
      To me our vain precautions make no sense.
      My fear for you springs from your mocking scorn,
      Which countless hapless husbands now have borne;
      For as you know, your satire, after all,
      Has hit all benedicts, both great and small;
      And everywhere you go, your chief delight
20   Is in the secrets that you bring to light.

ARNOLPHE. Fine. Is there anywhere another town
      Where husbands take such mishaps lying down?
      Is there a species that we do not see?
      And all accommodated to a tee.
      One piles up wealth, with which his wife endows
      Those who cause horns to grow upon his brows;
      Another, happier but just as vile,
      Watches his wife take presents, with a smile;
      No jealous fancy ever gives him pause,
30   Because she says her virtue is the cause.
      One loudly—and as vainly—makes a scene,
      The other lets things go their way serene,
      And when she has a caller, never rude,
      Gets coat and gloves, not wanting to intrude.
      One clever female tells a soothing tale
      About her gallant to her doting male,
      Who pities his poor rival's labor lost,
      While that same rival labors to his cost.
      Another, strangely wealthy, stoutly claims
40   She won the extra money playing games;
      What games, the husband lacks the wit to know,

And thanks the Lord, from whom all blessings
    flow.
In short, when all around lies comedy,
May I not laugh at all these things I see?
When I see fools . . .

CHRYSALDE.   Yes, laugh at all the rest.
    But don't forget: he who laughs last laughs best.
    I hear how people talk; some make a sport
    Of passing on each scandalous report;
    But though I hear stories I might well quote,
    I never do allow myself to gloat.   50
    I hold my peace; and though upon occasion
    I may condemn some kinds of toleration,
    Although I've no intention to abide
    The things that leave some husbands satisfied,
    I prefer not to speak my mind straight out;
    For all of us must fear a turnabout,
    And we should never, since each case is new,
    Swear rashly what we will, or will not, do.
    Therefore if fortune, which ignores our vows,
    Should plant a cuckold's horns upon my brows,   60
    My past behavior makes me almost sure
    I'd have just quiet laughter to endure,
    And that a few good people in this city
    Might even say they thought it was a pity.
    But you, my friend, would find it otherwise;
    You run a real risk of a rude surprise.
    Since you have been prolific in your sneers
    At husbands too indulgent to their dears,
    Since you have always been so quick to blast,
    Beware of giving them their turn at last;   70
    For if you offer them the slightest ground,
    They'll trumpet it to hear for miles around,
    And . . .

ARNOLPHE. Lord, my friend, please don't be so upset:
    The one who catches *me* is not born yet.
    I know each cunning trick that women use
    Upon their docile men, each subtle ruse,
    And how they exercise their sleight-of-hand.
    And so against this mishap I have planned.

My guarantee against such accident
80   Is marriage to a perfect innocent.

CHRYSALDE. Why such reliance on a simpleton?

ARNOLPHE. A man's no simpleton to marry one.
No doubt your wife's virtue matches her charm,
But a smart woman is cause for alarm;
And I know just what certain men have paid
For marrying an overgifted maid.
I should take on some lady of *esprit,*
Full of her literary coterie,
Dashing off prose and verse in tender bits,
90   Attended by the marquises and wits,
While I, known as "the husband of Madame,"
Play the unworshiped saint *ad nauseam?*
No, you can have your lofty minds and such;
A woman who's a writer knows too much.
I mean that mine shall not be so sublime,
And shall not even know what's meant by rhyme;
If she plays *corbillon**—that parlor game
Where everything in the basket ends the same—
Let her reply "Cream tart" to "What goes in?"
100   In short, I'd have her ignorant as sin;
And frankly, it's enough for her to know
How to spin, love me, say her prayers, and sew.

CHRYSALDE. To have a stupid wife, then: that's your
          whim?

ARNOLPHE. She can be ugly, so her wits are dim,
But not a brain, even if she's a beauty.

CHRYSALDE. Beauty and wit . . .

*The popular game of *corbillon* ("basket"), much like the English crambo, involved answering the question *"Dans mon corbillon qu'y met-on?"* ("What do we put in my basket?") by a
word ending in -*on*—which *"tarte à la crème"* ("cream tart") of
course is not.

ARNOLPHE.   I'll take a sense of duty.

CHRYSALDE. But how do you expect an idiot
  To learn what is her duty and what's not?
  For one thing, it must be a dreadful bore
  To have a fool around you evermore.   *110*
  Then, do you think your theory is sound
  And will protect your brow from being crowned?
  Now, when a clever woman goes astray,
  At least she knows, and means it just that way;
  A stupid one may fall in the same snare
  Not wishing to and wholly unaware.

ARNOLPHE. That profound thought is met by
    Rabelais,*
  Who to Panurge has Pantagruel say:
  "Urge on me any but a witless bride,
  Talk me to death, preach on till Whitsuntide: *120*
  When you're all done, you'll be amazed to find
  That nothing you have said has changed my mind."

CHRYSALDE. I say no more.

ARNOLPHE.   Right. Every man his way.
  I have my own to choose a fiancée.
  I'm rich enough, I think, to have felt free
  To have my wife owe everything to me.
  From her dependency has come submission;
  She cannot flaunt her wealth or her position.
  When she was four, one of a numerous brood,
  I came to love her modest rectitude;   *130*
  Seeing her mother too poor to afford
  Her care, I asked to take her for my ward;
  And that good peasant woman acquiesced
  With much relief, finding it for the best.
  In a small convent, undisturbed by man,
  I had her raised according to my plan,

---

*Chapter 5 of Book III of *Gargantua and Pantagruel* is the
source of lines 120–2, but not of 119. Arnolphe takes from Rabelais only what he can use.

Which was to have them try as best they could
To keep her ignorant and therefore good.
Thank God, the outcome answered my intent,
140   And now she has grown up so innocent
That I bless Heaven for having been so kind
As to give me the wife I had in mind.
And so I brought her out; and since my home
Is one to which all kinds of people come,
Since we must never trust the wayward heart,
I've put her in this other house, apart,
And, to preserve her native purity,
Given her servants as naïve as she.
Now you will ask me: why this long narration?
150   —To let you know of my deliberation.
So, as a faithful friend, I now invite
You to come sup with her and me tonight
To see if, when you've had a chance to tell,
You will not think that I have chosen well.

CHRYSALDE. Agreed.

ARNOLPHE.   And there you can, with con-
    fidence,
Judge of her person and her innocence.

CHRYSALDE. In that regard, what you have been
    relating
Cannot . . .

ARNOLPHE.   You'll see, I have been understanding.
I simply marvel at her naïvetés,
160   And could die laughing at the things she says.
Just fancy that, a day or two ago,
She came to me distraught, wanting to know—
So innocent, so candid and sincere—
If children are begotten through the ear.

CHRYSALDE. I'm glad, Seigneur Arnolphe . . .

ARNOLPHE.   Come
    now, for shame!
Must you forever call me by that name?

CHRYSALDE. It always will come out, do what I may,
  And never your Monsieur de La Forêt.
  At forty-two, what led you thus to dump
  The name Arnolphe, and take that of some
    stump—   *170*
  Rotten and old—upon your property,
  To make a title of nobility?

ARNOLPHE. Because that's now my name among my
    peers,
  Also because it better suits my ears.

CHRYSALDE. But why give up your true ancestral
    name
  To take this empty one? It seems a shame.
  Yet this is what most people itch to do;
  And, though this tale does not apply to you,
  I know a peasant whom they call Fat Pete,
  Who owned a tiny lot, a few square feet,   *180*
  Circled it with a ditch to be genteel,
  And from it took the name Monsieur de l'Isle.*

ARNOLPHE. Such an example I could gladly spare;
  But de La Forêt is the name I bear.
  It makes good sense to me; I like its flavor;
  And those who spurn it do me a disfavor.

CHRYSALDE. Yet most folk still address you as before,
  Even on letters coming to your door.

ARNOLPHE. I don't much mind from those who do
    not know;
  But you . . .

CHRYSALDE.   All right, agreed; it shall be so.   *190*
  And I shall try to school my mouth to say
  Not Arnolphe, but Monsieur de La Forêt.

_____

*The lesser Corneille, Thomas, a writer of tragedies like his
brother Pierre, had taken this name. This remark of Molière's
naturally intensified the bad feeling between him and the
Corneilles.

ARNOLPHE. Goodbye. I'll stop here for a word or two,
To tell them I am back and learn what's new.

CHRYSALDE (aside, leaving). My word, he is completely
daft, I swear!

ARNOLPHE. On certain matters he's just not all there.
How strange it is to see with how much passion
People see things only in their own fashion!
Hey, open up!

Scene 2.   ALAIN, GEORGETTE, ARNOLPHE

ALAIN (opens an upper window). Who's there?

ARNOLPHE.   I'm sure that
they
200 Will welcome me after ten days away.

ALAIN. Who's that?

ARNOLPHE.   Me.

ALAIN.   Georgette!

GEORGETTE (opens a lower window). Well?

ALAIN.   Open up,
see!

GEORGETTE. You open up!

ALAIN.   No, you!

GEORGETTE.   Oh no, not me!

(Slams window shut.)

ALAIN. Neither will I.

(Slams window shut.)

ARNOLPHE.   I could stand here and freeze
Through this routine of theirs. Hey, come on,
    please.

GEORGETTE *(opening window).* Who's there?

ARNOLPHE.   Your master.

GEORGETTE.   Alain!

ALAIN *(opening window).*   What?

GEORGETTE.   The squire.
Open.

ALAIN. No, you.

GEORGETTE.   I'm blowing on the fire.

ALAIN. I'm trying to save the sparrow from the cat.

            (Both windows shut.)

ARNOLPHE. Whichever doesn't open up like *that*
Shall get no food for four days, to the day.

    (ALAIN and GEORGETTE appear at the door.)

GEORGETTE. Why are you coming when I'm on my
    way?   *210*

ALAIN. Why you, not me? That's a fine strodegy!

GEORGETTE. Get out of here.

ALAIN.   No, you get out; let me.

    (ALAIN and GEORGETTE run to the gate.)

GEORGETTE. I want to open the gate.

ALAIN.   And I do too.

GEORGETTE. You will not.

ALAIN.   You won't either.

GEORGETTE.   Nor will you

ARNOLPHE. So, on they go, and I am waiting yet.

ALAIN. It's me, Alain, sir.

GEORGETTE.   No, it's me, Georgette.

ALAIN. If I did not respect our master's frown,
    I'd . . .

(Swings at GEORGETTE, *who ducks; hits* ARNOLPHE
instead.)

ARNOLPHE. Damn it!

ALAIN.   Pardon me.

ARNOLPHE.   You stupid clown!

ALAIN. She is too, sir . . .

ARNOLPHE.   Now, both of you, enough.
220 Listen and answer. No more silly stuff.
    Well, Alain, how is everybody here?

ALAIN. Why, sir . . .
    *(*ARNOLPHE *removes* ALAIN'S *hat;* ALAIN *replaces it.)*
                    Why, sir, we . . . *(Same
    business)*
    Thank the Lord, sir, we're . . . *(Same business)*

ARNOLPHE. Lord! Will you never learn how to
    behave?
    Take off your hat to me, you saucy knave!

ALAIN. You're right, I'm wrong.

ARNOLPHE *(to* ALAIN).   Ask Agnès down,
  then, lad.
          (To GEORGETTE)
  After I left, did she seem pretty sad?

GEORGETTE. Sad? No.

ARNOLPHE.   No?

GEORGETTE.   Yes, she did.

ARNOLPHE.   Then why . . . ?

GEORGETTE.   Good lack,
  She kept thinking she saw you coming back;
  Each time a horse or mule or donkey passed
  She was quite sure that it was you at last.   *230*

Scene 3.   AGNÈS, ALAIN, GEORGETTE, ARNOLPHE

ARNOLPHE. Her work in hand! That's a good sign.
  Well then!
  Agnès, my trip is done; I'm back again.
  Do you like that?

AGNÈS.   God be praised, sir, I do.

ARNOLPHE. And I am very pleased to see you too.
  I trust you're well, just as you seem to be?

AGNÈS. Yes, but those fleas: all night they bothered
  me.

ARNOLPHE. You'll soon have someone to drive them
  away.

AGNÈS. You'll do me pleasure.

ARNOLPHE.   Yes, I trust I may.
  What are you doing?

AGNÈS.   Some caps that I've begun.
240   Your nightshirts and your nightcaps are all done.

ARNOLPHE. Well! Very good. Now, go on back
    upstairs.
  I'll soon be back; I'm off for some affairs;
  Then we'll talk seriously for a bit.

(Exeunt AGNÈS, ALAIN, GEORGETTE.*)*

  You learned ladies, paragons of wit,
  Spouters of sentiment and tenderness,
  I challenge all your treasured cleverness,
  And every letter, love-note, poem, romance,
  To match this decent, modest ignorance.

Scene 4.   HORACE, ARNOLPHE

ARNOLPHE. We must not set our minds on property;
250   And if our honor is . . . What? Can it be . . . ?
  Yes . . . No, I'm wrong . . . It *is* . . . Yes. My dear
    boy,
  Horace!

HORACE. Monsieur Arnolphe!

ARNOLPHE.   Why, what a joy!
  How long have you been here?

HORACE.   Nine days.

ARNOLPHE.   Where, pray?

HORACE. I came to see you, but you were away.

ARNOLPHE. Yes, in the country.

HORACE.   You'd left two days past.

ARNOLPHE. My! When young people grow, they do
   grow fast!
  I can't believe the stage I see him at,
  When I remember him as small as *that*.

HORACE. Well, here I am.

ARNOLPHE.   Tell me: Oronte, my dear
  Old friend, your father, whom I so revere: 260
  What is he up to? Is he still robust?
  He knows I care about these things, I trust.
  We haven't seen each other for four years.

HORACE. Nor written to each other, it appears.
  Monsieur Arnolphe, he is as gay as ever.
  I have a letter from him to deliver;
  But now he writes he's coming here, although
  His reason for it I still do not know.
  Do you know someone from this neighborhood
  Returning from America for good   270
  With wealth it took him fourteen years to seek?

ARNOLPHE. I don't. Didn't he say his name?

HORACE.   Enrique.

ARNOLPHE. No.

HORACE.   Father speaks about him in the tone
  He'd use of someone I had always known,
  And says they will discuss, along the way,
  Something important—what, he does not say.
     (Hands ORONTE'S *letter to* ARNOLPHE.*)*

ARNOLPHE. When he returns, I hope to make it plain
  How glad I'll be to see my friend again.
     (Reads the letter.)
  Friends should not be so ceremonious;

280   These compliments are pointless between us.
He did not need to ask me; please make free,
For any funds you wish, to call on me.

HORACE. I'll take you at your word, if you'll permit.
A hundred pistoles would help quite a bit.

ARNOLPHE. Believe me, you oblige me, I avow,
And I am glad I have them on me now.
Keep the purse too.

HORACE.   But . . .

ARNOLPHE.   Let me have my way.
Now then. How do you like our city, pray?

HORACE. Fine buildings; an impressive population;
290   And fun, I think, beyond my expectation.

ARNOLPHE. As regards pleasures, every man his own.
And for gallants (for thus I think they're known)
This town offers delights beyond compare.
The women here are ripe for an affair:
Blonde or brunette, all are exceeding kind,
And all their husbands suitably resigned.
It is sport for a prince; and what I see
Is an unfailing source of comedy.
Already you have smitten one, I'll bet.
300   Haven't you had some such adventure yet?
Good looks achieve much more than purses do,
And cuckolds owe their horns to such as you.

HORACE. Well, since you want the whole truth, I
    declare
I am involved here in a love affair
Which, as a friend, I'll tell you if you wish.

ARNOLPHE. Another spicy tale! They're just my dish,
And I'll add this one to my growing list.

HORACE. This is in confidence; I must insist.

ARNOLPHE. Oh!

HORACE.   You must be aware that in these
      matters
    If anything leaks out, the whole thing shatters.   *310*
    Frankly, then, here is what I have to tell:
    My heart's been captured by a local belle.
    My first attentions had enough success
    To lead the girl to grant me some access;
    And, not to boast too much or do her wrong,
    I really think my chances now are strong.

ARNOLPHE *(laughing)*. But who?

HORACE *(pointing to* AGNÈS'S *house)*. A young girl
      who, it so befalls,
    Lives over in that house with the red walls;
    Naïve, indeed, thanks to some simpleton
    Who hides her from the sight of everyone,   *320*
    While she, brought up to be an ignorant slave,
    Shows charms designed to make an angel rave,
    A most engaging manner, something tender,
    To which any man's heart can but surrender.
    But you are probably not ignorant of
    This lovely creature, this young star of love.
    Her name's Agnès.

ARNOLPHE *(aside)*.   I'll burst!

HORACE.   The man, they say,
    Is Monsieur de la Roche . . . de La Forêt . . .
    I paid little attention to his name;
    Not very bright, it seems, but rich, they claim;   *330*
    And, so I gather, quite an imbecile.
    Surely you know him?

ARNOLPHE *(aside)*.   What a bitter pill!

HORACE. But you don't answer.

ARNOLPHE.   Yes, he's known to me.

HORACE. Surely he's crazy?

ARNOLPHE.   Well . . .

HORACE.   Don't you agree?
   Does that mean yes? A fool? A jealous clown?
   I see: just as they told me here in town.
   In short, I've come to love the fair Agnès.
   She is a perfect jewel, I confess.
   'Twould be a sin for someone so unique
340 To languish in the power of such a freak.
   My every effort, every aim shall go
   To win her heart despite my jealous foe;
   And what I borrow from you in this wise
   Shall serve this honorable enterprise.
   In great affairs, as you know better than I,
   Gold is the key, whatever else we try;
   And that sweet metal aids the conqueror
   In every case, in love as well as war.
   But you seem gloomy; can this be a sign
350 That you do not approve this plan of mine?

ARNOLPHE. No, I was thinking . . .

HORACE.   How I do go on!
   Goodbye. I've tired you. I will call anon
   To thank you.

ARNOLPHE (to himself). Can it be . . . ?

HORACE (returning).   Please be discreet.
   Mine is a secret you must not repeat.

ARNOLPHE (aside). My aching soul . . . !

HORACE.   To father above
   all:
   I fear his anger, and what might befall.

ARNOLPHE (thinking HORACE is returning). Oh!
                              (Exit HORACE.)
            How I suffered through that conversation!

Never has anyone known such vexation.
What haste and what imprudence, I declare,
He showed in telling *me* the whole affair!   360
Although my other name leads him astray,
He is a giddy fool to act this way.
Having endured, I had to persevere
Until I learned just what I had to fear,
And had to listen to his heedless chatter
To reach the center of this secret matter.
I'll try to catch him; he will not take wing;
I need to have him tell me everything.
I hate to think of what may be in store;
We often seek more than we bargain for.   370

ACT II

Scene 1.　ARNOLPHE

ARNOLPHE. I couldn't find Horace, but who can tell?
　Now that I think of it, it's just as well;
　I would have been unable to conceal
　From him the deep anxiety I feel:
　My gnawing perturbation would have shown;
　And what he does not know is best not known.
　But I'm not one to take this lying down
　And leave the field open to that young clown.
　I want to break this up, and I intend
380　To learn how far their friendship may extend.
　My honor is as precious as my life;
　I look on her already as my wife;
　A lapse of hers would cover me with shame;
　Her acts may be imputed to my name.
　Why was I absent? Why did I go away?
(Knocks at his gate. ALAIN *and* GEORGETTE *open the
door and come out.)*

Scene 2.　ALAIN, GEORGETTE, ARNOLPHE

ALAIN. Ah, this time, sir . . .

ARNOLPHE.　　　　Enough. Come here, I say,
　Both of you. This way, this way. Just come here.

GEORGETTE. You frighten me; my blood runs cold
　from fear.

112

ARNOLPHE. When I am gone, this is how you obey
  me?
  You put your heads together to betray me?   390

GEORGETTE. Don't eat me, sir. You give me quite a
  scare.

ALAIN *(aside)*. Some mad dog must have bitten him,
  I swear.

ARNOLPHE. I cannot say a word, I am so bothered:
  I'd like to shed my clothes, not to be smothered.
  So you permitted, you accursed scum—
                (To ALAIN, *who starts to run)*
  Oh, so you want to flee—a man to come?
                (To GEORGETTE*)*
  Right now, you . . .
                    (To ALAIN*)*
                If you move . . .
                                Upon your oath,
  I want you both to tell me . . . Yes, you both . . .

(Both ALAIN *and* GEORGETTE *rise and try to run
              away.)*

  If either of you moves, you're dead, d'you hear?
  Now! How did that man ever get in here?   400
  Well, well, speak up now, promptly, quick and
    smart.
  Speak up, will you?

ALAIN and GEORGETTE *(on their knees)*. Oh! Oh!

GEORGETTE.   Oh, sir! My heart!

ALAIN. I'm dying.

ARNOLPHE *(aside)*. Lord! I'm soaked with sweat. I
  swear
  I need a cooling walk, a breath of air.
  When he was little, how was I to know

He would grow up—to this? I suffer so!
I think my first step is to have recourse
To her, and draw her out, gently, of course.
I'll try to moderate my irritation.
410   Gently, my heart, gently; hide your vexation.
(Aloud) Get up. Go in and send me down Agnès.
No, stop. *(Aside)* That way I would surprise her less.
They'd tell her my distress. No, no, much better
That I myself go in right now and get her.
(Aloud) Wait for me here.

Scene 3.   ALAIN, GEORGETTE

GEORGETTE.   Lord, what an awful sight!
The way he looks at you gives me a fright!
I never saw a Christian look so grim.

ALAIN. That gentleman, I tell you, maddened him.

GEORGETTE. But why the devil treat his future spouse
420   So rough, and make us keep her in the house?
How come he hides her in seclusion here
And won't let anyone at all come near?

ALAIN. Because such things arouse his jealousy.

GEORGETTE. But where did he get such a fantasy?

ALAIN. Because . . . because he is a jealous cuss.

GEORGETTE. Yes, but why is he? And why all the fuss?

ALAIN. Well, jealousy . . . You understand,
Georgette . . .
Is something that . . . well . . . makes a man upset,
And makes him chase all other men away.

I'll give you a comparison, which may   *430*
Help you to see the point. Now then, when you
Have got a bowl of soup, isn't it true
That if some hungry man came up to eat it,
You would be angry, and you'd make him beat it?

GEORGETTE. I can see that.

ALAIN.   Good girl, of course you can:
Well, woman is in effect the soup of man.
When one man sees others ready to swoop
And try to dip their fingers in his soup,
He flies into a fury right away.

GEORGETTE. Yes; but why don't all men react that
  way?   *440*
And why do some seem perfectly content
To see their wife go out with some fine gent?

ALAIN. Not everyone is of the greedy kind
That wants all for himself.

GEORGETTE.   Unless I'm blind,
He's coming back.

ALAIN.   Your eyes are good; that's him.

GEORGETTE. He's angry!

ALAIN.   He has reason to look grim.

Scene 4.   ARNOLPHE, AGNÈS, ALAIN, GEORGETTE

ARNOLPHE. A Greek once gave the Emperor
  Augustus
This advice, full of usefulness and justice:
That when some mishap puts us in a fret,
The first thing is to say the alphabet,   *450*
So as to give us time to grow less hot

And not do anything that we should not.
So for Agnès, rather than be severe,
I'm having her come down and join me here
Upon the pretext of a little stroll,
That the suspicions of my ailing soul
May deftly lead her on and sound her out,
And I may learn what this is all about.
                    (*To* AGNÈS)
Come out.
          (*To* ALAIN *and* GEORGETTE)
          Go in.

          Scene 5.   ARNOLPHE, AGNÈS

ARNOLPHE.   It's nice to walk with you.

AGNÈS. Yes, nice.

ARNOLPHE.   A lovely day!

AGNÈS.   Lovely.

460 ARNOLPHE.   What's new?

AGNÈS. The little kitten died.

ARNOLPHE.   Too bad she's gone,
But we're all mortal, and we're on our own.
Didn't it rain while I was gone, my lamb?

AGNÈS. No, no.

ARNOLPHE.   And were you bored?

AGNÈS.   I never am.

ARNOLPHE. In those nine or ten days, what did you
    do?

AGNÈS. Six shirts, I think; yes, and six nightcaps too.

ARNOLPHE *(after musing a bit)*. The world is a strange
    place, my dear Agnès.
  People talk about anything, I guess.
  Just think: some neighbors came to me to say
  That a young man came while I was away,   470
  That you received, and listened to, this male.
  But I would not believe this wicked tale,
  And I proposed to bet them, to their cost . . .

AGNÈS. Good Lord, don't bet! Oh, my! You would
    have lost.

ARNOLPHE. You mean to say a man . . . ?

AGNÈS.   Indeed I do.
  He hardly left here once, I swear to you.

ARNOLPHE *(aside)*. Such candor, I confess, is quite
    disarming,
  And her simplicity at least is charming.
                        (Aloud)
  But I had said, Agnès, if I recall,
  That you must not see anyone at all.   480

AGNÈS. Oh yes. I saw him, but you don't know why;
  I'm sure you would have done the same as I.

ARNOLPHE. Perhaps. Let's hear about it, by your
    leave.

AGNÈS. It's quite amazing, quite hard to believe.
  Out on the balcony to get the air,
  I saw, under those trees right over there,
  A most attractive young man passing by,
  Who bowed most humbly when he caught my eye.
  And I, not wishing to be impolite,
  Returned a deep bow, as was only right.   490
  Promptly he makes another bow, and then,
  I naturally bow to him again;
  And since he then goes on to number three,

Without delay he gets a third from me.
He passes by, comes back . . . well, anyhow,
Each time he does he makes another bow.
And I, observing this most carefully,
Returned him every bow he made to me.
The fact is, if the light had not grown dim,
500   I would have gone on trading bows with him,
Because I did not want to yield, and be
Inferior to him in courtesy.

ARNOLPHE. All right.

AGNÈS.   When I was at the door, next day,
An old woman comes up to me to say:
"My child, God keep you in his loving care,
And make you always look so young and fair!
Now, all his bounties constitute a duty:
You must not make a bad use of your beauty.
You have wounded a heart, which now, in pain,
510   Is forced at last to cry out and complain."

ARNOLPHE (aside). That tool of Satan! Witch! Accursed scum!

AGNÈS. "I? Wounded someone?" I was overcome.
—"Yes," she said, "wounded, wounded terribly:
The man you bowed to from your balcony."
—"Alas!" said I. "I meant no harm, I swear.
Did I drop something on him unaware?"
—"Oh no, your eyes performed the deadly deed,"
She said, "and caused the damage and his need."
—"Good Lord!" I said. "I do not understand:
520   Have they some fatal power at their command?"
—"Fatal?" she said. "Oh yes, indeed they do.
They have a poison, dear, unknown to you.
In short, he's dying, and he's nearly gone.
And if," that kind old woman then went on,
"You are so cruel as not to give him aid,
They'll bury him in two days, pretty maid."
—"Good Lord!" I said. "That I don't want to see.
But just what help then does he ask of me?"
—"My child," she said, "he only wants to gain

The right to see and talk to you again.   *530*
Your eyes alone can end what they've begun,
Prevent his death, undo the harm they've done."
—"Alas! Of course," I said. "Now that that's clear,
He can come all he likes to see me here."

ARNOLPHE *(aside)*. Ah, poisoner of souls! Accursed
    witch!
May hell repay your plots in boiling pitch!

AGNÈS. That's how he came to see me: as a cure.
Don't you think I did right? I did, I'm sure.
And after all, was I to let him die,
And always have to live with that, when I   *540*
Have such compassion on all suffering here,
And when they kill a chicken, shed a tear?

ARNOLPHE *(aside)*. There speaks a soul that's inno-
    cent and pure;
I was a fool to go away, that's sure,
And leave alone this girl, so free from guile,
Exposed to tempters and their every wile.
Now what I fear is that this noxious pest
Has carried matters . . . well, beyond a jest.

AGNÈS. What ails you? Why, you seem a little mad.
In what I've told you, was there something bad?   *550*

ARNOLPHE. No. But . . . after you met, what *did*
    ensue?
And when the young man came, what did he do?

AGNÈS. Alas! If you had witnessed his delight,
How he was cured when he came in my sight,
The casket for which I am in his debt,
His gifts of cash to Alain and Georgette,
You'd surely love him, and say, as we do . . .

ARNOLPHE. Yes. But what did he do, alone with you?

AGNÈS. He swore his love for me was *sans pareil*,
And oh! he had the nicest things to say,   *560*

Incomparable things, that make me weak,
Whose sweetness, every time I hear him speak,
Tickles my heart, and somehow, in a word,
Stirs in me feelings hitherto unstirred.

ARNOLPHE *(aside)*. O painful probing of a fatal riddle
In which the examiner is on the griddle!
                    (To AGNÈS*)*
Now. Besides all this talk, these tendernesses,
Didn't he also give you some caresses?

AGNÈS. Indeed he did! My hands and arms he seized,
570   And kissed and kissed them, seeming very pleased.

ARNOLPHE. Agnès, was there anything else he took?
                    (Seeing her taken aback)
    Ouf!

AGNÈS. Well, he . . .

ARNOLPHE.   What?

AGNÈS.   Took . . .

ARNOLPHE.   Ugh!

AGNÈS.   The . . .

ARNOLPHE.   Well?

AGNÈS.   Now look.
    I'm sure you will be angry. I don't dare.

ARNOLPHE. No.

AGNÈS.   Yes.

ARNOLPHE.   Good Lord, no!

AGNÈS.   Promise me, then, swear.

ARNOLPHE. I swear.

AGNÈS.   He took . . . You'll be mad, I
know you.

ARNOLPHE. No.

AGNÈS.   Yes.

ARNOLPHE.   No, no. Damn it, what an ado!
What did he take?

AGNÈS.   He . . .

ARNOLPHE *(aside)*.   I'm in agony.

AGNÈS. He took the ribbon that you'd given me.
I couldn't help it, he insisted so.

ARNOLPHE *(breathing again)*. All right, the ribbon.
But I want to know   *580*
If kiss your arms is all he ever did.

AGNÈS. What? Are there other things?

ARNOLPHE.   No, God forbid.
But as a cure for his so-called disease,
Didn't he press for . . . other remedies?

AGNÈS. Oh, no. You can imagine, if he had,
To help him, I'd have done it and been glad.

ARNOLPHE *(aside)*. I got off easy then, thanks be to
God!
If I do that again, call me a clod.
Hush.
                    (Aloud)
This, Agnès, comes of your innocence.
What's done is done. I've spoken. No offense.   *590*
Your lover only wishes to deceive,
Win your good graces, and then laugh and leave.

AGNÈS. Oh, no! He told me twenty times and more.

ARNOLPHE. You do not know what empty oaths he
    swore.
    But learn this: to accept caskets—or candies—
    And listen to the sweet talk of these dandies,
    Languidly acquiesce in their demands,
    And let them stir your heart and kiss your hands,
    This is a mortal sin, one of the worst.

600 AGNÈS. A sin, you say? And why is it accursed?

ARNOLPHE. Why? Why, there is a sacred declaration
    That Heaven regards these acts with indignation.

AGNÈS. With indignation? Why, then? I repeat,
    It's all, alas, so pleasant and so sweet!
    I marvel at the joy that all this brings,
    And I had never known about such things.

ARNOLPHE. Yes, there's great pleasure in this
    tenderness,
    In each nice word and in each sweet caress;
    But these have need of honor's discipline,
610   And only marriage can remove the sin.

AGNÈS. It's not a sin when you are married, pray?

ARNOLPHE. No.

AGNÈS.   Please let me be married right away.

ARNOLPHE. Oh, if you want that, so do I, my dear,
    And in fact that is why I've come back here.

AGNÈS. Can this be?

ARNOLPHE.   Yes.

AGNÈS.   You will delight me so!

ARNOLPHE. You will like marriage; that I think I
    know.

AGNÈS. You want us two . . . ?

ARNOLPHE.   I do, assuredly.

AGNÈS. How I'll caress you, if that comes to be!

ARNOLPHE. Believe me, you won't be the only one.

AGNÈS. I never know when someone's making fun.   620
   You really mean it?

ARNOLPHE.   Yes, you'll see all right.

AGNÈS. We shall be married?

ARNOLPHE.   Yes.

AGNÈS.   But when?

ARNOLPHE.   Tonight.

AGNÈS *(laughing)*. Tonight?

ARNOLPHE.   Tonight. It makes you laugh?

AGNÈS.   Oh, yes.

ARNOLPHE. My greatest wish is for your happiness.

AGNÈS. I shall be grateful to you all my life!
   And how I shall enjoy being his wife!

ARNOLPHE. Whose?

AGNÈS.   His, of course.

ARNOLPHE.   His . . . No. Let's get this
   straight.
You're pretty quick to pick yourself a mate.
The husband for you is another man.
As for that gentleman, here is my plan   630
(And if he really dies of it, too bad):
You are to end all dealings with the lad.

Now, if he comes to see you in this place,
You'll shut the door politely in his face,
And if he knocks and tries another tack,
Throw him a stone so that he won't come back.
You understand, Agnès? I'll hide right near.
Do as I say, for I shall see and hear.

AGNÈS. Alas! He is so handsome!

ARNOLPHE.   Hush! Enough.

AGNÈS. I shall not have the heart . . .

640 ARNOLPHE.   Now, stop that stuff.
Go on upstairs.

AGNÈS.   What? Do you mean to say . . . ?

ARNOLPHE. Enough. I'm master: when I speak, obey.*

---

*Another quip at Pierre Corneille, from whose contemporary
play *Sertorius* (Act V, scene 6) Molière borrows—and thus
parodies—this line.

ACT III

Scene 1. ARNOLPHE, AGNÈS, ALAIN, GEORGETTE

ARNOLPHE. Yes, all went well; I can't contain my glee:
  You all followed my orders to a tee,
  And put to rout that prince of libertines.
  Now that is what good generalship means.
  He had abused your innocence, Agnès.
  See the result of just such thoughtlessness;
  For you were, but for my interposition,
  Right on the road to hell and to perdition.   650
  The ways of all these boys are known to me:
  Their ribbons, feathers, canions at the knee,
  Their pretty talk, great wigs, and shining teeth;
  But take my word, they all have claws beneath.
  Oh yes, insatiable fiends are they,
  And women's honor is their favorite prey.
  But, once again, under my careful guard,
  You have come off with decency unscarred.
  Your manner, when I saw you cast that stone
  By which his wicked hopes were overthrown,   660
  Convinces me that I should not delay
  Our scheduled marriage for one single day.
  But first of all, I think it would be nice
  To let you have a little sound advice.
            (To ALAIN*)*
  A chair here, where it's cool.
            (To GEORGETTE*)*
                    If ever you . . .

GEORGETTE. We know our lesson now, indeed we do.
  That gentleman, he took us in; but then . . .

ALAIN. If he gets in, may I never drink again!
  And he's a fool: those two gold crowns he gave
  To us that time were underweight, the knave!   670

125

ARNOLPHE. Supper as ordered, then; get what we
    lack.
And for the contract, stop on your way back,
One of you, get the corner notary,
And ask him to come here with you to me.

          Scene 2.   ARNOLPHE, AGNÈS

ARNOLPHE *(seated)*. Agnès, take heed. Now, no more
    work tonight.
Head up, now; turn your face a bit. That's right.
        (He puts his finger on his forehead.)
Look at me when I talk—there, that's the way—
And take good note of everything I say.
Agnès, I'm marrying you; and you ought
680   A hundred times a day to bless your lot,
To keep your former low estate in mind
And marvel that a man can be so kind
As I, who found you just a country lass,
And raise you to the honored middle class,
There to enjoy the bed and the embraces
Of one who's always kicked against such traces,
Denying to all parties hitherto
The honor that he now reserves for you.
Always you ought to keep before your eyes
690   Your little worth without this splendid prize,
So that you may be all the more intent
On meriting this glorious ascent,
Knowing your place, and acting so that I
Never repent of raising you so high.
Marriage is not a joke, Agnès, my dear!
Its laws are stern, its duties are severe;
And you're not going into it, I claim,
As if it were a pastime or a game.
For frailty your sex is made and reared;
700   Authority is vested in the beard.
Although you form half of society,
Between our halves is no equality;

One is supreme, the other one abject;
One must submit, the other one direct;
And the obedience a soldier must
Show to his leader to deserve his trust,
That which a servant, monk, or little tot
Owes his lord, abbot, father, by his lot,
Comes nowhere near to the docility,
To the obedient humility   710
And deep respect a wife should harbor toward
Her husband, as her master, chief, and lord.
Now, when he glances at her seriously,
She should cast down her eyes immediately,
And never dare to look him in the face
Unless his glance is kind and full of grace.
Wives will not understand this nowadays;
But do not follow their abandoned ways.
Don't imitate all those flirtatious jades
Who make the town ring with their escapades;   720
And guard against the Evil One's attacks,
Who uses handsome fops to make girls lax.
Note that in giving you my life to share,
Agnès, I place my honor in your care;
It is a tender thing, easy to hurt,
Which will not tolerate a playful flirt;
And in hell there are caldrons in which wives
Will boil forever, if they lead bad lives.
This is no idle talk that I impart,
And you should take these lessons to your heart.   730
Heed them, don't flirt, and then your soul is sure
To be forever lily-white and pure;
But if you let dishonor stain your soul,
Then it will promptly turn as black as coal;
People will shrink in horror, and one day
You will go down to hell, the devil's prey,
And there for all eternity you'll stew.
May Heaven not reserve that fate for you!
Now, make a curtsy. As a novice must
Master her convent's laws, and know her trust,   740
A future bride must know the marriage pact.
Here in my pocket is a useful tract
(Rising) In which to learn what is to be your role.
The author I don't know: some worthy soul.

On this alone I want your mind to dwell.
Here. Let's just see if you can read it well.

AGNÈS (reads). *The Maxims of Marriage, or, The
Duties of the Married Woman, with Her Daily
Practice*

Maxim I.
When a woman, duly wed,
Comes to share her husband's bed,
She must keep one thing in mind:
750   Even in these times she'll find
He takes her for himself alone, not for mankind.

ARNOLPHE. I will explain that later, yes indeed;
But for the present, go ahead and read.

AGNÈS (reads on).

Maxim II.
She should be nicely dressed
Only to interest
Her husband—not some swain.
His satisfaction must be paramount.
It is of no account
That others find her plain.

Maxim III.
760   Not for her the ogling glance
Or cosmetics, to enhance
Her loveliness, and set off her complexion:
These are the bane of honor and of duty;
Wives rarely fuss about their beauty
To guarantee their mate's affection.

Maxim IV.
Decently she must hide her eyes, that gleam so,
Under her coif, soon as she leaves the house,
Since, to seem lovely to her spouse,
To no one must she seem so.

Maxim V.

All visitors but those who come to see   770
    Her lord and master, she
    In honor must deter.
    Those who, with gallant whim,
    Come only to see her,
    Are sure to displease him.

Maxim VI.

    When men, in a pleasant way,
    Offer gifts, she must say no;
    All men of the present day
    Count upon a *quid pro quo*.

Maxim VII.

In her possessions, though this rouse her spite,   780
Must be no desk, no paper, pen, or ink;
    It is the husband's job to think,
    And what needs writing he will write.

Maxim VIII.

    Those giddy blatherings
    Called social gatherings
Are places for the wives to plot and plan.
    To ban them all would be good policy
    As a conspiracy
    Against the married man.

Maxim IX.

Gambling a wife must shun: its specious charm   790
    Should fill her with alarm
    For her dear honor's sake:
    Luck comes and goes away
    And often makes her play
    Her one remaining stake.

Maxim X.

    Let a country promenade
    Or a picnic in a glade
    Not be something she essays:
    Men of prudent counsel find
    That for pastimes of this kind   800
The husband is the one who pays.

Maxim XI. . . .

ARNOLPHE. Now, finish it alone; and in a while
          I will explain all this in thorough style.
          I've just remembered something I must do:
          It won't take long; I'll come right back to
               you.
          Go in; I leave this booklet in your care.
          If the notary comes, I'll soon be there.

Scene 3.   ARNOLPHE

ARNOLPHE. No, I could never find a better wife.
          I'll shape her soul at will, and mold her life.
810   Between my hands she's like a piece of clay,
          And I can fashion her in any way.
          They nearly caught me, though, when I was gone,
          Using her innocence to lead her on.
          But truly it is better that a bride,
          If err she must, should err upon that side.
          Such failings are no reason for concern:
          A simple person is disposed to learn;
          And if she's left the straight and narrow lane,
          Two words will bring her back to it again.
820   A clever woman is another dish;
          Our fate depends upon her slightest wish.
          Nothing can budge her from her chosen course,
          And all our teaching does is make us hoarse.
          Her wit helps her make sport of our advice,
          Portray as virtuous her every vice,
          And, to fulfill her bad intentions, find
          Devices to deceive the shrewdest mind.
          To try to fend the blow is vain fatigue:
          A clever wife's a devil for intrigue;
830   Her husband's honor hangs upon her whim:
          Its verdict reached, there's no appeal for him.
          Many good men could amplify that theme.
          Well, my young fool will have no cause to beam.
          He talked too much, and now he pays the price.

That is our Frenchmen's ordinary vice:
When they are lucky in a love affair,
Secrecy is a thing they cannot bear;
And vanity holds them so much in thrall,
They'd rather hang themselves than not tell all.
Oh! How a woman takes the devil's bait   840
When she picks up with such an addlepate,
And how ...! But here he is ... Let's play our part,
And learn what disappointment fills his heart.

Scene 4.   HORACE, ARNOLPHE

HORACE. I've just come from your house. You know,
    I swear
Fate simply will not let me find you there.
But still I'll try to pay a proper call ...

ARNOLPHE. Lord! Please don't think about such things
    at all.
These ceremonies are a thing I hate,
And I would like to ban them from the state.
Most people waste some two thirds of their days   850
Quite stupidly, on these accursed ways.
So, let's put on our hats. *(Puts on his.)* No more
    ado.
Now, in your love life, Sir Horace, what's new?
Just now I had my mind on other things,
I fear; but with the thoughts that leisure brings,
I marvel at your progress from the start,
And I take your successes to my heart.

HORACE. Well, since I told you all I had to tell,
    My love, I must admit, has not fared well.

ARNOLPHE. Oho! How so?

HORACE.   It's Fortune's cruel frown   860
    Which brought my lady's master back to town.

ARNOLPHE. Oh, what bad luck!

HORACE.   What's more, to my chagrin,
He's learned about the state affairs are in.

ARNOLPHE. Why, how the devil did he come to know?

HORACE. I've no idea; but it is surely so.
I planned, at just about my usual hour,
To pay a visit to my lovely flower,
When, with a wholly altered tone and face,
The maid and valet barred me from the place,
870   Saying "You can't come back here any more,"
And then—in my face, mind you—slammed the
    door.

ARNOLPHE. Right in your face!

HORACE.   My face.

ARNOLPHE.   That *is* severe.

HORACE. Still from outside I tried to make them hear;
But every time I spoke, they answered faster:
"You can't come in, by order of the master."

ARNOLPHE. They didn't open?

HORACE.   No. From up above
I then had confirmation from my love,
Who sent me packing in a haughty tone,
And from her window threw me out a stone.

ARNOLPHE. How's that? A stone?

880 HORACE.   A stone of no small size,
With her own hands, to greet my enterprise.

ARNOLPHE. The devil take it! That was pretty cruel,
And I'm afraid you've lost your little jewel.

HORACE. It's too bad that man should come back
    right now.

ARNOLPHE. It makes me sorry for your sake, I vow.

HORACE. He breaks up everything.

ARNOLPHE.   Well, never mind,
    There must be a way out that you will find.

HORACE. By some device, I certainly must try
    Some way to dodge this jealous fellow's eye.

ARNOLPHE. That should be easy. And the girl, you
    say,   *890*
    Loves you.

HORACE.   Indeed she does.

ARNOLPHE.   You'll find a way.

HORACE. I hope I shall.

ARNOLPHE.   That stone put you to rout,
    But that should not astonish you.

HORACE.   No doubt,
    And I knew right away my man was there,
    Unseen, but managing the whole affair.
    What I did marvel at—and you will too—
    Was something else I must report to you:
    That lovely girl hit on a bold device
    Startling for one so innocent and nice.
    Love is a great teacher, you must agree,   *900*
    Making us what we never thought to be;
    And in a moment, under his direction,
    Our character can change its whole complexion.
    He breaks down even natural obstacles,
    And seems to manage sudden miracles;
    In no time he can make a miser kind,
    A coward valiant, and a boor refined;
    He makes the dullest soul agile and fit,

And gives the most naïve its share of wit.
910 That miracle has happened to Agnès;
Her terms in breaking with me were express:
"I want no further visits, so goodbye;
I've heard you out, and this is my reply."
And then the stone—and this was really neat—
Fell, with this note attached, right at my feet.
And I'm amazed at how, in sense and tone,
This note goes with her throwing of the stone.
Aren't you surprised at how her action fits?
And isn't love a sharpener of wits?
920 Can one deny its power to impart
Wondrous resources to the human heart?
Come! How about this letter and her trick?
Don't you admire her wit? Wasn't she quick?
And what about my jealous rival's role
In all this nonsense? Don't you find it droll?
Tell me.

ARNOLPHE. Yes, very droll.

HORACE.   Then how about
A laugh?

(ARNOLPHE *forces a laugh.*)

                         This man, in arms to keep me out,
Entrenched at home, with stones for ammunition,
As if I were a storming expedition;
930 Who goads his servants, in his antic fear,
To hinder me from even coming near;
And whom this girl, that he's kept so naïve,
Through his own scheme has managed to deceive!
I must say that although his coming back
Forces my love to take another tack,
I never heard of anything so funny;
I can't help laughing, not for love or money.
But you're not laughing very hard, I'd say.

ARNOLPHE (*forcing a laugh*). I'm laughing—pardon
me—as best I may.

HORACE. But here's her note. Please read it, as my
    friend.   *940*
  All that was in her heart, her hand has penned,
  But that in touching terms of kindliness,
  Of simple innocence and tenderness.
  In short, in just the way I'm speaking of,
  Nature expresses the first pangs of love.

ARNOLPHE *(aside)*. So that's why you were taught to
    write, you tart!
  I never wanted you to learn the art.

HORACE *(reads)*.

"I want to write you, and I am at a loss how to set
about it. I have thoughts that I would like you to
know; but I don't know how to go about telling them
to you, and I mistrust my own words. As I am beginning to realize that I have always been kept in ignorance, I am afraid of putting down something that
may not be right and saying more than I ought. Truly,
I don't know what you've done to me; but I feel that
I am mortally unhappy over what they're making me
do to you, that it will be terribly hard for me to get
along without you, and that I would be very glad to
be yours. Perhaps it's a bad thing to say that; but anyway I can't help saying it, and I wish it could be done
without its being wrong. They keep telling me that all
young men are deceivers, that I mustn't listen to
them, and that everything you say to me is only to
take advantage of me; but I assure you that I have
not yet been able to imagine that of you, and I am so
touched by your words that I cannot possibly believe
they are lies. Tell me frankly what the truth is in all
this; for after all, since there is no malice in me, you
would be doing a terrible wrong if you deceived me,
and I think I would die of sorrow."

ARNOLPHE *(aside)*. Hellcat!

HORACE.   What's wrong?

ARNOLPHE.   I coughed; just a sore throat.

HORACE. Could anything be sweeter than that note?
950   The tyrant's damned precautions are in vain;
          This letter makes her lovely nature plain.
          Shouldn't it be a punishable crime
          To smother such a spirit all this time,
          And to have tried to dim her brilliant mind
          By keeping her ignorant and confined?
          Love has begun to tear away the veil;
          And if some lucky star lets me prevail,
          I hope to teach him what it's all about,
          That traitor, hangman, scoundrel, brutish lout . . .

ARNOLPHE. Goodbye.

HORACE.   So soon?

960 ARNOLPHE.   Something I have to do,
          Which I'd forgotten as I talked to you.

HORACE. But since they keep close watch, could you
          suggest
          How to get to her; who could help me best?
          I'm free in asking favors without end;
          I hope I'm not imposing on a friend.
          I've only foes inside; their eyes are keen;
          And maid and servant, whom I just have seen,
          No matter what cajoleries I try,
          Keep me away with a suspicious eye.
970   I used to have, for such things, an old woman
          Whose gifts, to tell the truth, were superhuman.
          It helped at first to have her on my side;
          But just four days ago the poor thing died.
          Can't you see any way to help me out?

ARNOLPHE. You don't need me; you know what
          you're about.

HORACE. Goodbye then. See how I confide in you.

Scene 5. ARNOLPHE

ARNOLPHE. What torment that young fellow put me
    through!
  How I have struggled to conceal my hurt!
  How could a simple girl be so alert?
  Either her innocence is just a role,   *980*
  Or Satan breathed this cunning in her soul.
  That cursed note of hers! I could have died.
  I see the traitor's got her on his side.
  He rules her mind; he's firmly anchored there;
  And that's my mortal pain and my despair.
  The stealing of her heart afflicts me twice:
  My honor and my love both pay the price;
  I'm furious that he's usurped my domain,
  And furious that my schemes have been in vain.
  She will be punished for her lewd romance,   *990*
  I know, by the sheer force of circumstance:
  And she will give herself her just deserts;
  But still, to lose the one you love—it hurts.
  I made my choice like a philosopher.
  Heavens! Why am I so bewitched by her?
  She has no relatives, wealth, or protection;
  She spurns my cares, my kindness, my affection;
  Yet I love her, for all this turnabout:
  Her love is something I can't do without.
  You fool, you make me mad; you're a disgrace!   *1000*
  A thousand times I'd like to slap my face.
  I'll go indoors awhile, only to see
  The face she puts upon such treachery.
  Heaven, keep my forehead free from any horn;
  Or, if it was for that that I was born,
  Grant me at least, to help me bear the shame,
  The fortitude of some whom I could name!

ACT IV

Scene 1. ARNOLPHE

ARNOLPHE. I cannot seem to stay put anywhere,
And my poor mind is torn with many a care,
1010 Trying, indoors and out, to put a stop
To the designs of that obnoxious fop.
With what aplomb the traitress met my gaze!
No care about the error of her ways!
And though she nearly was the death of me,
You never saw such peaceful purity.
The more I saw her sweet and tranquil smile,
The more I felt the boiling of my bile;
And as these angry transports racked me harder,
They seemed to reinforce my loving ardor;
1020 Of bitter, hopeless spite my heart was full:
Yet never has she looked so beautiful.
Her eyes have never seemed so much afire,
Nor ever roused in me such keen desire;
And I shall burst—I feel it deep inside—
If I cannot have Agnès for my bride.
Shall I have trained her under close direction,
With such precautions and with such affection,
Brought her up in my house from infancy,
Cherished the tenderest expectancy,
1030 Admired her budding charms, now almost grown,
Pampered her thirteen years, for me alone,
Only to watch while some young popinjay,
With whom she's smitten, carries her away?
And *that* when she is half married to me?
No, by God! No, by God! It shall not be!
My silly little friend, I'll take such care
That I will wreck your foolish hopes, I swear,
And we shall see which one of us laughs best.

138

Scene 2. NOTARY, ARNOLPHE

NOTARY. Ah, here you are! I've come at your behest
To draw that contract that you want. Good day.   *1040*

ARNOLPHE *(not seeing him)*. How shall I do it?

NOTARY.   In the regular way.

ARNOLPHE *(not seeing him)*. Now, what are the precautions I must take?

NOTARY. I'll not forget your interests are at stake.

ARNOLPHE *(not seeing him)*. I must protect myself
against surprises.

NOTARY. I'll handle any problem that arises.
Your worries can be easily allayed:
Don't sign the contract till the money's paid.

ARNOLPHE *(not seeing him)*. My fear is that, if anything gets out,
All over town it may be noised about.

NOTARY. It's easy to prevent publicity;   *1050*
Your contract can be drawn up privately.

ARNOLPHE *(not seeing him)*. But for this, how can I
win her assent?

NOTARY. Jointure and dowry should be congruent.

ARNOLPHE *(not seeing him)*. I love her, and by love
my hands are tied.

NOTARY. Then one may give some extra to the bride.

ARNOLPHE *(not seeing him)*. How shall I treat her
    now?
What shall I say?

NOTARY. The husband to his fiancée shall pay
    One third her dowry; but one may ignore
    This rule and, if one wants to, pay her more.

ARNOLPHE *(not seeing him)*. Now if . . . *(He sees the
    notary.)*

1060 NOTARY.   Survivors' shares concern them both.
    He may endow his bride, if he's not loath,
    Just as he likes.

ARNOLPHE.   Eh?

NOTARY.   Set her up for life
    (If he adores and wants to please his wife)
    By stipulated jointure, as they say,
    Which would be lost if she should pass away;
    It could go to the heirs of the said bride;
    Or else by common law, as specified;
    Or further, by contractual stipulation,
    Through simple or through mutual donation.
    Why do you shrug? Don't I make sense? Do you
1070   doubt
    I know my marriage contracts inside out?
    Who is to teach me? Just name anyone.
    Don't I know spouses hold in unison
    Property, chattels, monies, real estate,
    Save what they formally repudiate?
    And that one third of the fiancée's share
    Enters the joint estate . . . ?

ARNOLPHE.   Yes, I'm aware
    You know that; but who asked to hear about it?

NOTARY. You seemed as though you could not do
    without it:
1080   You with your shoulder shrugs and your grimace.

ARNOLPHE. A plague upon him and his ugly face!
  Goodbye: I hope that makes you disappear.

NOTARY. Isn't the contract why you called me here?

ARNOLPHE. Yes, I did send for you; but it's deferred,
  And when the time is set I'll send you word.
  What can possess the man, with all his chatter?

NOTARY. He's had a bellyful, that's what's the matter.

Scene 3. NOTARY, ALAIN, GEORGETTE, ARNOLPHE

NOTARY. Wasn't it you your master sent for me?

ALAIN. Yes.

NOTARY.   I don't know what you take him to be,
  But give this message to that imbecile: *1090*
  That he's an arrant fool.

GEORGETTE.   We surely will.

Scene 4. ALAIN, GEORGETTE, ARNOLPHE

ALAIN. Monsieur . . .

ARNOLPHE.   Come here: you both are tried
  and true,
  My real, good friends; and I've had news of you.

ALAIN. The notary . . .

ARNOLPHE.   Wait; time for him anon.
  Now hear me. Someone has designs upon
  My honor. Children, what would be your shame

If your master were robbed of his good name!
Nowhere in public would you dare appear,
And everyone would point you out and jeer.
1100   So, since you are involved in this affair
As much as I, keep watch with such great care
That this young gallant never may get through.

GEORGETTE. A while ago you showed us what to do.

ARNOLPHE. Don't listen to a word he has to say.

ALAIN. Of course we won't.

GEORGETTE.   We'll send him on his way.

ARNOLPHE. Suppose he's very sweet: "Alain, please
    deign
To help me out a bit and ease my pain."

ALAIN. You are a fool.

ARNOLPHE.   That's good.
                    (To GEORGETTE*)*
                        "My sweet Georgette,
You seem as kind a person as I've met."

GEORGETTE. You are an ass.

1110 ARNOLPHE *(to* ALAIN*).*   "How can you blame
My virtuous and honorable aim?"

ALAIN. You are a rascal.

ARNOLPHE. Fine. *(To* GEORGETTE*)* "My death is sure
Without your pity for what I endure."

GEORGETTE. You're an impudent booby.

ARNOLPHE.   Good enough.
                    (To ALAIN*)*
"I do not ask for favors on the cuff.
I've a good memory for service done.

Here's an advance, Alain; go have some fun.
Here's for another petticoat, Georgette.
(He holds out money; both reach out and take it.)
　That's just a sample; I'll do better yet.
　And in return I merely ask to see   *1120*
　Your lovely mistress; that's my only plea."

GEORGETTE *(pushing him)*. Try someone else.

ARNOLPHE.   That's good.

ALAIN *(pushing him)*.   Out!

ARNOLPHE.   Good.

GEORGETTE *(pushing him)*.   But quick!

ARNOLPHE. Good. Hey! Enough.

GEORGETTE.   Oh, did I miss a
　trick?

ALAIN. Is that the way? Aren't we pretty adept?

ARNOLPHE. The money, though, you never should
　have kept.

GEORGETTE. Oh yes, that is a point that we forgot.

ALAIN. Shall we begin again?

ARNOLPHE.   I should say not.
　Enough. Go on back in.

ALAIN.   One word from you . . .

ARNOLPHE. I tell you, no; go in, I want you to.
　There, keep the money; I'll be right along.   *1130*
　Keep watch, and see that not a thing goes wrong.

Scene 5. ARNOLPHE

ARNOLPHE. I need to get a careful, keen-eyed spy;
    The corner cobbler is the man to try.
    I mean to hold her under lock and key
    At all times, and to keep the household free
    Of hairdressers, wigmakers, ribbon peddlers,
    Milliners, glovers, and assorted meddlers,
    All those who make a covert business of
    Encouraging the mysteries of love.
1140 I've been around, and I know every trick.
    In short, this fellow will be very slick
    If he can get a message past my guard.

Scene 6. HORACE, ARNOLPHE

HORACE. What luck to find you in your own back
    yard!
    I had a really narrow squeak, I swear.
    Just after leaving you, all unaware,
    I saw Agnès come to her balcony,
    Alone, in the cool shade of the nearby tree.
    She, having given me a sign to wait,
    And got downstairs, opened the garden gate;
1150 But when we'd barely got inside her room,
    Up the stairs came her jealous would-be groom;
    And all that she could do in such a plight
    Was shut me in a wardrobe good and tight.
    He came right in; I could not see, but heard;
    He strode around the room without a word,
    Uttering frequent sighs that spoke his woes,
    Beating the tables with horrendous blows,
    Striking a friendly dog, and when he found
    Some things of hers, tossing them all around.
1160 He knocked some vases, with a furious hand,
    From off the mantel where they used to stand.

This horned goat, I'm very much afraid,
Has got some inkling of the trick she played.
When he had vented his discomfiture
At length upon the helpless furniture,
At last, speechless and vexed, he went away,
And I came out into the light of day.
Fearing my rival, we decided not
To stay together longer in that spot:
His jealousy would make the risk too great;   1170
But tonight I shall come to see her late.
I'll cough three times, and she, upstairs, inside,
Will at the signal open the window wide.
A ladder and her help are all I need,
I trust, to reach her side with loving speed.
I tell you all this as to my sole friend.
With joy, it seems, to share is to extend;
And perfect happiness, if it's unknown,
Tastes flat; we cannot savor it alone.
I trust that my success will please you too.   1180
Goodbye. I have some urgent things to do.

Scene 7.   ARNOLPHE

ARNOLPHE. What? Shall the star that drives me to
     despair
    Not give me time to catch a breath of air?
    Blow upon blow! Then must my vigilance
    Be overcome by their intelligence?
    And at my age, am I to be the dupe
    Of a young girl and a young nincompoop?
    For twenty years, a philosophic sage,
    I've watched the hapless husbands of this age,
    Studied all their disasters, tried to know   1190
    How even the most prudent are brought low.
    Applying all these lessons learned from life,
    I sought a way, wanting to take a wife,
    To escape the dismal horns of cuckoldry
    Which on so many other brows I see.

To serve this noble aim, I put to use
All that human invention can adduce;
And as if fate had chosen to ordain
That men seek such security in vain,
1200   After all my experience, my cares,
My hard-won insight into these affairs,
After twenty-odd years of meditation
Leading to caution and deliberation,
I shall have left the other husbands' route
Just to fall into the same disrepute?
No! Hangman fate, I'll still prove you a liar.
I hold her still, in spite of his desire;
If I have lost her heart to this blond pest,
At least I'll see he shall not have the rest;
1210   And this night, which they count on to elope,
Shall not go by as sweetly as they hope.
I take some pleasure, amid so much pain,
To learn about the snares he sets in vain,
And see my foe, this rattle-brained gallant,
Take his own rival for his confidant.

Scene 8.   CHRYSALDE, ARNOLPHE

CHRYSALDE. Well then? Before our walk, suppose we
    sup?

ARNOLPHE. I shall not eat this evening.

CHRYSALDE.   Why, what's up?

ARNOLPHE. I've problems on my mind; excuse me,
    pray.

CHRYSALDE. Why, have your marriage plans then
    gone astray?

1220 ARNOLPHE. You're too intent on other men's affairs.

CHRYSALDE. Oho! So angry! Well, what are your
   cares?
  Old chap, your love has not, by any chance,
  Encountered some unhappy circumstance?
  From your expression, I would almost swear it.

ARNOLPHE. Whatever happens, I shall have the merit
  Of not resembling certain folk I know
  Who meekly watch the suitors come and go.

CHRYSALDE. I marvel that, with your philosophy,
  These matters cause you such anxiety,
  That you equate security with bliss,   1230
  And think the test of honor is just this.
  For you, a man may be a wicked brute,
  So long as he avoids this disrepute;
  His honor's safe, no matter what his life,
  Provided he enjoys a faithful wife.
  Come now, how can you make our reputation
  Depend on such a chance consideration?
  Why should a well-born soul have to repent
  Brooking a wrong that no one can prevent?
  When we select a wife, why should her ways   1240
  Decide whether we merit blame or praise?
  Why make a bugbear out of the offense
  We suffer from her lack of continence?
  Know that a gentleman may possibly
  Take a much milder view of cuckoldry,
  That since none can ward off this accident,
  It should be, by itself, indifferent,
  And that the harm, whatever people say,
  Comes from our viewing it with such dismay;
  For in this plight, as everywhere, it seems   1250
  That we should find our way between extremes:
  Not imitate the overdebonair
  Who pride themselves on every such affair,
  Are always mentioning their wives' young gallants,
  Singing their praises, dwelling on their talents,
  Who take them and their interests to their heart,
  And in their treats and parties have their part,
  Till, when they turn up in some public place,
  Men wonder that they dare to show their face.

1260 But, even as we blame such silliness,
      We must condemn the opposite excess.
      Friendship with suitors seems a sorry joke;
      Yet neither do I praise those stormy folk
      Whose reckless anger and tempestuous cries
      Bring their anxiety to all men's eyes,
      Whose outbursts seem intended to invite
      The world's attention to their sorry plight.
      Between these courses lies a proper way
      In which a prudent man will often stay.
1270 We need not blush, if we are men of sense,
      Not even at our partner's worst offense.
      In short, say what men will, then, cuckoldom
      Is not as frightful as it seems to some;
      And our ability, just as I say,
      Consists in taking it the proper way.

      ARNOLPHE. After that pretty speech, your lordship
          should
        Be thanked by all the cuckolds' brotherhood;
        And anyone who hears your rhapsody
        Will soon enroll in their society.

1280 CHRYSALDE. I don't say that; I look at that askance.
        But since we owe our choice of wives to chance,
        As in a game of dice we should behave,
        Where, when you do not get the roll you crave,
        You must reduce your stakes, control your play,
        And change your luck by caution and delay.

      ARNOLPHE. In short, sleep and eat well; don't fret a
          minute;
        And make yourself believe there's nothing in it.

      CHRYSALDE. You think you're joking; but, pretense
          aside,
        We have more reason to be terrified
1290 At countless sources of much greater woe
        Than at this accident that scares you so.
        For if I had to choose, do you suppose
        I would not rather be—well, one of *those*—
        Than have one of those wives without a taint

Whose life is one perpetual complaint,
Dragons of virtue, devils full of piety,
Entrenched in their self-satisfied propriety,
Who, for the one fault they're not guilty of,
Assume the right to look down from above,
And on the grounds that they are chaste and pure, *1300*
Indulge their tempers, which we must endure?
Once more, my friend, the state of cuckoldry
Is only what we make it out to be;
It even may be in our interest,
And has its compensations, like the rest.

ARNOLPHE. Then go ahead, if you're contented by it;
But as for me, I have no wish to try it;
And rather than endure the cuckold's horn . . .

CHRYSALDE. Good Lord! Don't swear, lest you
    should be forsworn.
If fate has willed it, nothing you can do   *1310*
Can change it; it won't come consulting you.

ARNOLPHE. What, *I* a cuckold?

CHRYSALDE.   You're not making sense.
A thousand people are—please, no offense—
Whose wealth, birth, courage, and attractive air
Make them literally beyond compare.

ARNOLPHE. I crave comparison with no such folk.
But come, I'm tired of your elaborate joke:
Let's let it go at that.

CHRYSALDE.   My, how you fret!
I don't know why. Goodbye. But don't forget,
Whatever oaths your honor may suggest,   *1320*
You're halfway toward the fate that you detest
As soon as you have sworn it shall not be.

ARNOLPHE. Again I swear it, and immediately
I'll test my preparations for loose ends.

Scene 9. ALAIN, GEORGETTE, ARNOLPHE

ARNOLPHE. It's now that I implore your aid, my
    friends.
Your loyalty gives me great satisfaction.
Now I must see it manifest in action;
And if your service now repays my trust,
Your recompense shall be secure and just.
1330 Now—not a word—the man you know about
Intends, I've learned, to try to catch me out
And enter Agnès' room by escalade;
But you and I will set an ambuscade.
I want each one of you to take a stick,
And when he's at the topmost rung, be quick—
(At the right time I'll open the window wide)
—And set upon the traitor from inside;
Give him a thorough lesson on his back,
So that he won't return to the attack;
1340 But in all this you must not speak my name
Or hint that I'm a party to this game.
Have you the wit to do what I desire?

ALAIN. If beating, sir, is all that you require,
    Trust us. Now, when I hit, I hit. You'll see.

GEORGETTE. My blows are harder than they look to
    be,
And in a thrashing they will play their role.

ARNOLPHE. Go in then, and don't tell this to a soul.
    Ah, this will teach the neighbors and this clown!
And if each husband living in this town
1350 Gave this response to suitors' provocation,
It would reduce the cuckold population.

ACT V

Scene 1.   ALAIN, GEORGETTE, ARNOLPHE

ARNOLPHE. Traitors, what have you done? He may
  be dead.

ALAIN. But, sir, we did exactly what you said.

ARNOLPHE. You try such an excuse on me in vain:
  I said he should be beaten up, not slain,
  And ordered that the brunt of your attack
  Should fall not on his head but on his back.
  Heavens! What disaster fate reserved for me!
  And with him dead, what is my course to be?
  Go back into the house, and not a word   1360
  Of any harmless order that you heard.
  It's almost dawn, and I must make my plans
  On how I should behave in this mischance.
  What will become of me in my despair?
  What will his father say to this affair?

Scene 2.   HORACE, ARNOLPHE

HORACE. I must try to find out who that can be.

ARNOLPHE. Could I have known . . . ? Who goes
  there?
  Answer me.

HORACE. Seigneur Arnolphe?

ARNOLPHE.   Yes, but . . .

HORACE.   Horace. It's true.
    I was just coming to get help from you.
    You are up early!

1370 ARNOLPHE *(aside)*. What is my confusion!
        Is it enchantment? Can it be illusion?

    HORACE. Really, I was in great distress of mind,
            And I bless Heaven, which was extremely kind
            To let me find you now. I came to say
            That things turned out in a delightful way,
            Both better than I could have hoped, and faster,
            Thanks to a plan that seemed to bring disaster.
            I can't imagine how the man—can you?
            Got his suspicions of our rendezvous;
1380   But, near the window, ready to climb in,
            I found some people there, to my chagrin;
            And when I saw them swing, and their intent,
            I lost my footing—and then down I went.
            Though I was bruised, I have no doubt at all
            That I was spared a drubbing by my fall.
            These folk—my foe among them, I suppose—
            Assumed my tumble followed from their blows;
            And since for quite a while I did remain
            Motionless in considerable pain,
1390   They obviously thought that I was dead—
            A notion which filled all of them with dread.
            I heard each hold the other ones at fault
            For the intensity of their assault;
            Cursing their fate, they came, without a light,
            To check, and judged that I was dead all right:
            And in the darkness, be it understood,
            I played a corpse's part as best I could.
            Then, terrified, they disappeared from view,
            And as I thought about withdrawing too,
1400   Hearing of the disaster, young Agnès
            Came down to me in haste and in distress;
            For from the outset she had overheard
            These people's conversation, every word,
            And had, in the confusion, made her way
            Out of the house to me without delay;
            But finding me uninjured, her relief

Displayed itself in joy beyond belief.
How can I tell you? Well, that charming creature
Followed the counsels of her loving nature,
Flatly refused to go on back in there, 1410
And placed her fate, her honor in my care.
Think how that madman's utter lack of sense
Exposes her in all her innocence,
And of the perils that she might go through
If I did not adore her as I do.
But it is far too purely that I love her;
I'd rather die than take advantage of her.
Her charms are worthy of a better fate,
And death alone can make us separate.
My father, I foresee, will be displeased; 1420
But in due time his wrath can be appeased.
This is the girl I always shall adore;
A man would be a fool to ask for more.
Now I beg leave to give my lady fair,
In utter secrecy, into your care;
Please make her welcome under your protection
A day or two, to favor my affection.
Her flight must be concealed from everyone,
Though soon a search will surely be begun;
And such a beauty, seen with a young male, 1430
Is promptly thought to be beyond the pale.
Now, since, from the beginning to the end,
I've told you everything, my trusted friend,
I come to ask you this one favor more:
To guard for me the woman I adore.

ARNOLPHE. Believe me, I will serve you all I can.

HORACE. You'll help me carry out this cherished
    plan?

ARNOLPHE. Most willingly; I feel the greatest joy
    To have this chance to help you out, my boy;
    Heaven be praised you trust me with Agnès: 1440
    Nothing could give me greater happiness.

HORACE. My debt to you is great in every way.
    This is one step I feared you might gainsay;

But you have been around, and from above
You understand the ardor of young love.
She's at the corner, and my man stands guard.

ARNOLPHE. It's getting light; this will be rather hard.
Someone may see me if I take her here;
And at my house, if you were to appear,
1450   Servants are sure to talk. No, just in case,
You'd better bring her to some darker place.
My garden alley's hid from prying eyes.

HORACE. All these precautions you suggest are wise.
I'll simply turn her over then to you
And go back home without further ado.

                                        (Exit.)

ARNOLPHE (alone). Ah, fortune! This propitious accident
Makes up for all the troubles you have sent!
            (He muffles his face in his cloak.)

Scene 3.   AGNÈS, ARNOLPHE, HORACE

HORACE. Don't worry at my bringing you this way;
I had to find you some safe place to stay.
1460   All would be ruined if you stopped with me.
Go in this door and you'll be safe; you'll see.

(ARNOLPHE, unrecognized by her, takes her hand.)

AGNÈS (to HORACE.) Why are you leaving me?

HORACE.   I must, my dear.

AGNÈS. Then come back soon and end my waiting
    here.

HORACE. My love will bring me back soon, dear
   Agnès.

AGNÈS. When you're away I have no happiness.

HORACE. Out of your presence, I too am in pain.

AGNÈS. Alas! If that were so, you would remain.

HORACE. What? Can you doubt then that my love is
   true?

AGNÈS. You don't love me as much as I love you.

   (ARNOLPHE *pulls her away.*)

He pulls too hard.

HORACE.   It's dangerous, my dear,   1470
   For us two to be seen together here;
   This is a perfect friend, who knows what's best,
   And will act wisely in our interest.

AGNÈS. But I don't know him, and . . .

HORACE.   Don't worry, please:
   In hands like his you should feel quite at ease.

AGNÈS. Those of Horace would give me more delight.
   And I would . . .*
       (*To* ARNOLPHE, *still pulling her*)
               Wait.

HORACE.   Goodbye; it's getting light.

AGNÈS. When shall I see you?

---

*These three words ("And I would . . .") are assigned by some
editions to Horace, by others to Agnès. The latter reading seems
to me clearly preferable.

HORACE.   Soon. Depend on me.

AGNÈS. Until that time, how wretched I shall be!

1480 HORACE. My happiness, thank Heaven, now is sure,
    And I can go at last and sleep secure.

Scene 4.   ARNOLPHE, AGNÈS

ARNOLPHE (concealed in his cloak and disguising his
    voice).
    Come on now, you will not be living *there*,
    And lodgings are prepared for you elsewhere.
    I mean to put you in a safer place.
    (Throwing back his cloak, in his normal voice)
    You recognize me?

AGNÈS.   Oh!

ARNOLPHE.   You wretch, my face
    Frightens your senses more than you'll allow,
    And you're dismayed to see me here and now.
    I'm interrupting all your amorous schemes.

(AGNÈS looks around for HORACE.)

    You can't bring back the sweetheart of your
        dreams;
1490 He's too far off to help in such a fix.
    Oh! Oh! So young still, and so full of tricks!
    Your innocence, that seems without a peer,
    Asks whether we make children through the ear;
    But you know how to set a midnight tryst
    And join your lover without being missed!
    Lord! How your tongue can twitter on with him!
    Your schooling can't have been so very prim.
    Who the devil taught you so much so fast?
    And is your fear of ghosts a thing of the past?

Was it he gave you such temerity?   *1500*
Cruel girl, how could you show such perfidy?
And after all my kindness! I'm distressed.
You serpent, whom I fostered at my breast,
And who, at your first thankless inclination,
Pursue your benefactor's ruination!

AGNÈS. Why do you shout so?

ARNOLPHE.   Wouldn't anyone?

AGNÈS. I see no wrong in anything I've done.

ARNOLPHE. Follow a suitor? That's not infamy?

AGNÈS. That suitor says he wants to marry me.
I've heard you preach; your lessons have sunk in: *1510*
One must be married to avoid the sin.

ARNOLPHE. Yes, but married to me was what I
    meant,
And I believe you knew of my intent.

AGNÈS. Yes, but to speak quite frankly, *entre nous,*
He suits my taste for this better than you.
With you, marriage is tiresome and austere;
You always represent it as severe.
But he makes it so pleasureful instead,
He really makes me eager to be wed.

ARNOLPHE. Traitress, you love him then?

AGNÈS.   I love him; yes. *1520*

ARNOLPHE. You have the gall to tell me that, Agnès?

AGNÈS. Since it is true, shouldn't I be sincere?

ARNOLPHE. And ought you to have loved him, minx?

AGNÈS.   Oh, dear!
He made it happen. What am I to do?
And when it did, I wasn't meaning to.

ARNOLPHE. You should have banned that amorous
    desire.

AGNÈS. How can you ban what sets your heart on fire?

ARNOLPHE. Didn't you know I'd frown on this affair?

AGNÈS. I? Not at all. Why on earth should you care?

ARNOLPHE. Oh, this should fill my cup with
1530   happiness!
    In short, you do not love me then.

AGNÈS.   You?

ARNOLPHE.   Yes.

AGNÈS. Alas! No.

ARNOLPHE.   What, no?

AGNÈS.   Would you have me lie?

ARNOLPHE. And why not love me, hussy? Tell me
    why.

AGNÈS. He made me love him; I am not to blame.
    Why couldn't you have tried to do the same?
    I surely didn't stop you, did I now?

ARNOLPHE. Really, I did the best that I knew how;
    But all my pains were wasted, I confess.

AGNÈS. He must know how better than you, I guess;
1540   He made me love him without half a try.

ARNOLPHE. Just hear this peasant argue and reply.
    Damn it! Would a *précieuse* say any more?
    Oh, I've misjudged her; or else, on that score,
    A stupid girl knows more than any sage.
    Since disputation is your present rage,

My pretty reasoner, does it make sense
To bring you up, for him, at my expense?

AGNÈS. Oh, no. He'll pay each penny back again.

ARNOLPHE *(aside)*. She finds expressions that increase
   my pain.
         (Aloud)
Will he discharge, able as he may be,   *1550*
The obligations, minx, you have to me?

AGNÈS. You find these great; I find them rather small.

ARNOLPHE. I've brought you up; is that nothing at all?

AGNÈS. Indeed, that was a wondrous operation,
And you gave me a pretty education!
Do you think I fool myself, and fail to see
That I'm as ignorant as I can be?
I am ashamed, myself; and at my age,
It's time for me to leave the idiot stage.

ARNOLPHE. You're tired of ignorance, and, come
   what may,   *1560*
Want lessons from this dandy?

AGNÈS.   I should say.
It is from him I know all that I know:
Much more than you, he is the one I owe.

ARNOLPHE. Lord, what bravado! I don't understand
Why I don't take revenge with this right hand.
Her tantalizing coldness drives me mad,
And a few cuffs would make my spirit glad.

AGNÈS. Alas! You have the power, if you desire.

ARNOLPHE *(aside)*. Her words, her glance, how they
   disarm my ire!
How they bring back my tenderness to stay,   *1570*
And drive my evil thoughts of her away!
How strange a thing is love! How soft the male

Is proven by each feminine betrayal!
All are aware of women's frailties,
Their indiscretion, their absurdities,
Their fragile soul and their pernicious spirit;
Nothing could be more weak, devoid of merit,
Nothing more faithless: why, they're hardly human!
Yet man does almost anything for woman.
                        (Aloud)
1580   Well, let's make peace. Traitress, live and let live.
Take back my heart; I'm ready to forgive.
Thus you may judge the love with which I burn,
And, seeing me so good, love me in turn.

AGNÈS. I'd like to grant your wish, I really would:
What would it cost me—if I only could?

ARNOLPHE. Poor little doll, you can if you just try.
                        (He sighs.)
Consider well that tender, loving sigh,
That dying glance, the person that I am;
Give up that urchin and his love, my lamb.
1590   He must have charmed you by some sorcery,
And you will be far happier with me.
Clothing and finery are your great passion:
I swear you shall be always in the fashion.
I will caress you always, night and noon,
Fondle you, kiss you, eat you with a spoon;
And you may do whatever you like best.
I've said enough; you can work out the rest.
                        (Aside)
How far passion can lead a man astray!
                        (Aloud)
Nothing can match my love in any way.
1600   Ungrateful girl, what proof would you suggest?
Am I to weep for you, or beat my chest?
Tear out half of my hair for love of you?
Or kill myself? Just tell me what to do.
I'll prove my love to you in any way.

AGNÈS. My soul is deaf to all these things you say,

And two words from Horace would have more
   weight.

ARNOLPHE. You've flouted me too long. Let's get
      things straight.
I'll carry out my plan, you stubborn pretty,
And pack you off this instant from this city.
You scorn my suit and put me on the rack;   *1610*
But now a convent cell shall pay you back.

Scene 5.   ALAIN, ARNOLPHE, AGNÈS

ALAIN. I don't know how it is, sir, but I guess
The corpse must have departed with Agnès.

ARNOLPHE. Here she is. Shut her up inside my room.
He won't go looking there, her would-be groom;
And in just half an hour we'll take the road
To carry her to some secret abode.
I'll get a carriage. Lock yourselves up tight,
And never let her get out of your sight.
                   (Exeunt ALAIN *and* AGNÈS.)
She may be of the sort that one can wean   *1620*
From her affection by a change of scene.

Scene 6.   ARNOLPHE, HORACE

HORACE. Seigneur Arnolphe! I've had a frightful
      blow!
Heaven has certainly decreed my woe.
A deadly plot seeks to drive us apart
And tear from me the darling of my heart.
My father traveled hither all last night.
I met him here, just ready to alight.
And listen to the reason why he's here—

Which, as I said, had never been made clear—
1630 All unbeknownst he's made a match for me,
And comes to honor this solemnity.
Imagine—you will sympathize, I know—
If I could suffer any greater blow!
Enrique, whom I inquired about of late,
Has been the cause of my disastrous fate.
He comes here with my father, on his side;
His only daughter is my destined bride.
I thought I'd faint at what they had to say;
And soon, finding I could not bear to stay,
1640 Since Father planned to visit you, he said,
In consternation I came on ahead.
I beg you, do not say a word about
My new attachment which might put him out.
And, since he has great faith in you, please try
To change his mind about this other tie.

ARNOLPHE. Of course.

HORACE.   Just show him the advantage of
A short delay, and thus assist my love.

ARNOLPHE. I shall.

HORACE.   I put my trust in you alone.

ARNOLPHE. Good.

HORACE.   You're a truer father than my own.
1650 Say that my age . . . He's here! Let's step aside.
Listen: I've many reasons to provide.

(They move to a corner of the stage.)

Scene 7. ENRIQUE, ORONTE, CHRYSALDE, HORACE,
                        ARNOLPHE

ENRIQUE *(to* CHRYSALDE*)*. The moment I first saw
      you, I could tell
There's something in your face that I know well.
I find in you your lovely sister's features,
My wife, dearest to me of all God's creatures;
And happy I would be if cruel fate
Had let me bring back home that faithful mate,
After our miseries, to join me in
The happiness of seeing all her kin.
But since the fatal power of destiny   *1660*
Has taken her away from you and me,
Let us accept our loss, and spend our pains
On planning for the one child that remains.
You are concerned; and therefore I would not,
Without your full consent, decide her lot.
The choice of Oronte's son is glorious,
Provided that it pleases both of us.

CHRYSALDE. You pay my judgment no great
      compliment
If you can doubt my unreserved assent.

ARNOLPHE *(to* HORACE*)*. Yes, I shall serve your inter-
      ests as I must.   *1670*

HORACE. Be sure to keep . . .

ARNOLPHE.   I shall repay your trust.

      (ARNOLPHE *leaves* HORACE, *joins the others, and
                  embraces* ORONTE.*)*

ORONTE. How full of tenderness is this embrace!

ARNOLPHE. What a joy once again to see your face!

ORONTE. I have come here . . .

ARNOLPHE.   You need not say a word;
  I know what brings you.

ORONTE.   You've already heard?

ARNOLPHE. Yes.

ORONTE.   Very good.

ARNOLPHE.   Your son has set his heart
  Against this marriage from the very start.
  He even begged me to defend his side;
  But here's all the advice I can provide:
1680 Do not put off these nuptials, but rather
  Exercise the authority of a father.
  Young people must be shown that we know best;
  Indulgence is against their interest.

HORACE *(aside)*. Traitor!

CHRYSALDE.   I urge you not to have recourse,
  Against his wishes, to the use of force.
  My brother feels as I do, I believe.

ARNOLPHE. What? Shall he have to beg his young-
      ster's leave?
  And should a father be so soft and bland
  That he would let his son flout his command?
1690 I cannot think that he'd be such a fool
  As to be ruled by one whom he should rule!
  No, he's my friend, I share in his repute:
  His word is given, let him execute,
  Show that he can be firm, not merely fond,
  And make his son break off this other bond.

ORONTE. I quite agree with everything you say
  About this match; I warrant he'll obey.

CHRYSALDE *(to ARNOLPHE)*. I am astonished at your
      eagerness

To see these young folks married, I confess;
And I can't guess what's brewing in your head . . . *1700*

ARNOLPHE. I know what must be done and must be
    said.

ORONTE. Seigneur Arnolphe . . .

CHRYSALDE.   Not that name, *s'il vous plaît*;
    I told you, it's Monsieur de La Forêt.

ORONTE. No matter.

HORACE.   How is that?

ARNOLPHE.   Yes, now you know,
    And that is why I had to treat you so.

HORACE. In what confusion . . .

        Scene 8.   GEORGETTE, ENRIQUE, ORONTE,
            CHRYSALDE, HORACE, ARNOLPHE

GEORGETTE.   Sir, come quick; I fear
    We can't restrain Agnès unless you're here;
    She's dying to escape, and possibly
    Might jump right out the window to get free.

ARNOLPHE. Bring her to me; my plans are fully made *1710*
    To take her promptly off.
                        (*To* HORACE)
                        Don't be dismayed.
    Success may well bring pride, do what one may.
    The proverb says that turnabout's fair play.

HORACE. Can any troubles, Heaven, match my woe?
    And has a man ever been brought so low?

ARNOLPHE *(to* ORONTE*).* Schedule the ceremony soon,
   old friend:
  I am concerned, and eager to attend.

ORONTE. Just what we plan.

Scene 9.   AGNÈS, ALAIN, GEORGETTE, ORONTE, EN-
          RIQUE, ARNOLPHE, HORACE, CHRYSALDE

ARNOLPHE *(to* AGNÈS*).* Come, beautiful, come here,
  You whom we couldn't hold, you mutineer.
1720 Here he is: curtsy nicely to your swain
  As his reward for all his zeal and pain.
          (To HORACE*)*
  Farewell. Your aspirations are belied;
  But lovers are not always satisfied.

AGNÈS. Horace, you'd let me be abducted so?

HORACE. I don't know where to turn, so great is my
   woe.

ARNOLPHE. Come, chatterbox.

AGNÈS.   I want to stay right here.

ORONTE. This mystery will have to be made clear.
  Try as we may, we cannot comprehend.

ARNOLPHE. I'll tell you when I have some time to
   spend.
  Goodbye for now.

1730 ORONTE.   Where are you going, pray?
  You're not explaining in the proper way.

ARNOLPHE. I urge that you, despite his discontent,
  Put on the wedding.

ORONTE.   But for that intent,
  If you heard everything, did you not hear
  That this same girl is staying with you here,
  The daughter of the lovely Angélique,
  Who married, secretly, Seigneur Enrique?
  So all your talk—what was it getting at?

CHRYSALDE. I was vastly astonished too at that.

ARNOLPHE. What's this . . . ?

CHRYSALDE.   My sister bore, a secret bride,   *1740*
  One daughter, whose fate she contrived to hide.

ORONTE. The father sent the child, with a false name,
  To be the nursling of a country dame.

CHRYSALDE. And then, while she was there, a hostile fate
  Made of the father an expatriate.

ORONTE. A thousand different risks he underwent
  Across the seas in a far continent.

CHRYSALDE. And there he won what in his native land
  Deceit and envy formerly had banned.

ORONTE. And back in France, he promptly went to
      see   *1750*
  The one who had his daughter's custody.

CHRYSALDE. This peasant woman told him all she
      knew:
  That she had passed the girl, aged four, to you.

ORONTE. Since you were noted for your charity,
  And she was in the throes of poverty.

CHRYSALDE. Enrique, transported with relief and
      bliss,
  Has brought the woman here to witness this.

ORONTE. And you shall see her soon arriving here
So that this mystery may at last be clear.

1760 CHRYSALDE. I think I can imagine your despair;
But fate is kind to you in this affair.
Since you so fear your marriage may miscarry,
Your surest policy is not to marry.

ARNOLPHE. Ouf!

        (Exit overcome, unable to speak.)

ORONTE.   What! Without a word?

HORACE.   You soon shall know
In full, Father, what mystifies you so.
In all this, chance has managed, as you'll find,
Exactly what your wisdom had in mind:
By the sweet ties of mutual love and duty,
I had become engaged to this same beauty;
She, whom you came to seek and whom you
1770   choose,
Is just the one I thought I must refuse.

ENRIQUE. I had no doubt about this at first sight;
And ever since she fills me with delight.
My daughter, I have loved you from the start.
        (Embraces AGNÈS.)

CHRYSALDE. I'd do the same, brother, with all my
    heart;
But this is not the place. So, if you please,
Let's go in and resolve these mysteries,
Repay Arnolphe for all his interest,
And thank Heaven, which does all for the best!

The Critique of
The School for Wives

THE CRITIQUE OF
THE SCHOOL FOR WIVES

A prose comedy in seven scenes, first performed June 1, 1663, at the Théâtre du Palais-Royal, by Molière's company, the Troupe de Monsieur. Élise was played by Mlle. Molière, Climène by Mlle. du Parc, Dorante by Brécourt, Lysidas by Du Croisy, the Marquis probably by Molière himself.

The great success of *The School for Wives* was an affront to those who disliked it, and they attacked it on devious and trivial grounds. Molière's younger friend Boileau urged him to let the critics talk, but he preferred to strike back. He chose three main targets, the ostentatious prudes, the empty-headed fops, and the jealous pedantic authors, personified them in Climène, the Marquis, and Lysidas, showed them and their criticisms up as ridiculous, and defended his play and his sense of comedy.

Tragedy, he argues (thinking of Corneille, with whom he was on bad terms at the time), is relatively easy; the imagination has free play; comedy alone is responsible to truth and realism. Against the foolish prudes, fops, and pedants, he appeals to the sound good sense of the pit and the still more discerning taste of the court. From the artificial rules that sterile theorists sought to apply, like Procrustean beds, to living works, he appeals to the one great rule: to please. On this ground and that of good sense, he readily shows that no rules are violated by *The School for Wives*.

Not one of his greatest plays, *The Critique* has great interest for us. It gives us a sense of living in his time, listening to his critics, and hearing him reply. We can allow for bias in his account and still—knowing his power of observation and his basic fairness—be very grateful to have it. Besides general observations on the nature and problems of tragedy and comedy, it offers interesting insights of detail, such as Dorante's explanation (scene 6) that the merit of a phrase such as "children through the ear" is not at all in the phrase itself but in what we learn about Arnolphe from his delight that Agnès should have used it.

Molière gives more space to the criticisms than to the refutations, and leaves his critics still talking and by no means convinced. To be sure, he makes his points; but it is rare in didactic drama or dialogue that the fools have so good a say and are left so untouched by the voices of good sense. Thus the effect of the play is rather wry. Molière's purpose was presumably to suggest that no amount of reason would convert the fools, to annoy the spectators with them, and thus in effect to enlist the sympathy of his public and ask them to bring in, by their attendance and applause, the final favorable verdict. His strategy seems to have worked well.

THE CRITIQUE OF THE
SCHOOL FOR WIVES

CHARACTERS

URANIE
ÉLISE
CLIMÈNE
GALOPIN, *a lackey*
THE MARQUIS
DORANTE, or THE CHEVALIER
LYSIDAS, *a poet*

The scene is Uranie's drawing room, in Paris

Scene 1.   URANIE, ÉLISE

URANIE. What, cousin, has no one come to call on you?

ÉLISE. Not a soul.

URANIE. Really, I'm amazed; we've both been alone all day.

ÉLISE. I'm amazed too, for it's hardly our custom; and your house, thank the Lord, is the ordinary refuge of all the court loafers.

173

URANIE. To tell the truth, the afternoon has seemed very long to me.

ÉLISE. As for me, I have found it very short.

URANIE. That, cousin, is because clever people like solitude.

ÉLISE. You're very kind, but no: you know I have no pretensions to cleverness.

URANIE. For my part, I like company, I confess.

ÉLISE. I like it too, but I like it select; and the quantity of stupid visits that you have to put up with among the others makes me very often take pleasure in being alone.

URANIE. Delicacy is too great if it cannot endure any but choice people.

ÉLISE. And complaisance is too general if it endures all kinds of people indiscriminately.

URANIE. I enjoy those that are reasonable, and those that are characters amuse me.

ÉLISE. My word, the characters don't take long to become bores, and most of those people aren't funny any more by the second visit. But speaking of characters, won't you get me rid of that bothersome marquis of yours? Do you mean to leave him on my hands forever, and do you think I can live through his everlasting puns?

URANIE. That's the fashionable way to talk, and they think it's very funny at court.

ÉLISE. Too bad for those who do, and who kill themselves all day long talking that obscure jargon. What a fine thing, to bring into the conversations at the Louvre* a

*In Molière's day, the royal palace.

lot of old double meanings picked up in the mud of Les
Halles* and of the Place Maubert!† What a pretty way
to be funny, for courtiers! And how witty a man is when
he comes up and says to you: "Madame, you are in the
Place Royale, and everyone sees you from three
leagues out of Paris, for everyone sees you *de bon
œil*,"‡ because Bonneuil is a village three leagues from
here! Isn't that mighty gallant and clever? And those
who hit upon such sparkling finds, haven't they good
reason to be proud of them?

URANIE. Well, but they don't say that as something witty;
and most of those who affect that language know very
well themselves that it's ridiculous.

ÉLISE. Then again, too bad, to take pains to say stupid
things and to be bad jokers on purpose. I hold them all
the less excusable for that; and if I were their judge, I
know just how I'd sentence all these gentlemen pun-
sters.

URANIE. Let's drop this subject; it gets you a little too
heated up; and let's take note that Dorante is quite late,
it seems to me, in coming to have supper with us.

ÉLISE. Perhaps he's forgotten, and . . .

Scene 2.   GALOPIN, URANIE, ÉLISE

GALOPIN. Madame, here's Climène to see you.

URANIE. Oh, my Lord! What a visit!

ÉLISE. Well, you were complaining of being alone; Heaven
is punishing you.

*The great markets of Paris.
†Then a noisy rendezvous for students and delinquents.
‡Sees you with a favorable eye, looks on you with favor.

URANIE. Quick, go say I'm not at home.

GALOPIN. She's already been told you are.

URANIE. And who's the idiot who told her that?

GALOPIN. Me, Madame.

URANIE. The devil take the little wretch! I'll teach you to give your own answers!

GALOPIN. I'll tell her, Madame, that you want to be out.

URANIE. Stop, you dolt, and show her up, since the damage is done.

GALOPIN. She's still talking to a man in the street.

URANIE. Oh, cousin, how embarrassing this visit is at this hour!

ÉLISE. It's true that the lady is a bit embarrassing by nature. I've always had a frightful aversion for her; and with all respect to her rank, she's the stupidest animal that ever undertook to reason.

URANIE. The epithet is a bit strong.

ÉLISE. Come, come, she certainly deserves that, and something more, to do her justice. Is anyone a better example of what we mean by a *précieuse,** taking the word in its worst sense?

URANIE. Yet she strongly objects to that term.

ÉLISE. That's true: she objects to the term, but not to the thing; for after all she *is* one from head to foot, and the most affected woman in the world. It seems as though her whole body is unhinged, and as though she moves her thighs, her shoulders, and her head only by springs.

*For a fuller portrait of two such affectedly refined ladies, see *The Ridiculous Précieuses*.

She always affects a languishing, simpering tone of voice, she pouts to make her mouth look small, and she rolls her eyes to make them look big.

URANIE. *Softly:* if she should hear you . . .

ÉLISE. No, no, she's not coming up yet. I still remember the evening when she wanted to see Damon,* because of the reputation he has and the things of his that the public has seen. You know the man, and his natural laziness about keeping up a conversation. She had invited him to supper as a wit, and never did he appear so stupid, among half a dozen people to whom she had played him up, and who were staring at him wide-eyed as a person who must be not made like other men. They all thought he was there to entertain the company with witty remarks, that every word that came out of his mouth must be extraordinary, that he must make impromptu epigrams about everything that was said, and not ask for a drink except with a quip. But he let them down hard by his silence; and the lady was as dissatisfied with him as I was with her.

URANIE. Quiet. I'm going to the door to receive her.

ÉLISE. One word more. I'd really like to see her married to the marquis we were talking about. That would be a fine match: a *précieuse* and a punster!

URANIE. Will you be quiet? Here she is.

Scene 3.   CLIMÈNE, URANIE, ÉLISE, GALOPIN

URANIE. Really, it's very late that . . .

CLIMÈNE. Oh! Please, my dear, have them bring me a chair, quick.

* Possibly meant to represent Molière.

URANIE. A chair, promptly.

CLIMÈNE. Oh! My heavens!

URANIE. Why, what is it?

CLIMÈNE. I'm exhausted.

URANIE. What's the matter?

CLIMÈNE. My heart fails me.

URANIE. Is it vapors that have struck you?

CLIMÈNE. No.

URANIE. Do you want to be unlaced?

CLIMÈNE. Good Lord, no. Oh!

URANIE. Then what is your trouble? And when did it strike you?

CLIMÈNE. Over three hours ago. I got it at the Palais-Royal.*

URANIE. How's that?

CLIMÈNE. I've just seen, for my sins, that wretched rhapsody *The School for Wives*. I'm still all weak, it made me so sick; and I don't think I'll get over it for more than a fortnight.

ÉLISE. Just look at the way illnesses come on without our thinking about it!

URANIE. I don't know what temperament my cousin and I share, but we went to the same play day before yesterday and both came back hale and hearty.

CLIMÈNE. What? You've seen it?

*The theater where Molière's *School for Wives* was playing.

URANIE. Yes, and listened from beginning to end.

CLIMÈNE. And it didn't give you convulsions, my dear?

URANIE. I'm not so delicate, thank the Lord! And for my part I think that comedy would be more likely to cure people than to make them sick.

CLIMÈNE. Oh, good heavens! What are you saying? Can such a proposition be advanced by a person who has some stock of common sense? Can one enter the lists with impunity against reason, as you do? And in all truth, is there a mind so starved for drollery that it can relish the insipidities with which that comedy is seasoned? For my part, I confess to you that I did not find the slightest grain of salt in the whole thing. *The children through the ear* seemed to me in the most detestable taste; the *cream tart* made my gorge rise; and I almost vomited at the *soup*.*

ÉLISE. My word! How elegantly put! I would have thought that the play was good; but Madame's eloquence is so persuasive, she turns things in so charming a way, that one has to agree with her in spite of oneself.

URANIE. For my part, I'm not so complaisant; and to speak my mind, I think this comedy is one of the most amusing the author has produced.

CLIMÈNE. Oh! I pity you for talking so; and I cannot bear such obscurity of discernment in you. Can anyone with some claim to virtue find charm in a play which keeps modesty perpetually in alarm and sullies the imagination at every moment?

ÉLISE. Those are pretty ways of speaking! How rough you play in criticism, Madame! And how I pity poor Molière for having you as an enemy!

CLIMÈNE. Believe me, my dear, correct your judgment in

*The School for Wives, lines 164, 99, 436.

good earnest; and for the sake of your honor, don't go saying in society that you liked that comedy.

URANIE. Well, *I* don't know what you found in it to wound anyone's modesty.

CLIMÈNE. Alas, everything! And I maintain that a decent woman could not see it without confusion, I discovered so much dirt and filth in it.

URANIE. Then you must have an eye for filth that others have not; for I didn't see any myself.

CLIMÈNE. Certainly, that's because you wouldn't see any; for after all, thank heaven, all the dirty parts are barefaced. They haven't the slightest wrap to cover them, and even the boldest eyes are horrified at their nudity.

ÉLISE. Ah!

CLIMÈNE *(reminiscent)*. Hee, hee, hee!

URANIE. But once again, please point me out one of these dirty parts you speak of.

CLIMÈNE. Alas! Is it necessary to point them out to you?

URANIE. Yes. I ask you for just one place that really shocked you.

CLIMÈNE. Do you need any other than the scene with that Agnès, when she says what was taken from her?

URANIE. Well! What do you consider dirty in that?

CLIMÈNE. Ah!

URANIE. Please?

CLIMÈNE. Fie!

URANIE. But still?

CLIMÈNE. I have nothing to say to you.

URANIE. For my part, I see no harm in it.

CLIMÈNE. All the worse for you.

URANIE. Rather all the better, it seems to me. I look at things in the way they are shown me, and I don't turn them around to look for what shouldn't be seen.

CLIMÈNE. A woman's decency . . .

URANIE. A woman's decency does not reside in grimaces. It is unbecoming to want to seem more virtuous than the virtuous. Affectation in this matter is worse than in any other; and I see nothing so ridiculous as that delicacy of honor which takes everything amiss, gives a criminal sense to the most innocent words, and takes offense at the shadow of things. Believe me, these women who make such a fuss are not esteemed more upright for that. On the contrary, their mysterious severity and affected grimaces provoke everyone's censure upon the actions of their life. People are delighted to discover whatever is open to criticism in them; and to give you an example, the other day at this comedy there were some women right across from the box we were in, who, by the looks they affected during the whole play, the way they would turn their heads away and hide their faces, provoked on every side a hundred foolish remarks about their behavior which would not have been made otherwise; and even one of the lackeys called right out that they were more chaste in the ears than in all the rest of their bodies.

CLIMÈNE (ironic). In short, you have to be blind to watch that play, and seem not to see what's there.

URANIE. You shouldn't insist on seeing what isn't there.

CLIMÈNE. Oh! Once more, I maintain that the dirty parts knock your eyes out.

URANIE. And *I* do not agree on that.

CLIMÈNE. What? Modesty isn't obviously wounded by what Agnès says in the place we're talking about?

URANIE. No, really. She doesn't say a word that isn't perfectly decent in itself; and if you want to understand something else hidden underneath, you are the one who's making it dirty, not she, since she is only speaking of a ribbon that has been taken from her.

CLIMÈNE. Oh! Ribbon all you like; but that *the*,* which she stops at, is not put in for peanuts. That *the* gives rise to strange thoughts. That *the* is frantically scandalizing; and say what you may, you cannot possibly defend the insolence of that *the*.

ÉLISE. It's true, cousin, I am for Madame against that *the*. That *the* is insolent to the uttermost degree, and you are wrong to defend that *the*.

CLIMÈNE. It has an intolerable salacity.

ÉLISE. How do you say that word, Madame?

CLIMÈNE. Salacity, Madame.

ÉLISE. Oh! My goodness, salacity!† I don't know what that word means, but I think it is as pretty as can be.

CLIMÈNE. There, you see how your own flesh and blood takes my side.

URANIE. Oh, my word! She's a talker who doesn't say what she thinks. If you'll take my word for it, don't trust her much.

ÉLISE. Oh, how mean you are to try to make me suspect to Madame! Just see where I'd be if she went and be-

---

*The School for Wives, ll. 572, 578.
†The French word, obscénité (obscenity), was evidently a précieux neologism in Molière's time.

lieved what you say! Could I be so unfortunate, Madame, as to have you think this of me?

CLIMÈNE. No, no. I don't take her remarks seriously, and I think you are more sincere than she says.

ÉLISE. Ah! How right you are, Madame, and how you will do me justice when you believe that I find you the most engaging person in the world, that I enter into all your sentiments and am charmed with all the expressions that issue from your mouth!

CLIMÈNE. Alas! I speak without affectation.

ÉLISE. This is easy to see, Madame, and that everything in you is natural. Your words, the tone of your voice, your glances, your walk, your gestures and your dress, have an indefinable air of distinction about them that enchants everyone. I am studying you with eyes and ears; and I am so full of you that I try to ape you and imitate you in everything.

CLIMÈNE. You are making fun of me, Madame.

ÉLISE. Pardon me, Madame. Who would want to make fun of you?

CLIMÈNE. I am not a good model, Madame.

ÉLISE. Oh yes, you are, Madame!

CLIMÈNE. You flatter me, Madame.

ÉLISE. Not at all, Madame.

CLIMÈNE. Spare me, please, Madame.

ÉLISE. Indeed I do spare you, Madame, and I do not say half of what I think, Madame.

CLIMÈNE. Oh, good heavens! Let's drop the subject, pray. You would plunge me into the most frightful embarrassment. (*To* URANIE) Now, here we are both against you, and obstinacy is unbecoming to clever people . . .

Scene 4.   THE MARQUIS, CLIMÈNE, GALOPIN, URANIE, ÉLISE.

GALOPIN. Stop, sir, please!

MARQUIS. You don't know me, obviously.

GALOPIN. Oh yes, I know you; but you shan't come in.

MARQUIS. Oh! What a lot of noise, little lackey!

GALOPIN. It's not proper to try to come in in spite of people.

MARQUIS. I want to see your mistress.

GALOPIN. She's not at home, I tell you.

MARQUIS. There she is in the room.

GALOPIN. That's true, there she is; but she isn't there.

URANIE. What's the trouble here?

MARQUIS. It's your lackey, Madame, playing the fool.

GALOPIN. I tell him you're not at home, Madame, and he won't stop coming in.

URANIE. And why tell the gentleman I'm not at home?

GALOPIN. You scolded me the other day for telling him you were.

URANIE. Look at that insolence! I beg you, sir, not to believe what he says. He's a little scatterbrain, who took you for someone else.

MARQUIS. I saw that clearly, Madame; and but for my respect for you, I would have taught him to recognize people of quality.

ÉLISE. My cousin is much obliged to you for this deference.

URANIE. Well, then, a chair, malapert.

GALOPIN. Isn't that one?

URANIE. Bring it here.

(GALOPIN *pushes the chair up roughly, and exits.*)

MARQUIS. Your little lackey, Madame, is scornful of my person.

ÉLISE. He would be very wrong, unquestionably.

MARQUIS. Perhaps that's because I'm paying damages for my bad appearance—hee, hee, hee, hee!

ÉLISE. Age will make him more discerning of gentlemen.

MARQUIS. What were you talking about, ladies, when I interrupted you?

URANIE. The comedy *The School for Wives*.

MARQUIS. I've just been to see it.

CLIMÈNE. Well, sir, what do you think of it, pray?

MARQUIS. Absolutely impertinent.

CLIMÈNE. Oh! I'm delighted to hear it!

MARQUIS. It's the worst thing you ever saw. Why, what

the devil! I could hardly get a seat; I was nearly smothered going in, and I've never had my feet so stepped
on. I beg you, just see the condition my knee ruffles and
ribbons are in!

ÉLISE. It's true, that calls for vengeance on *The School for
Wives,* and you are quite right to condemn it.

MARQUIS. Never, I think, was such a bad comedy written.

URANIE. Ah! Here's Dorante, whom we were expecting.

Scene 5.   DORANTE, THE MARQUIS, CLIMÈNE, ÉLISE, URANIE

DORANTE. Please don't move and don't interrupt your
talk. You're on a subject which for four days has been
practically the topic of every house in Paris; and you've
never seen anything so amusing as the variety of judgments that are passed on it. For to sum it up, I've heard
this comedy condemned by some people for the same
things that I have seen others esteem the most.

URANIE. Monsieur le Marquis here speaks very ill of it.

MARQUIS. That's true, I think it's detestable. Egad, detestable as detestable can be; what you may call detestable.

DORANTE. And I, my dear Marquis, I consider that judgment detestable.

MARQUIS. What? Chevalier, do you mean to defend that
play?

DORANTE. Yes, I mean to defend it.

MARQUIS. By Jove! I guarantee it's detestable.

DORANTE. That's no average guarantee. But pray, Marquis, for what reason is this comedy—what you say?

MARQUIS. Why it's detestable?

DORANTE. Yes.

MARQUIS. It's detestable, because it's detestable.

DORANTE. After that, there'll be nothing more to say; the case against it is closed. But still inform us, and tell us the faults it has.

MARQUIS. How do I know? I didn't even take the trouble to listen. But anyway, I know very well I've never seen anything so bad, damme! And Dorilas, who was next to me, agreed with me.

DORANTE. There's a fine authority, and you are well supported.

MARQUIS. All you have to do is observe the continual roars of laughter from the pit. That's all I want, to prove that it's worthless.

DORANTE. So, Marquis, you are one of those gentlemen of fashion who won't allow that the pit has any common sense, and who would be sorry to have joined in its laughter, even at the best thing in the world? The other day I saw one of our friends sitting on the stage who made himself ridiculous in that way. He listened to the whole play with the gloomiest seriousness in the world; and everything that amused the others made him frown. At every burst of laughter he would shrug his shoulders and look with pity on the pit; and sometimes again he would look at it with vexation and say aloud: "Go ahead and laugh, pit, go ahead and laugh." Our friend's chagrin was a second comedy. As a gallant man, he offered it to the whole gathering, and everyone agreed that no one could play it better than he did. I pray you, Marquis, and the others too, learn that good sense has no special seats at a play; that the difference between a gold half-louis and a fifteen-sou piece has no effect on good taste. Standing or sitting, a man can pass a bad judgment; and in short, generally speaking, I would be rather willing to trust the approval of the pit, for this reason: that there are many in it who are capable of judging a play according to the rules, and the others judge it as it should be judged, by letting themselves be gripped by what's in it without either blind prejudice, affected indulgence, or ridiculous delicacy.

MARQUIS. So now, Chevalier, you're the defender of the pit? Gad! I'm delighted, and I shan't fail to inform it that you are one of its friends. Hee, hee, hee, hee, hee, hee!

DORANTE. Laugh all you like. I am for good sense, and I can't abide the ebullitions of the brain of our Marquises de Mascarille.* It drives me mad to see these people who make themselves ridiculous in spite of their rank; these people who are always decisive and talk boldly about everything without knowing anything about it; who at a play cry out in enthusiasm at the bad parts, and don't stir at the good ones; who when they see a painting or listen to a concert, likewise blame and praise all the wrong things, pick up wherever they can and mimic the technical terms of the art in question, and never fail to mangle them and use them in the wrong place. Oh good Lord, gentlemen, when God has not given you knowledge about something, keep quiet! Don't give those who hear you a laugh; and consider that if you don't say a word, maybe people will think you are clever.

MARQUIS. By Jove, Chevalier, the way you talk . . .

DORANTE. Oh heavens, Marquis, I'm not saying this to you. This is for a dozen of these gentlemen who dishonor court society by their exaggerated manners and make the people think that we're all alike. For my part, I'll do all I can to avoid that reputation; and I'll belabor

---

*A comic character in *The Ridiculous Précieuses*.

them so at every encounter that in the end they'll behave sensibly.

MARQUIS. Just tell me, Chevalier, do you think Lysandre is a clever man?

DORANTE. Yes indeed, very much so.

URANIE. That cannot be denied.

MARQUIS. Ask him what he thinks of *The School for Wives*. You'll see, he'll tell you he doesn't like it.

DORANTE. Oh Lord! Many people are spoiled by being too clever, see things poorly because they are too bright, and would even be very sorry to agree with others, because they want the glory of making the decisions.

URANIE. That's true. Our friend is one of those people, beyond a doubt. He wants to be the first one to hold his opinion, and for others to wait for his judgment out of respect. Any approval that is given before his own is an offense to his brilliance, which he avenges loudly by taking the opposite side. He wants to be consulted about all matters of intelligence; and I am sure that if the author had shown him his comedy before exhibiting it to the public, he would have thought it the finest in the world.

MARQUIS. And what will you say of the Marquise Araminte, who proclaims everywhere that the play is frightful, and says she could never endure the filth it's full of?

DORANTE. I will say that this is worthy of the character she has assumed, and that there are people who make themselves ridiculous by wanting to have too much honor. Although she has some intelligence, she has followed the bad example of those women who, having reached a certain age, want something to replace what they see they are losing, and imagine that the grimaces of a scrupulous prudery will take the place of youth and beauty for them. This lady carries the matter further than anyone, and the astuteness of her scruples discovers dirty meanings where no one else had ever seen them. They say that this scrupulosity of hers goes so far as to disfigure our language, and that there are almost no words from which this lady's severity would not lop off either the head or the tail because of the indecent syllables that she finds in them.

URANIE. You're a mad one, Chevalier.

MARQUIS. In short, Chevalier, you think you are defending your comedy by satirizing those who condemn it.

DORANTE. Not at all; but I maintain that that lady is wrong to be scandalized . . .

ÉLISE. Gently, Sir Chevalier; there might be others besides her who have the same feelings.

DORANTE. I know very well that you're not one, at least; and when you saw the performance . . .

ÉLISE. That's true; but I've changed my mind; and Madame supports her opinion by such convincing reasons that she has won me over to her side.

DORANTE (to CLIMÈNE). Ah! Madame, I ask your pardon; and if you wish, for love of you, I'll unsay everything I've said.

CLIMÈNE. I don't want you to for love of me, but for love of reason; for after all, that play, if you take it rightly, is wholly indefensible; and I can't conceive . . .

URANIE. Ah! Here is Monsieur Lysidas the author. He comes at just the right time for this matter. Monsieur Lysidas,* bring up a chair yourself and sit down there.

---

*The salutation "Monsieur" followed by the proper name is at best slighting, at worst contemptuous. People to reckon with are addressed as "Monsieur" or "Madame" and nothing more unless it is a title, as in "Madame la Marquise."

Scene 6. LYSIDAS, DORANTE, THE MARQUIS, ÉLISE,
URANIE, CLIMÈNE

LYSIDAS. Madame, I'm coming a little late; but I had to read my play at Madame la Marquise's—the one I told you about; and the praise it received kept me an hour longer than I expected.

ÉLISE. Praise is a potent charm to detain an author.

URANIE. Do sit down, Monsieur Lysidas; we'll read your play after supper.

LYSIDAS. All who were there are to come to the première and have promised me that they would do their duty as they should.

URANIE. I can well believe it. But again, sit down, please. We are on a subject here that I would like to have us carry further.

LYSIDAS. I trust, Madame, that you too will reserve a box for that day.

URANIE. We shall see. Pray, let's go on with our talk.

LYSIDAS. I warn you, Madame, that they are nearly all taken.

URANIE. Well and good. Anyway, when you came in I was needing you, and everyone here was against me.

ÉLISE (to URANIE, indicating DORANTE). At first he was on your side; but now that he knows that Madame is at the head of the opposite party, I think you have to look for other help.

CLIMÈNE. No, no, I wouldn't want him to fail to pay his

court to your cousin, and I permit his mind to be on the same side as his heart.

DORANTE. With that permission, Madame, I shall make bold to defend myself.

URANIE. But first let's find out Monsieur Lysidas' sentiments.

LYSIDAS. About what, Madame?

URANIE. On the subject of *The School for Wives*.

LYSIDAS. Ha, ha!

DORANTE. What do you think of it?

LYSIDAS. I have nothing to say about that; and you know that among us authors, we must speak of one another's works with great circumspection.

DORANTE. But still, just between us, what do you think of this comedy?

LYSIDAS. I, sir?

URANIE. Tell us your honest opinion.

LYSIDAS. I think it is very fine.

DORANTE. Really?

LYSIDAS. Really. Why not? Isn't it indeed the finest in the world?

DORANTE. Umhumh, you're a sly devil, Monsieur Lysidas: you're not saying what you think.

LYSIDAS. I beg your pardon?

DORANTE. Good Lord, I know you! Let's not play games.

LYSIDAS. I, sir?

DORANTE. I see very well that the good you say about this play is only out of politeness, and that at the bottom of your heart you agree with the many people who think it is bad.

LYSIDAS. Hee, hee, hee!

DORANTE. Come now, admit that this comedy is a wretched piece of work.

LYSIDAS. It is true that it is not approved by the connoisseurs.

MARQUIS. My word, Chevalier, there you are, and you're paid back for your raillery. Ha, ha, ha, ha, ha!

DORANTE. Go to it, my dear Marquis, go to it!

MARQUIS. You see, we have the intellectuals on our side.

DORANTE. It's true, Monsieur Lysidas' judgment is something considerable. But Monsieur Lysidas will allow me not to surrender for that alone; and since I do indeed have the audacity to defend myself against Madame's sentiments, he will not take it ill if I combat his.

ÉLISE. What? You see against you Madame, Monsieur le Marquis, and Monsieur Lysidas, and still you dare resist? Fie! How ungracious you are!

CLIMÈNE. As for me, that's what confounds me: that reasonable people can take it into their heads to stand up for the stupidities of that play.

MARQUIS. Damme, Madame, it's miserable from beginning to end.

DORANTE. That's soon said, Marquis. Nothing is easier than to settle things that way; and I don't see anything that can be protected from the sovereignty of your decisions.

MARQUIS. Gad! All the other comic actors who were there to see it said the worst possible things about it.

DORANTE. Oh! I've nothing more to say; you're right, Marquis. Since the other actors speak ill of it, of course we must take their word for it. They are all enlightened people speaking without partiality. There is nothing more to say, I give up.

CLIMÈNE. Give up or not, I know very well that you will never persuade me to endure the immodest parts of that play, any more than the disagreeable satire in it against women.

URANIE. As for me, I shall be very careful not to take offense at them or charge anything that is said to my own account. This kind of satire falls directly on modes of behavior, and hits people only indirectly. Let's not go and apply the details of a general censure to ourselves; and let's profit by the lesson, if we can, without pretending it is addressed to us. All the ridiculous portrayals that are exhibited on the stage should be viewed by everyone without chagrin. They are public mirrors, in which we should never show that we see ourselves; and we accuse ourselves publicly of a fault when we take offense at its being reproved.

CLIMÈNE. As for me, I am not talking about these things for any part I may have in them; and I think I live in society in such a way as to have no fear that anyone would think of me in those portrayals of ill-behaved women.

ÉLISE. Certainly, Madame, no one will think of you in them. Your behavior is sufficiently known, and this sort of thing is incontestable.

URANIE (to CLIMÈNE). That is why, Madame, I said nothing that applies to you; and my words, like the satire in comedy, remain within the general thesis.

CLIMÈNE. I don't doubt it, Madame. But let's get off this subject at last. I don't know how you take the insults cast at our sex at a certain point in the play; and for my part, I confess I am frightfully angry to see that this impertinent author calls us *animals*.

URANIE. Don't you see that he has a ridiculous character say this?

DORANTE. And then, Madame, don't you know that lovers' insults never offend? That love can be violent as well as sweetish? And that on such occasions the wildest words—and even worse—are very often taken as marks of affection by the very women who receive them?

ÉLISE. Say all you please, I can't stomach that, any more than the *soup* and the *cream tart,* which Madame was just speaking about.

MARQUIS. Ah! My word, yes, *cream tart!* That's what I had noted a while ago: *cream tart!* I'm so obliged to you, Madame, for reminding me of *cream tart!* Are there enough apples in Normandy to salute *cream tart?** *Cream tart,* by Jove, *cream tart!*

DORANTE. Well, what do you mean, *cream tart?*

MARQUIS. Good heavens! Why, *cream tart,* Chevalier.

DORANTE. But what then?

MARQUIS. *Cream tart!*

DORANTE. Just tell us some of your reasons.

MARQUIS. *Cream tart!*

*Baked apples were sold at theaters and often thrown at bad actors.

URANIE. But it seems to me people should explain what they mean.

MARQUIS. *Cream tart,* Madame!

URANIE. What do you say is wrong with that?

MARQUIS. I? Nothing. *Cream tart!*

URANIE. Oh! I give up.

ÉLISE. Monsieur le Marquis goes about it deftly and trounces you in proper fashion. But I wish Monsieur Lysidas would finish these off with a few little blows of his own.

LYSIDAS. It is not my custom to blame anything, and I am pretty indulgent to other people's works. But after all, with no offense to Monsieur le Chevalier's evident friendship for the author, you will grant me that this sort of comedy is not properly a comedy, and that there is a great difference between all these trifles and the beauty of serious drama. However, everybody is going in for this nowadays; it's the only thing that people flock to see; and there's a frightful solitude at the great works, while nonsensicalities capture all Paris. I must admit my heart sometimes bleeds at this, and it is shameful for France.

CLIMÈNE. It's true, people's taste is strangely corrupted in that regard, and our times are growing frantically scummified.

ÉLISE. That's a pretty one too, *scummified!* Was it you who invented that, Madame?

CLIMÈNE. Oh!

ÉLISE. I certainly suspected it.

DORANTE. So you think, Monsieur Lysidas, that all wit and

beauty are in serious verse drama, and that comic plays are tomfooleries that deserve no praise at all?

URANIE. As for me, that's not my feeling. No doubt, tragedy is a beautiful thing when it's well done; but comedy has its own charms, and I think the one is no less difficult to create than the other.

DORANTE. Certainly, Madame; and if you were to put a *plus* for difficulty on the side of comedy, perhaps you would be making no mistake. For after all, I think it is much easier to strike a lofty pose upon grand sentiments, to brave fortune in rhyme, accuse destiny, and hurl insults at the gods, than to enter into the ridiculous side of men in the right way and represent everybody's defects agreeably on the stage. When you paint heroes, you do what you like. These are portraits drawn at pleasure, in which no one looks for resemblance; and you have only to follow the flights of a soaring imagination, which often abandons the true to seize the marvelous. But when you paint men, you must paint from nature. These portraits are expected to be lifelike; and you've accomplished nothing if you don't make people recognize the men of your day. In a word, in serious plays, to avoid blame it is enough to say things that are sensible and well written; but in the other kind this is not enough, you have to be funny; and it's quite an undertaking, to make people of breeding laugh.

CLIMÈNE. I think I'm numbered among people of breeding; and yet I didn't find a thing to laugh at in all I saw.

MARQUIS. My word, neither did I.

DORANTE. As for you, Marquis, I'm not surprised: you didn't find any puns in it.

LYSIDAS. Faith, sir, what you do find in it isn't much better, and in my opinion all the witticisms are pretty insipid.

DORANTE. The court didn't think so.

LYSIDAS. Ah, sir, the court!

DORANTE. Go ahead, Monsieur Lysidas. I can see you mean that the court is no judge of these things; and the ordinary refuge of you authors, when your works have no success, is to accuse the injustice of the times and the dim discernment of the courtiers. Please learn, Monsieur Lysidas, that courtiers have as good eyes as anyone else; that a person can be as able with plumes and a Venetian lace collar as with a short wig and a plain little neckcloth; that the great test of all your plays is the judgment of the court; that it is *its* taste you must study to learn the art of succeeding; that there is no place where the decisions are so just; and, without putting into account all the learned men who are there, that, from plain natural good sense and the contact with all high society, people there develop a kind of intelligence which judges things with incomparably greater finesse than all the rusty erudition of the pedants.

URANIE. It is true that if you stay there even a little, enough things pass before your eyes every day for you to acquire some habit of discernment, especially as regards good and bad humor.

DORANTE. The court has its follies, I admit, and as you see, I am the first to attack them. But my word, there are plenty of them among the professional wits; and if the plays lampoon a few marquises, I think there is much more reason to lampoon the authors, and that it would be a funny thing to put on the stage their learned grimaces and ridiculous refinements, their vicious custom of boring people to death with their works, their greediness for praise, the expedient caution of their ideas, their deals for getting a reputation, and their offensive and defensive leagues, as well as their wars of wit and their battles of prose and verse.

LYSIDAS. Molière is very fortunate, Monsieur, to have so warm a protector as you. But anyway, to come to the point, the question is whether his play is good; and I will undertake to indicate a hundred evident defects in it everywhere.

URANIE. It's a curious thing about you playwrights that you always condemn the plays that everybody flocks to, and never say anything good except about those that nobody goes to see. You display for the first an invincible hatred, and for the others an inconceivable tenderness.

DORANTE. That's because it's noble to be on the side of the afflicted.

URANIE. But pray, Monsieur Lysidas, show us these defects that I did not notice.

LYSIDAS. Those who know their Aristotle and their Horace see first of all, Madame, that this comedy sins against all the rules of the art.

URANIE. I admit I am not at all familiar with those gentlemen, and I don't know the rules of the art.

DORANTE. You people are funny with your rules, with which you embarrass the ignorant and deafen the rest of us every day. To hear you talk, it seems as though these rules of the art are the greatest mysteries in the world; and yet they are merely a few simple observations which good sense has made about what can take away the pleasure one finds in this sort of poem;* and the same good sense which made these observations once, still makes them easily every day without the help of Horace and Aristotle. I would really like to know whether the great rule of all rules is not to please, and whether a play that has attained its purpose has not followed a good path. Do these people think that an entire public is deluded about this kind of thing, and that each person is not the judge of the pleasure he takes in it?

URANIE. I've noticed one thing about these gentlemen:

*Throughout his discussion of drama in this play, Molière has verse drama in mind.

that those who talk the most about the rules, and know them better than anyone else, write comedies that nobody considers good.

DORANTE. And that, Madame, is what shows how little attention we should pay to their involved disputes. For after all, if the plays that are according to the rules are not liked, and if those that are liked are not according to the rules, then the rules must necessarily have been badly made. So let's laugh off this chicanery which they want to impose on the public's taste, and consult nothing about a play but the effect it has on us. Let's let ourselves go wholeheartedly to the things that grip us by the entrails, and let's not seek out arguments to keep ourselves from having pleasure.

URANIE. As for me, when I see a comedy, I consider only whether the things in it touch me; and when I have been really amused, I don't go asking whether I was wrong and whether Aristotle's rules forbade me to laugh.

DORANTE. That's just as if a man had found an excellent sauce and wanted to examine whether it was good according to the precepts of *The French Cook.* *

URANIE. That's true; and I marvel at some people's refinements upon things that we should feel for ourselves.

DORANTE. You are right, Madame, to consider all these mysterious refinements strange. For after all, if they take place, we are reduced to no longer believing our own selves; our own senses will be slaves in all matters; and even to food and drink, we will no longer dare to think that anything is good without permission from my lords the experts.

LYSIDAS. In short, sir, your entire reason is that *The School for Wives* was liked; and you don't care whether it stays within the rules, provided . . .

DORANTE. Gently, Monsieur Lysidas, I don't grant you

*La Varenne, *Le Cuisinier françois* (1651).

that. I do indeed say that the great art is to please, and
that since this comedy pleased those for whom it was
written, I think that that is enough for it and that it
shouldn't worry much about the rest. But at the same
time, I maintain that it does not sin against any of the
rules you speak of. I have read them, thank God, as
often as the next man; and I could easily demonstrate
that we have perhaps no play in the theater more regular than that one.

CLIMÈNE. Courage, Monsieur Lysidas! We are lost if you
draw back.

LYSIDAS. What, sir? The protasis, the epitasis, and the
peripety . . . ?

DORANTE. Oh, Monsieur Lysidas, you belabor us with
your big words. Don't appear so scholarly, pray. Hu-
manize your talk, and speak to be understood. Do you
think a Greek name gives more weight to your reasons?
And wouldn't you think it sounded as good to say the
exposition of the subject as the protasis, the plot development as the epitasis, and the denouement as the
peripety?

LYSIDAS. Those are technical terms which it is permissible
to use. But since those words offend your ears, I shall
explain myself in another way, and I ask you to give me
a positive reply to three or four comments I shall make.
Can one put up with a play which sins against the very
definition of a theatrical play? For after all, the term
dramatic poem comes from a Greek word meaning "to
act," showing that the nature of this sort of poem consists in action. And in this comedy no actions take place,
and everything consists of the accounts related by either
Agnès or Horace.

MARQUIS. Aha, Chevalier!

CLIMÈNE. That is shrewdly observed indeed, and gets to
the heart of things.

LYSIDAS. Is there anything so devoid of wit, or, to put it

better, anything so low, as certain phrases at which everybody laughs, and especially the one about *children through the ear?*

CLIMÈNE. Very good.

ÉLISE. Ah!

LYSIDAS. Isn't the scene between the valet and the maid inside the house* tediously long and completely irrelevant?

MARQUIS. That's true.

CLIMÈNE. Indeed it is.

ÉLISE. He's right.

LYSIDAS. Doesn't Arnolphe give his money too freely to Horace? And since he is the ridiculous character in the play, should he have been made to perform the act of a man of breeding?

MARQUIS. Good! Another good point!

CLIMÈNE. Admirable!

ÉLISE. Marvelous!

LYSIDAS. The sermon and the *Maxims:* aren't they ridiculous things, which offend the very respect that we owe to these mysteries of ours?

MARQUIS. That's well said!

CLIMÈNE. That's the way to talk!

ÉLISE. Nothing could be better!

LYSIDAS. And finally that Monsieur de La Forêt, who is represented to us as an intelligent man, and who ap-

*Act I, scene 2.

pears so serious in so many places: doesn't he descend to something too comical and too exaggerated in the fifth act, when he explains to Agnès the violence of his love, with that preposterous rolling of his eyes, those ridiculous sighs, and those idiotic tears which make everybody laugh?

MARQUIS. Gad! A marvel!

CLIMÈNE. A miracle!

ÉLISE. Long live Monsieur Lysidas!

LYSIDAS. I omit a thousand other things, for fear of being tedious.

MARQUIS. By Jove, Chevalier, you're in a bad way!

DORANTE. We shall see.

MARQUIS. My word, you've found your match!

DORANTE. Perhaps.

MARQUIS. Answer, answer, answer, answer!

DORANTE. Gladly. He . . .

MARQUIS. Go on and answer, I beg you.

DORANTE. Then let me speak. If . . .

MARQUIS. Gad, I defy you to answer!

DORANTE. Of course, if you keep talking.

CLIMÈNE. Please, let's hear his arguments.

DORANTE. In the first place, it is not true to say that the entire play is in nothing but accounts. Many actions are seen taking place on the stage, and the accounts themselves are actions, according to the nature of the subject;

for they are all given innocently to the person concerned, who is thereby thrown at every turn into a confusion that delights the spectators, and who, at each further piece of news, takes all the measures he can to ward off the calamity he fears.

URANIE. For my part, I think the very beauty of the subject of *The School for Wives* consists in these perpetual confidences; and what seems to me quite funny is that a man of some intelligence, who is warned of everything by an innocent girl whom he wants to marry and by a scatterbrained boy who is his rival, cannot even so avoid what happens to him.

MARQUIS. Trifles, trifles.

CLIMÈNE. Weak reply.

ÉLISE. Bad reasons.

DORANTE. As regards the *children through the ear*, that is funny only in relation to Arnolphe; and the author didn't put it in as being a witty remark in itself, but only as something which characterizes the man and portrays his absurdity all the better for that; since he reports a trivial foolish remark of Agnès as the funniest thing in the world, which gives him inconceivable joy.

MARQUIS. That's a poor answer.

CLIMÈNE. That's not satisfactory.

ÉLISE. That doesn't say a thing.

DORANTE. As for the money he gives freely, besides the fact that his best friend's letter is sufficient security, there is nothing incompatible about a person's being ridiculous in certain things and a man of breeding in others. And as for the scene with Alain and Georgette in the house, which some people have found long and flat, it certainly has its reasons. For even as Arnolphe finds himself caught, during his absence, by the pure inno-

cence of his beloved, so on his return he is detained a
long time outside his own door by the innocence of his
servants, that he may be punished throughout by the
very things by which he thought to make his precautions sure.

MARQUIS. There are some worthless arguments for you!

CLIMÈNE. All that makes no difference.

ÉLISE. That's pitiful.

DORANTE. As for the moral speech that you call a sermon,
it is certain that some really devout people who have
heard it did not find it offensive to the things you speak
of; and surely the words *hell* and *boiling caldrons* are
sufficiently justified by the eccentricity of Arnolphe and
the innocence of the girl he is speaking to. And as for
the amorous transport in the fifth act, which is accused
of being too exaggerated and too comical, I would like
to know if that is not a satire of lovers, and if even the
most serious men of breeding, on similar occasions,
don't do things . . . ?

MARQUIS. My word, Chevalier, you'd do better to be
silent.

DORANTE. Very well. But after all, if we looked at our
own selves, when we are really in love . . . ?

MARQUIS. I don't even want to listen to you.

DORANTE. Listen to me, if you will. Isn't it true that in the
violence of passion . . . ?

MARQUIS *(sings)*. La, la, la, la, lare, la, la, la, la, la, la.

DORANTE. What . . . ?

MARQUIS. La, la, la, la, lare, la, la, la, la, la, la.

DORANTE. I don't know whether . . .

MARQUIS. La, la, la, la, lare, la, la, la, la, la, la, la.

URANIE. It seems to me that . . .

MARQUIS. La, la, la, lare, la, la, la, la, la, la, la, la, la, la.

URANIE. Some pretty funny things happen in our dispute. I think someone might well make a little comedy out of it, and that it wouldn't go too badly to follow up *The School for Wives*.

DORANTE. You're right.

MARQUIS. By Jove, Chevalier, you'd play a part in it that would not be to your advantage!

DORANTE. That's true, Marquis.

CLIMÈNE. For my part, I would like to see that done, provided the affair was treated just as it happened.

ÉLISE. And I would furnish my own character, with all my heart.

LYSIDAS. I would not refuse my own, I don't think.

URANIE. Since each of us would be happy, Chevalier, make a note of everything and give it to Molière, since you know him, to put into a comedy.

CLIMÈNE. He wouldn't do any such thing, of course; it would not be any rhymed eulogy of him!

URANIE. No, no; I know his temperament: he doesn't care if his plays are attacked, as long as people come to see them.

DORANTE. Yes. But what denouement could he find for all this? For there can't be a marriage or a recognition; and I don't know how one could finish off the dispute.

URANIE. We must dream up some incident for that.

Scene 7.   GALOPIN, LYSIDAS, DORANTE, THE MARQUIS,
CLIMÈNE, ÉLISE, URANIE

GALOPIN. Madame, supper is on the table.

DORANTE. Ah! That's just what we need for the denouement we were looking for, and you couldn't find anything more natural. Everyone will argue hot and heavy
on each side, as we have done, without anyone's giving
in; a little lackey will come to say that supper is served;
and everyone will get up and go to supper.

URANIE. The comedy cannot end better, and we shall do
well to leave it at that.

The Versailles
Impromptu

THE VERSAILLES IMPROMPTU

A prose comedy in eleven scenes, first performed for the King at Versailles, October 14, 1663, and first performed publicly at the Théâtre du Palais-Royal, November 4, 1663, by Molière's company, the Troupe de Monsieur. The characters bear the names of the actors.

Molière's second critical play is again a minor one, but remarkable and fascinating. Composed on the King's orders (as Molière is at pains to point out) and apparently in no more than a week or two, it is an extraordinary proof of his readiness and invention. What he does is to make his play out of the business of making a play under pressure. Thus it consists of a rather short, incomplete play-within-a-play, a kind of continuation of the *Critique,* that his troupe is supposed to be preparing to perform; and mainly of a quasi-documentary representation of Molière rehearsing his company. The play-within-a-play seems to serve two main functions besides that of subject or pretext for the rest: it adds the variety of a change of pace, and it makes the other, "real" part seem all the more real and convincing.

The main interest is in the "real" part, which is the nearest thing we have to an actual glimpse of Molière at grips with the myriad problems that were his life. Though any such self-portrait in a polemical piece is self-serving and thus suspect, this one has the ring of truth and is a treasured source of insights for Molière scholars. Molière's Molière is no idealized hero but a harassed director trying to do the job he has to do, prodding each of the rather self-absorbed individuals of his troupe into the teamwork required for a good performance. Under such stress, the attacks on him as author, even his own performance as actor, can have only minor claims to his attention. He can be irritable, as he shows in his sharp "Be quiet, wife, you're a fool"; though he suppresses digressiveness in others in the interest of the task at hand, he lets himself be lured, by the admiring Mlle. de Brie, into acting out his "abandoned" plan to parody at length the pompous actors of the Hôtel de Bourgogne.

His framework allows him to tell us much that we are glad to know: how he sees his own life, his co-workers, and himself at work among them; his views, both theoretical and applied, on acting; his sense of the tactics appropriate—and inappropriate—to controversy; the place of this in his life; his attitude toward his principal critics; the obstacles offered by even the best-intentioned meddlers; and above all the constant pressure of wearing so many hats and meeting so many stiff deadlines. We may hope that it gave him some satisfaction to show the King—and us—just how hard it was to do everything he did.

THE VERSAILLES IMPROMPTU

CHARACTERS

MOLIÈRE, *a ridiculous marquis*
BRÉCOURT, *a man of quality*
LA GRANGE, *a ridiculous marquis*
DU CROISY, *a dramatic poet*
LA THORILLIÈRE, *a marquis and a bore*
BÉJART, *a busybody*
MLLE.* DU PARC, *a ceremonious marquise*
MLLE. BÉJART, *a prude*
MLLE. DE BRIE, *a prudent coquette*
MLLE. MOLIÈRE, *a satirical wit*
MLLE. DU CROISY, *a sweetish pest*
MLLE. HERVÉ, *a précieuse ladies' maid*
FOUR BUSYBODIES

The scene is the royal theater at Versailles.

Scene 1.   MOLIÈRE, BRÉCOURT, LA GRANGE, DU
CROISY, MLLE. DU PARC, MLLE. BÉJART, MLLE. DE
BRIE, MLLE. MOLIÈRE, MLLE. DU CROISY, MLLE. HERVÉ

MOLIÈRE. Come on now, ladies and gentlemen, are you
trying to be funny, being so slow? *Will* you come here,

---

*In Molière's day, women of the middle class, whether married or
not, were referred to and addressed as Mademoiselle.

213

all of you? A plague on these people! Hi, hello! Monsieur de Brécourt!

BRÉCOURT. What?

MOLIÈRE. Monsieur de La Grange!

LA GRANGE. What is it?

MOLIÈRE. Monsieur du Croisy!

DU CROISY. Yes?

MOLIÈRE. Mademoiselle du Parc!

MLLE. DU PARC. Well?

MOLIÈRE. Mademoiselle Béjart!

MLLE. BÉJART. What's up?

MOLIÈRE. Mademoiselle de Brie!

MLLE. DE BRIE. What do you want?

MOLIÈRE. Mademoiselle du Croisy!

MLLE. DU CROISY. What's going on?

MOLIÈRE. Mademoiselle Hervé!

MLLE. HERVÉ. Coming.

MOLIÈRE. I think I'll go mad with all these people. Damnation! Gentlemen, do you want to drive me crazy today?

BRÉCOURT. What do you want us to do? We don't know our parts, and you're the one that's driving *us* crazy by making us play this way.

MOLIÈRE. Oh! Actors are strange creatures to manage!

MLLE. BÉJART. Well, here we are. What do you aim to do?

MLLE. DU PARC. What do you have in mind?

MLLE. DE BRIE. What is it all about?

MOLIÈRE. For pity's sake, let's take our places; and since we are all in costume, and the King isn't due to come for two hours, let's use this time to rehearse our business and see how things have to be played.

LA GRANGE. How can you play what you don't know?

MLLE. DU PARC. As for me, I tell you, I don't remember a word of my part.

MLLE. DE BRIE. I know perfectly well I'll have to be prompted from beginning to end.

MLLE. BÉJART. And *I'm* just about ready to hold my lines in my hand.

MLLE. MOLIÈRE. Me too.

MLLE. HERVÉ. Well, *I* don't have much to say.

MLLE. DU CROISY. Neither do I; but even so, I can't guarantee not to miss anything.

DU CROISY. I'd give ten pistoles to be out of this.

BRÉCOURT. And I'd take twenty good lashes, I swear.

MOLIÈRE. So you're all mighty sick over having a wretched little part to play; so what would you do if you were in my place?

MLLE. BÉJART. Who, you? There's no reason to feel sorry for you. You wrote the play; you're not afraid of missing anything.

MOLIÈRE. And haven't I anything to fear but a lapse of

memory? Aren't you forgetting my worry over the result, which concerns me alone? And do you think it's a small matter to put on something comic before a gathering like this one, to try to get a laugh from people who fill us with respect and who laugh only when they please? Is there an author who isn't bound to tremble when he comes to this test? And am I not the one to say that *I'd* give anything in the world to be out of this?

MLLE. BÉJART. If that did make you tremble, you'd take better precautions, and you wouldn't have undertaken to put this on in a week.

MOLIÈRE. How could I help it when a king ordered it?

MLLE. BÉJART. How? A respectful excuse based on the impossibility of the thing in the little time given you. Anyone else in your place would take better care of his reputation and would have been mighty careful not to commit himself as you do. Where will you be, I ask you, if the thing goes off badly? And think of the advantage all your enemies will get from it!

MLLE. DE BRIE. That's right: you should have excused yourself, respectfully, to the King, or else asked for more time.

MOLIÈRE. Good Lord, Mademoiselle, kings like nothing so much as prompt obedience, and they're not at all happy at encountering obstacles. Things are good only at the time when they crave them; and if you want to put off their entertainment, for them you're taking away all its charm. They want pleasures that don't keep them waiting; and those least prepared are always the ones they like best. We must never consider ourselves in what they want of us; we are there only to please them; and when they order something from us, it's up to us to profit by the desire they feel. It's better to do what they ask of us badly than not to do it soon enough; and if we have the shame of not making a real success of it, we still have the glory of obeying their commands promptly. But please, let's get our minds on rehearsing.

MLLE. BÉJART. How do you expect us to go about it if we don't know our parts?

MOLIÈRE. You'll know them, I tell you; and even if you shouldn't know them perfectly, can't you use your wits to fill in, since it's prose and you know your subject?

MLLE. BÉJART. No thanks: prose is even worse than verse.

MLLE. MOLIÈRE. Do you want to know what I think? You should have written a comedy you'd have acted in all by yourself.

MOLIÈRE. Be quiet, wife, you're a fool.

MLLE. MOLIÈRE. Thanks very much, my lord husband. That's the way it is: marriage certainly changes people, and you wouldn't have said that to me a year and a half ago.

MOLIÈRE. Be quiet, please.

MLLE. MOLIÈRE. It's a strange thing that one little ceremony can take away all our fine qualities, and that a husband and a suitor look at the same person with such different eyes.

MOLIÈRE. How you do talk!

MLLE. MOLIÈRE. Faith, if I were writing a comedy, I'd write it on this subject. I'd justify the wives for a lot of things that they're accused of; and I'd make the husbands fear the difference there is between their brusque manners and the civilities of suitors.

MOLIÈRE. Ouch! Let's drop it. This is no time for chitchat now; we have other things to do.

MLLE. BÉJART. But since you've been ordered to work on

the subject of the criticism made against you,* why didn't you do that comedy on the actors that you talked to us about a long time ago? That was a ready-made thing and fitted the situation very well—especially because, since the critics had undertaken to portray you, they left themselves open for you to portray them likewise; and that could have been called their portrait much more properly than all they've done can be called yours. For to try to mimic an actor in a comic role is not to portray him but to portray after him the characters he plays and to use the same strokes and the same colors that he is obliged to use for the various portraits of the ridiculous characters that he imitates from nature. But to mimic an actor in serious roles is to portray him by faults that are all his own, since characters of that sort do not call for the ridiculous gestures or tones of voice by which he is recognized.

MOLIÈRE. That's true; but I have my reasons for not doing so; and between you and me, I didn't think the thing was worth doing; and then I'd have needed more time to carry out that idea. Since the days they play are the same as ours, I've hardly been to see them more than three or four times since we've been in Paris; all I've caught of their delivery is what struck me right away; and I would have needed to study them further in order to draw really lifelike portraits.

MLLE. DU PARC. As for me, I've recognized some of them when you've imitated them.

MLLE. DE BRIE. I never heard about that.

MOLIÈRE. It's an idea that went through my mind once, and I let it go as a trifle, a little joke, that might not have made anyone laugh.

MLLE. DE BRIE. Tell me a little about it, since you've told the others.

*A reference to Boursault's *Le Portrait du peintre* (*The Portrait of the Painter*), recently acted at the rival Hôtel de Bourgogne.

MOLIÈRE. We haven't the time now.

MLLE. DE BRIE. Just a couple of words.

MOLIÈRE. I'd thought of a comedy where there would be a dramatic poet—I would have played him myself—who would have come to offer a play to a troupe of players just arrived from the country. He would say: "Do you have any actors and actresses who are capable of doing justice to a work? For my play is a play . . . !" "Well, sir," the actors would reply, "we have men and women who have been found adequate everywhere we've been." "And which one of you plays the kings?" "There's an actor who manages those now and then." "Who? That handsome young man? Are you joking? You need a king as big and fat as four, a king—my Lord!—with the right kind of potbelly, a king of vast circumference, who can fill a throne in the grand manner.* That's a fine thing, a king with an elegant figure! That's one big defect already; but just let me hear him recite a dozen lines." Thereupon the actor would recite, for example, a few lines of the King in *Nicomède*—†

"Shall I tell you, Araspe? He has served me too well;
By adding to my power . . ."

—just as naturally as he possibly could. Then the poet: "What? You call that reciting? You've got to say the words grandiloquently. Listen to me *(Imitating Montfleury, an excellent actor of the Hôtel de Bourgogne)*

'Shall I tell you, Araspe? . . .'

Do you see that posture? Take good note of it. Now, blast out that last line properly. That's what brings out the applause and makes them roar." "But, sir," the actor would reply, "it seems to me that a king talking

---

*An allusion to Montfleury, an actor of the Hôtel de Bourgogne whom Molière presently imitates.
†A tragedy by Pierre Corneille, as are the works quoted subsequently: *Horace, Le Cid, Sertorius, Œdipe.* Molière seems to have recited all these speeches entire.

in private with the captain of his guards speaks a little more humanly and doesn't sound quite so much like a man possessed." "You don't know what it's all about. You just go and recite the way you're doing, and see if you draw a single 'Oh!' Now let's have a look at a scene between two lovers." Thereupon an actor and an actress would do a scene together, the one between Camille and Curiace—

"Camille: Then will you go ahead, dear heart, and acquiesce
In this dread honor which destroys our happiness?
Curiace: Alas! I see only too well . . ."

—in exactly the same way as the other, and just as naturally as they could. Then the poet, right away: "You're joking; that's no good; here's the way you have to deliver that: (*Imitating Mlle. Beauchâteau, an actress of the Hôtel de Bourgogne*)

'Then will you go ahead . . .
No, I know you too well . . .'

You see how natural and passionate that is? Just admire that smiling face that she keeps in her greatest afflictions."—In short, that's the idea; and he would have gone through all the actors and actresses in the same way.

MLLE. DE BRIE. I think that idea is pretty funny, and I recognized some of them from the very first line. Go on, please.

MOLIÈRE (*imitating Beauchâteau, another actor, in the stanzas from Le Cid*).

"Pierced to my very heart . . ."

And this one, do you recognize him playing Pompey in *Sertorius*? (*Imitating Hauteroche, another actor*)

"The enmity that reigns between the rival camps
Does not annul the claims . . ."

MLLE. DE BRIE. Yes, I think I recognize him a bit.

MOLIÈRE. And this one? *(Imitating Villiers, another actor)*

"My lord, Polybe is dead . . ."

MLLE. DE BRIE. Yes, I know who that is. But there are some of them, I think, that you would have trouble taking off.

MOLIÈRE. Good Lord, there isn't one of them that I couldn't catch by some quirk, if I had studied them well. But you're making me lose time that is precious to us all. Let's get our minds on our business, please, and not waste any more time on idle talk. *(To* LA GRANGE*)* You, take good care to play your marquis part properly along with me.

MLLE. MOLIÈRE. Marquises still!

MOLIÈRE. Yes, marquises still. Who the devil do you expect us to use on the stage to keep people happy? The marquis today is the butt of comedy; and just as in all the old comedies you always see a clownish servant who makes the spectators laugh, so in all our plays nowadays you always need a ridiculous marquis to keep the audience amused.

MLLE. BÉJART. That's true, you can't do without them.

MOLIÈRE *(to* MLLE. DU PARC*)*. As for you, Mademoiselle . . .

MLLE. DU PARC. Good Lord, as for me, I'll play my part very badly, and I don't know why you gave me that affected role.

MOLIÈRE. Good Lord, Mademoiselle, that's what you said when you were given the one in *The Critique of the*

*School for Wives;** yet you brought it off wonderfully, and everybody agreed that it couldn't be done better than you did it. Believe me, it'll be the same with this one, and you'll play it better than you think.

MLLE. DU PARC. How could that be, when there's nobody in the world less affected than I am?

MOLIÈRE. That's true; and that's how you show best that you're an excellent actress, by portraying to the life a character so opposed to your temperament. So all of you, try to really assume the character of your part, and to imagine that you actually are what you are representing.

(*To* DU CROISY) Now you, you play the dramatic poet, and you must fill yourself with the character, stress that pedantic manner which remains even in his dealings with high society, that sententious tone of voice, and that exactitude in pronunciation that emphasizes every syllable and doesn't miss a single letter of the strictest spelling.

(*To* BRÉCOURT) As for you, you play a well-bred courtier, as you did already in *The Critique of the School for Wives;†* that is, you should maintain a calm manner, a natural tone of voice, and use as few gestures as you can.

(*To* LA GRANGE) As for you, I have nothing to tell you.

(*To* MLLE. BÉJART) Now you, you represent one of those women who, provided they don't make love, think that anything else is permissible, those women who always entrench themselves proudly in their prudery, look down on everyone, and think that all the finest qualities possessed by others are nothing in comparison with their own wretched honor—which nobody cares a rap about. Keep that character always before your eyes, so as to make the right grimaces.

(*To* MLLE. DE BRIE) As for you, you play one of those women who think they are the most virtuous people in the world provided they preserve appearances, those

* The part of Climène.
† The part of Dorante.

women who think that the only sin lies in the scandal, who try to carry on the affairs they have quietly, under the guise of honorable friendships, and who call people their friends whom others call their lovers. Get well into that character.

(To MLLE. MOLIÈRE*)* Now you, you play the same character as in *The Critique*;* and I have nothing more to tell you, any more than to Mademoiselle du Parc.

(To MLLE. DU CROISY*)* As for you, you represent one of those persons who sweetly bestow their charity on everyone, those women who always give a little tongue-lash in passing and would be miserable at having allowed anyone to speak well of their neighbor. I think you won't do badly in that part.

(To MLLE. HERVÉ*)* And you, you're the *précieuse's* maid, who breaks into the conversation from time to time and picks up all her mistress's terms as best she can.

(To the troupe) I'm telling you all your parts, so that you will imprint them deeply on your minds. Now let's begin to rehearse, and see how it goes.—Oh! Sure enough, here comes a meddler! That's all we needed!

Scene 2.   LA THORILLIÈRE, MOLIÈRE, *et al*

LA THORILLIÈRE. Good day, Monsieur Molière.

MOLIÈRE. Your servant, sir. *(Aside)* Plague take the man!

LA THORILLIÈRE. How are things with you?

MOLIÈRE. Very well, at your service. *(To the actresses)* Ladies, don't . . .

LA THORILLIÈRE. I've just been in a place where I said some very nice things about you.

*There she had played Élise.

MOLIÈRE. I am obliged to you. *(Aside)* The devil take you! *(To the troupe)* Now be careful . . .

LA THORILLIÈRE. You're doing a new play today?

MOLIÈRE. Yes, sir. *(To the troupe)* Don't forget . . .

LA THORILLIÈRE. It's the King that's having you do it?

MOLIÈRE. Yes, sir. *(To the troupe)* For pity's sake, remember . . .

LA THORILLIÈRE. What's the name of it?

MOLIÈRE. Yes, sir.

LA THORILLIÈRE. I'm asking you what you call it.

MOLIÈRE. Oh, Lord, I don't know. *(To the troupe)* Now, please, you must . . .

LA THORILLIÈRE. What costumes will you wear?

MOLIÈRE. As you see. *(To the troupe)* I beg you . . .

LA THORILLIÈRE. When will you begin?

MOLIÈRE. When the King has arrived. *(Aside)* Devil take this inquisitor!

LA THORILLIÈRE. When do you think he'll come?

MOLIÈRE. Plague take me if I know, sir.

LA THORILLIÈRE. Don't you know . . . ?

MOLIÈRE. Look here, sir, I'm the most ignorant man in the world; I don't know anything about anything you may ask me, I swear to you. *(Aside)* I'm going crazy! This torturer comes, calm as you please, and asks questions, and isn't the least bit worried that someone may have other things on his mind.

LA THORILLIÈRE. Ladies, I am your servant.

MOLIÈRE. Oh, fine! Now he's on another tack.

LA THORILLIÈRE (to MLLE. DU CROISY). You look as beautiful as a little angel. (Glancing at MLLE. HERVÉ) Are you both playing today?

MLLE. DU CROISY. Yes, sir.

LA THORILLIÈRE. Without you two, the play wouldn't be worth much.*

MOLIÈRE (to the two actresses). Won't you send that man on his way?

MLLE. DE BRIE. Sir, we have something here to rehearse together.

LA THORILLIÈRE. Oh, Gad! I won't hinder you; just go right ahead.

MLLE. DE BRIE. But . . .

LA THORILLIÈRE. No, no, I would be sorry to disturb anyone. Be quite free to do what you have to do.

MLLE. DE BRIE. Yes, but . . .

LA THORILLIÈRE. I'm not a man to stand on ceremony, I tell you, and you can rehearse whatever you please.

MOLIÈRE. Sir, these ladies are finding it hard to tell you that they would much rather have no one here during this rehearsal.

LA THORILLIÈRE. Why? There's no danger for me.

MOLIÈRE. Sir, it's a custom they observe, and you will have more pleasure when things come as a surprise.

*Mlles. du Croisy and Hervé were considered the weakest actresses in the troupe; but La Thorillière is not being ironic, merely silly.

LA THORILLIÈRE. Then I'll go along and say you're ready.

MOLIÈRE. Not at all, sir; don't hurry, I beg you.

Scene 3. MOLIÈRE, LA GRANGE, *et al*

MOLIÈRE. Oh, what a lot of nuisances there are in the world! Now then, let's get started. So first of all, imagine that the scene is the King's antechamber; for that's a place where some rather funny things happen every day. There it's easy to bring on any person we want, and you can even find reasons to justify having the women I put on come there. The play opens with two marquises meeting.

(*To* LA GRANGE) Now, you, remember to come in *there*, the way I told you, with the manner they call high-class, combing your wig, and humming a little song between your teeth. La, la, la, la, la, la. The rest of you make way, will you, for two marquises need room; and these are not the kind of people to confine their persons to a small space. Let's go; speak.

LA GRANGE. "Good day, Marquis."

MOLIÈRE. Good Lord, that's not the tone of a marquis; you've got to make it a bit loftier; and most of these gentlemen affect a special way of talking to distinguish themselves from common folk: "Good day, Marquis." So, begin again.

LA GRANGE. "Good day, Marquis."

MOLIÈRE. "Ah! Marquis, your servant."

LA GRANGE. "What are you doing here?"

MOLIÈRE. "Gad! You can see: I'm waiting for all these gentlemen to unstop the door, to show my face there."

LA GRANGE. "Damme! What a crowd! I have no mind to rub up against them, and I'd rather be one of the last to enter."

MOLIÈRE. "There are twenty people there who are perfectly sure of not getting in, and who still don't give up crowding and occupying every avenue to the King's door."

LA GRANGE. "Let's call out our names to the usher, so he'll announce us."

MOLIÈRE. "That's fine for you; but for my part, I don't want to be taken off by Molière."

LA GRANGE. "And yet, Marquis, I think it's you he puts on in *The Critique*."

MOLIÈRE. "I? I'm your servant; it's your very self in person."

LA GRANGE. "Ah! My word, you're a funny one to apply your character to me."

MOLIÈRE. "Damme! I think you're amusing to give me what belongs to you."

LA GRANGE. "Ha, ha, ha! That *is* droll!"

MOLIÈRE. "Ha, ha, ha! That *is* comical!"

LA GRANGE. "What! You mean to maintain that you're not the one who's impersonated in the Marquis in *The Critique?*"

MOLIÈRE. "That's right, it's me. *Detestable, egad! Detestable! Cream tart!* It's me, it's me, of course, it's me."

LA GRANGE. "Yes, damme, it *is* you! There's no use your joking; and if you want, we'll make a bet, and see which of us is right."

MOLIÈRE. "And just what do you want to bet?"

LA GRANGE. "I'll bet a hundred pistoles it's you."

MOLIÈRE. "And I, a hundred pistoles it's *you*."

LA GRANGE. "A hundred pistoles cash?"

MOLIÈRE. "Cash: ninety pistoles that Amyntas owes me, and ten pistoles cash."

LA GRANGE. "You're on."

MOLIÈRE. "Done."

LA GRANGE. "Your money runs a great risk."

MOLIÈRE. "Yours is in much danger."

LA GRANGE. "Whom shall we ask to judge?"

Scene 4. MOLIÈRE, BRÉCOURT, LA GRANGE, *et al*

MOLIÈRE. "Here's a man who will judge us. Chevalier!"

BRECOURT. "What?"

MOLIÈRE. Fine! There goes the other man assuming the Marquis's tone of voice! (*To* BRÉCOURT) Didn't I tell you you're playing a part in which you must speak naturally?

BRÉCOURT. That's true.

MOLIÈRE. Let's go then. "Chevalier!"

BRÉCOURT. "What?"

MOLIÈRE. "Come and judge between us on a bet we've made."

BRÉCOURT. "And what is it?"

MOLIÈRE. "We're arguing over who is the Marquis in Molière's *Critique*. He bets it's me, and I bet it's him."

BRÉCOURT. "As for me, my judgment is that it's neither one of you. You're both crazy to try to apply this sort of thing to yourselves; and that's something I heard Molière complain about the other day, speaking to some people who were charging him with the same thing as you. He said that nothing gave him so much annoyance as being accused of having some one person in mind in the portraits he draws; that his purpose is to depict manners without wanting to touch individuals, and the characters he represents are characters in the air, and properly phantoms, whom he dresses up to his fancy to entertain the spectators; that he would be very sorry ever to have designated in them any real person whatever; and that if anything could make him lose his taste for writing plays, it was the resemblances that people always insisted on finding in them—an idea which his enemies maliciously tried to support, to do him a bad disservice with certain persons whom he never thought of.—Indeed I think he's right; for why, I ask you, should we try to apply all his gestures and words, and make trouble for him by announcing loudly 'He's taking off so-and-so!' when these are things that can fit a hundred people? Since the business of comedy is to represent in general all the defects of men, and principally of the men of our time, it's impossible for Molière to create any character that doesn't correspond to someone in society; and if he has to be accused of having had in mind all the people in whom we can find the defects he portrays, then beyond a doubt he will have to write no more comedies."

MOLIÈRE. "Faith, Chevalier, you're trying to justify Molière and spare our friend here."

LA GRANGE. "Not at all. You're the one he's sparing, and we'll find other judges."

MOLIÈRE. "All right. But tell me, Chevalier, don't you think your Molière has run out of subjects and will find no more material to . . . ?"

BRÉCOURT. "No more material? Ah, my poor Marquis, we'll always furnish him plenty, and we're hardly on the road to good sense, for all he does and all he says."

MOLIÈRE. Wait, you've got to bring out this whole passage more. Just listen to me say it. "And will find no more material to . . . ?"—"No more material? Ah, my poor Marquis, we'll always furnish him plenty, and we're hardly on the road to good sense, for all he does and all he says. Do you think he has exhausted all the ridiculousness of men in his comedies? And without going outside the court, doesn't he still have twenty characters of people he hasn't touched on? Doesn't he have, for example, those who show each other the greatest friendliness in the world and who, when their backs are turned, entertain others by tearing each other apart? Doesn't he have those dispensers of all-out adulation, those insipid flatterers, who use no salt to season the praises they bestow, and whose flatteries all have a sickly sweetness that nauseates their listeners? Doesn't he have those obsequious curriers of favor, those perfidious worshipers of fortune, who sing your praises when you prosper and trample you when you're down? Doesn't he have those who are always discontented with the court, those useless followers, those assiduous nuisances, those people, I say, who can count as services rendered only their importunities, and who want to be rewarded for having besieged the Prince ten years running? Doesn't he have those who caress everyone alike, who promenade their civilities right and left, and run up to everyone they see with the same embraces and the same protestations of friendship: 'Sir, your very humble servant.—Sir, I am entirely at your service.—Consider me entirely yours, dear chap.—Count on me, sir, as the warmest of your friends.—Sir, I am overjoyed to embrace you.—Ah! sir, I didn't see you! Do me the favor of asking me to help. Believe me, I am utterly yours. You are the man I revere most in the world. There is no one whom I honor as I do you. I conjure you to believe it. I beseech you to have no doubt of it.—Your servant.—Your very humble servitor.'* Come, come, Marquis, Molière will always have more subjects than he wants; and everything he has touched on up to now is only a trifle compared to what remains."

    That's about how that should be played.

BRÉCOURT. That's good enough.

MOLIÈRE. Go on.

BRÉCOURT. "Here are Climène and Élise."

MOLIÈRE. Thereupon you two come on. (To MLLE. DU PARC) Now you, be very sure to flounce properly and put on lots of airs. You'll have to strain yourself a little; but there you are: sometimes we have to do ourselves violence.

MLLE. MOLIÈRE. "To be sure, Madame, I recognized you from a distance, and I could see very well from your manner that it couldn't be anyone but you."

MLLE. DU PARC. "As you see. I've come to wait for a man to come out with whom I have business."

MLLE. MOLIÈRE. "And so have I."

MOLIÈRE. Ladies, there are some trunks that you can use for chairs.

MLLE. DU PARC. "Come, Madame, please sit down."

MLLE. MOLIÈRE. "After you, Madame."

*Compare *The Misanthrope*, Act I, especially scene 1, ll. 14–72.

MOLIÈRE. Good. After these little silent ceremonies, everyone will sit down and speak seated, except the marquises, who will now get up and now sit down, according to their natural restlessness. "Gad, Chevalier, you should have your knee ruffles take medicine."

BRÉCOURT. "How's that?"

MOLIÈRE. "They're in very poor shape."

BRÉCOURT. "My compliments on the pun!"

MLLE. MOLIÈRE. "Heavens, Madame, your complexion seems to me dazzlingly white, and your lips amazingly flame-colored!"

MLLE. DU PARC. "Oh! What's that you say, Madame? Don't look at me, I'm utterly ugly today."

MLLE. MOLIÈRE. "Ah, Madame, raise your veil a little."

MLLE. DU PARC. "Fie! I look frightful, I tell you, and I even terrify myself."

MLLE. MOLIÈRE. "You're so beautiful!"

MLLE. DU PARC. "Not at all, not at all."

MLLE. MOLIÈRE. "Let me see you."

MLLE. DU PARC. "Oh, fie on you! Please!"

MLLE. MOLIÈRE. "I beg you."

MLLE. DU PARC. "Good heavens, no!"

MLLE. MOLIÈRE. "Oh, yes!"

MLLE. DU PARC. "You drive me to despair."

MLLE. MOLIÈRE. "Just for a moment."

MLLE. DU PARC. "Ohhhhh . . ."

MLLE. MOLIÈRE. "Positively, you *shall* show yourself. We can't get along without seeing you."

MLLE. DU PARC. "Bless me, what a strange person you are! Whatever you want, you want furiously."

MLLE. MOLIÈRE. "Ah, Madame, you have nothing to lose by appearing in broad daylight, I swear to you. Those wicked people who insisted that you used makeup! Believe me, I'll really give them the lie now."

MLLE. DU PARC. "Alas! I don't even know what they mean by 'using makeup.' But where are these ladies going?"

Scene 5.   MLLE. DE BRIE, MLLE. DU PARC, *et al*

MLLE. DE BRIE. "You won't mind, ladies, if we give you, in passing, the most delightful news in the world. Here is Monsieur Lysidas* who has just informed us that a play has been written against Molière which the *grands comédiens*† will put on."

MOLIÈRE. "That's true; they wanted to read it to me; and someone by the name of Br . . . Brou . . . Brossaut‡ wrote it."

DU CROISY. "Sir, it is announced under the name of Boursault; but to let you in on the secret, many people have set their hand to this work, and much is to be expected of it. Since all the authors and all the actors regard Molière as their greatest enemy, we have all united to do him in. Each of us has contributed a brush stroke to his portrait; but we have taken good care not to set our names to it: it would have been too glorious for him to

*Du Croisy had played Lysidas in *The Critique.*
† The troupe of the Hôtel de Bourgogne.
‡Boursault, author of *Le Portrait du peintre.*

succumb, in the eyes of the public, to the efforts of all Parnassus; and to make his defeat the more ignominious, we decided to choose, on purpose, an author with no reputation."

MLLE. DU PARC. "As for me, I confess that I am unimaginably overjoyed with it."

MOLIÈRE. "Me too. By Gad! The mocker will be mocked; he'll get his knuckles rapped, my word!"

MLLE. DU PARC. "That will teach him to want to satirize everything. What? He has the impertinence not to grant that women have wit? He condemns all our noble expressions and wants us always to talk down to earth!"

MLLE. DE BRIE. "The language is nothing; but he censures all our acquaintanceships, however innocent they may be; and to hear him talk, it's criminal to have merit."

MLLE. DU CROISY. "It's unbearable! There's not one woman who can do anything any more. Why doesn't he leave our husbands in peace, instead of opening their eyes and making them watch out for things they never thought about?"

MLLE. BÉJART. "I'd let all that pass; but he even satirizes virtuous women, and that bad joker gives them the title of 'devils full of piety'!"*

MLLE. MOLIÈRE. "He's a wiseacre. He must get what's coming to him."

DU CROISY. "The performance of this play, Madame, will need support, and the actors of the Hôtel de Bourgogne . . ."

MLLE. DU PARC. "Good Lord, they have no reason to worry! I'll vouch for the success of their play with my person."

---

*The School for Wives, Act IV, scene 8, 1. 1296.

MLLE. MOLIÈRE. "You are right, Madame. Too many people have an interest in finding it good. I leave you to judge whether all those who think themselves satirized by Molière will not seize the chance to take revenge on him by applauding this comedy."

BRÉCOURT. "Undoubtedly. And for my part, I'll answer for twelve marquises, six *précieuses,* twenty coquettes, and thirty cuckolds, who will not fail to clap their hands off."

MLLE. MOLIÈRE. "Exactly. Why should he go and offend all those people, and especially the cuckolds, who are the nicest fellows in the world?"

MOLIÈRE. "By Gad! I'm told they're going to lay it on him in proper style, him and all his comedies, and that all the actors and authors, great and small, are devilishly provoked against him."

MLLE. MOLIÈRE. "That serves him good and right. Why does he write wretched plays that all Paris goes to see, in which he portrays people so well that everyone recognizes himself? Why doesn't he write comedies like those of Monsieur Lysidas? He would have no one against him, and all the authors would say nice things about them. It is true that such plays don't draw such very big crowds; but on the other hand, they are always well written, no one writes against them, and everyone who sees them is just dying to think they are beautiful."

DU CROISY. "It is true that I have the advantage of not making enemies, and that all my works have the approval of the learned."

MLLE. MOLIÈRE. "You are right to be pleased with yourself. That's better than all the applause of the public and all the money a person could make on Molière's plays. What does it matter to you whether people come to see your comedies, provided they are approved by your learned colleagues?"

LA GRANGE. "But when will they play *The Portrait of the Painter?*"

DU CROISY. "I don't know; but I'm getting all ready to appear among the first in line and shout: 'Now that *is* beautiful!' "

MOLIÈRE. "And so am I, by Jove!"

LA GRANGE. "Me too, Lord help me!"

MLLE. DU PARC. "As for me, I'll give my all, as I should; and I'll guarantee you a burst of applause that will put all hostile judgments to rout. Surely that's the least we should do, to support the avenger of our interests with our praise."

MLLE. MOLIÈRE. "That's very well said."

MLLE. DE BRIE. "And that's what we all must do."

MLLE. BÉJART. "Certainly."

MLLE. DU CROISY. "Beyond a doubt."

MLLE. HERVÉ. "No quarter to that caricaturist!"

MOLIÈRE. "Faith, my dear Chevalier, your Molière will have to go into hiding!"

BRÉCOURT. "Who him? I promise you, Marquis, that he intends to go sit on the stage and laugh with all the others at the portrait they have made of him."*

MOLIÈRE. "Egad! Then he'll laugh on the wrong side of his face."

BRÉCOURT. "Come, come, perhaps he'll find more to laugh at than you think. I've seen the script; and since the only good parts are in fact the ideas taken from Mo-

---

*Molière did attend a performance of the play. His enemies report that he watched it with chagrin; his friends, with amusement.

lière, he will certainly have no reason to be unhappy at any pleasure it may give. For as for the part where they try to blacken his character, I'll be much mistaken if anyone approves of it; and as for all the people they've tried to stir up against him, because they say he makes his portraits too lifelike, not only is that criticism very ungraceful, but I know of nothing more ridiculous and inappropriate; and I had not supposed until now that a comic author was subject to blame for portraying men too well."

LA GRANGE. "The actors told me they were just waiting for his answer, and that . . ."

BRÉCOURT. "His answer? Faith, I think he'd be a great fool if he took the trouble to answer their invectives. Everybody knows well enough what motive prompts them; and the best answer he can make is another comedy that will succeed like all the rest of his. That's the real way to take revenge on them properly; and judging by their character, I'm perfectly sure that a new play which will take away their audiences will annoy them much more than all the satires anyone might make of their persons."

MOLIÈRE. "But, Chevalier . . ."

MLLE. BÉJART. Let me interrupt the rehearsal for just a bit. Shall I tell you what I think? If I'd been in your place, I'd have really pressed matters. Everyone is expecting a vigorous retort from you; and after the way I'm told you were treated in that comedy, you had the right to say anything you wanted against those actors, and you shouldn't have spared a one of them.

MOLIÈRE. It drives me mad to hear you talk that way, and this is a mania with you women. You'd like to have me burst into flame against them right away, and follow their example and break out promptly in insults and abuse. Much honor I would get out of that, and much chagrin it would give them! Haven't they made ready hopefully for that sort of thing? And when they deliberated whether they would play *The Portrait of the Painter* or not, for fear of a riposte, wasn't this the response of some of them: "Let him pay us back all the insults he wants, provided we make money"? Isn't that the mark of a soul keenly sensitive to shame? And wouldn't I get a fine revenge on them by giving them what they are perfectly willing to take?

MLLE. DE BRIE. Still, they complained loudly over three or four remarks you made about them in *The Critique* and *The Précieuses*.*

MOLIÈRE. That's true, those three or four remarks are very offensive, and they're perfectly right to quote them.— No, come on, that's not the point. The greatest harm I've done them was having the good fortune to be a little more successful than they would have liked; and their entire behavior since we came to Paris has indicated only too well what irks them. But let them go on all they like; I've no reason to be worried about anything they undertake. They criticize my plays: so much the better, and Heaven preserve me from ever writing one they like! That would be a bad business for me.

MLLE. DE BRIE. Yet there's no great pleasure in seeing your works torn to pieces.

MOLIÈRE. And what difference does that make to me? Haven't I gotten everything out of my comedy that I wanted to get, since it has had the good fortune to please the august personages whom I am particularly trying to please? Haven't I reason to be satisfied with its fate, and don't all their censures come too late? Am I the one, I ask you, that is now mainly concerned? And when people attack a successful play, aren't they attacking rather the judgment of those who have approved of it than the art of the one who wrote it?

MLLE. DE BRIE. Faith, I would have shown up that petty

*The Critique of the School for Wives, scene 6; The Ridiculous Précieuses, scene 9.

little author, who makes it his business to write against
people who don't even think about him.

MOLIÈRE. You're crazy. That would be a fine subject to
entertain the court: Monsieur Boursault! I'd just like to
know how in the world anyone could fit him out to make
him amusing, and whether, if you made fun of him on
the stage, he would be fortunate enough to make people laugh. It would be too much of an honor for him
to be taken off before an august gathering; he would
ask nothing better; and he attacks me for no other
reason than to make himself known in any way he can.
He's a man who has nothing to lose, and the actors
turned him loose on me only to get me involved in a
stupid war and distract me, by this artifice, from the
other works I have yet to write; and yet you women
are all simple enough to fall into this trap. But anyway,
I'll declare myself publicly on this point. I don't intend
to make any reply to all their criticisms and count-
ercriticisms. Let them say all the bad things they want
about my plays, that's all right with me. Let them
snatch them up after we've done them, and turn them
inside out like a suit to put them on in their own theater,* and try to profit by whatever enjoyment people
find in them and by a bit of good fortune I enjoy—I
consent to that: they need it, and I shall be very happy
to contribute to keeping them alive, provided they content themselves with what I can decently grant them.
Courtesy must have its limits; and there are things that
make neither the spectators laugh, nor the person
whom they are said about. With all my heart I'll turn
over to them my works, my face, my gestures, my
words, my tone of voice, and my delivery, for them to
do and say all they like about, if they can derive some
advantage from that: I don't oppose all that sort of
thing, and I'll be delighted if that can entertain people.
But when I turn all that over to them, they should do
me the favor of leaving me the rest and not touching
on such matters as those on which I've been told they

---

*This is what Boursault did with Molière's *Critique of the School
for Wives* in his *Portrait of the Painter*.

were attacking me in their comedies.* That's the request I shall make, civilly, to this honorable gentleman who makes it his business to write for them; and that's all the reply they shall have from me.

MLLE. BÉJART. But after all . . .

MOLIÈRE. But after all, you'd drive me crazy. Let's not talk about that any more; we're wasting time making speeches instead of rehearsing our comedy. Where were we? I don't remember.

MLLE. DE BRIE. You were at the place . . .

MOLIÈRE. Good Lord! I hear some noise: that's the King coming, for certain; and I see very well that we won't have time to go any further. That's what we get for fooling around. Oh, well! For the rest, then, do the best you can.

MLLE. BÉJART. My word, I'm scared, and I can't possibly play my part unless I rehearse the whole of it.

MOLIÈRE. What do you mean, you can't possibly play your part?

MLLE. BÉJART. No.

MLLE. DU PARC. I can't play mine either.

MLLE. DE BRIE. Neither can I.

MLLE. MOLIÈRE. Nor I.

MLLE. HERVÉ. Nor I.

MLLE. DU CROISY. Nor I.

MOLIÈRE. Then just what do you intend to do? Are you all trying to make a fool of me?

---

*They attacked Molière's religion and his private married life.

Scene 6.   BÉJART, MOLIÈRE, *et al*

BÉJART. Gentlemen, I come to give you notice that the
King has arrived and is waiting for you to begin.

MOLIÈRE. Ah, sir, you see me in the worst possible trouble! Right now as I'm talking to you I'm desperate!
Here are these women all terrified and saying that they
have to rehearse their parts before they begin. For mercy's sake, we ask for a moment more. The King is kind,
and he knows full well that this thing has been done in
a rush. *(To the troupe)* Oh! for pity's sake, try to pull
yourselves together; take courage, I beg you.

MLLE. DU PARC. You should go and make an excuse.

MOLIÈRE. How can I make an excuse?

Scene 7.   MOLIÈRE, MLLE. BÉJART, *et al*

A BUSYBODY. Come on, gentlemen, begin.

MOLIÈRE. Just a minute, sir. I think I'll lose my mind over
this business, and . . .

Scene 8.   MOLIÈRE, MLLE. BÉJART, *et al*

ANOTHER BUSYBODY. Come on, gentlemen, begin.

MOLIÈRE. In a moment, sir. *(To the troupe)* Then what?
Do you want me to be disgraced by . . . ?

Scene 9.   MOLIÈRE, MLLE. BÉJART, *et al*

ANOTHER BUSYBODY. Come on, gentlemen, begin.

MOLIÈRE. Yes, sir, we're on our way. *(To the troupe)* Oh!
What a lot of people won't mind their own business,
and come and say "Come on, begin," when the King
hasn't ordered them to.

Scene 10.   MOLIÈRE, MLLE. BÉJART, *et al*

ANOTHER BUSYBODY. Come on, gentlemen, begin.

MOLIÈRE. As good as done, sir. *(To the troupe)* What,
then? Shall I have the humiliation . . . ?

Scene 11.   BÉJART, MOLIÈRE, *et al*

MOLIÈRE. Sir, you're coming to tell us to begin, but . . .

BÉJART. No, gentlemen, I come to tell you that the King
has been told of the plight you were in, and that by a
very special kindness he is putting off your new comedy
for another time, and contenting himself for today with
the first one you can give.

MOLIÈRE. Ah, sir, you give me back my life! The King
grants us the greatest possible boon by giving us time
for what he wanted; and now we are all going to thank
him for the extreme kindness he displays to us.

Tartuffe

TARTUFFE

A verse comedy in five acts. The original three-act version was first performed for the King at Versailles May 12, 1664. A five-act revision was first played for the Prince de Condé at the Château de Raincy (near Paris) November 29, 1664. The first public performance, under the title *The Impostor,* was in the Palais-Royal, August 5, 1667; the first (public) performance of the play that we know was in the same theater on February 5, 1669. In 1665 Molière's company had become the Troupe du Roi. Molière played the part of Orgon, Du Croisy of Tartuffe, Mlle. Molière of Elmire, and Béjart (in the tradition by which the duenna roles were played by men) of Mme. Pernelle. Molière's own title for the play is *The Tartuffe . . . ;* but most commentators, and at times Molière himself, refer to it as simply *Tartuffe.*

The quarrel over *The School for Wives* had gone Molière's way but had only infuriated his enemies. In the France of his day two views of Christian morality were at odds: a rather mild and tractable one which regarded human instincts ("passions" in the language of the time) and values benignly as part of God's creation; and an austere, puritanical one that condemned all instinct and pleasure as evil and that in many cases led to a police-state mentality exemplified by such groups as the Compagnie du Saint-Sacrement, officially suppressed by the Paris Parlement in 1660 but still strong. These purists viewed the increasing prevalence of worldliness, and especially the growing popularity of the stage, with horrified alarm. Molière's first open attack on what to him was a conspiracy of the professionally pious involved him in the greatest struggle of his life.

245

We do not know the nature of his first three-act version
of 1664; it may well have comprised roughly Acts I, III,
and IV of the play that we know. It was attacked with
almost incredible violence: Molière was portrayed as a
demon fit only for hanging; the approval of the Papal leg-
ate, Cardinal Chigi, was unavailing; even the King, Molière's strongest supporter, gave way and banned the play.
He did not abandon his author, however, but followed his
revisions with interest and on August 14, 1665, adopted
his company as the Troupe du Roi. Molière continued to
fight for his play with revisions, petitions, a few private
performances, and many private readings. He went on
writing other plays, as indeed he had to—*Don Juan,* with
its bitter attack on hypocrites and wicked noblemen, *The
Misanthrope, The Doctor in Spite of Himself,* and many
others—but meanwhile kept on fighting in every way he
could, to have *Tartuffe* performed. Revised under the title
The Impostor, with the hypocrite's name changed to Panulphe, it was played in August 1667 and promptly
banned. Not until a year and a half later, on February 5,
1669, after almost five years of struggle, after *Amphitryon,
George Dandlin,* and *The Miser,* after the "Peace of the
Church" between Pope Clement IX and Louis XIV, was
the ban lifted and the play performed. It has been a smash
hit ever since.

It is somewhat baffling, mostly because, like its central
character, it defies easy classification. Tartuffe, "the impostor" of the subtitle, is obviously an *homme sensuel in-
férieur* who counterfeits austerity; this much is clear. But
the play avoids tragedy or grim melodrama only by a
wholly unprepared *rex ex machina,* and to most people
Tartuffe is repulsive, a sort of moral monster, basically
alien to the ambiance of comedy. Molière seems to have
set himself this problem: how do I put the worst aspects
of my overpious enemies—rigorism, inhuman rejection of
"merely" human values, gullibility, sensuality, arrant
hypocrisy—into a play and keep it comic?

Part of his solution was of course to focus much attention on the dupe—Orgon—or rather the dupes; for Orgon's role is framed by that of his mother, Mme. Pernelle.
He comes by his bullheadedness honestly, and even his
impetuous son Damis is a chip off the old blockhead.

Without Orgon, the play would be grim; but of course
without Orgon there would be no play. Here and often
elsewhere Molière's finest comic and psychological effects
depend not on one character but on the interplay of two
or more: Tartuffe and Orgon, Alceste and Philinte—and
Célimène, Arnolphe and Agnès—and Horace, Don Juan
and Sganarelle.

The reader or spectator inevitably wants to define Tartuffe, and this is not easy. Some see him as the perfect
hypocrite, as Stendhal seems to when he makes him the
idol of Julien Sorel in *The Red and the Black*. Yet he fools
no one but the two obvious dupes; to everyone else his
game is apparent, even blatant. Should we then write him
off as inept? But if the play ended as it logically should,
without the turnabout of the final scene, Tartuffe would
have triumphed; the whole play up to then shows that he
must. The currently popular and persuasive theory about
many of Euripides' plays—that he offers us a logical harsh
ending, then adds, in case we prefer it, an unmotivated
happy one—fits nothing in Euripides any better than it
does Molière's *Tartuffe*.

Part of our difficulty here is of our own making. As
W. G. Moore so cogently reminds us, Molière's characters
are not *really* human beings, they are dramatis personae;
or as Hubert puts it, *Tartuffe* is "hypocrisy as spectacle."
One of the best ways to portray a dangerous religious
hypocrite in a comedy, perhaps the only safe way in Molière's time, is to give the audience fair warning of his
nature in advance and focus much attention on his
dupes—as Molière does for more than two acts before
Tartuffe ever appears; to make him successful only with
the dupes, not with all the characters and certainly not
with the audience. Moreover, whereas a novelist can tell
us or show us that one of his characters is a hypocrite, in
a play it is far preferable, if not actually necessary, for the
hypocrite to give himself away, by word or deed—and
right out in front of all those people. The nature of the
comic theater virtually denies him perfection in his role.

This suggests two likely conclusions. Molière is going
just about as far as he can to show, in a comic way, just
how dangerous a canting hypocrite can be when he meets
a perfect dupe; and his Tartuffe is not a perfect religious

hypocrite like La Bruyère's Onuphre, since he is a character created for the comic stage.

An often debated question is whether Molière is attacking only piety that is false or any that is excessive. It seems clear that—perhaps in the name of a genuine but milder type—he is striking back at both. The villain and his dupes are the only champions of extremist rigor; and the main dupe, Orgon, is a cruelly blind and selfish menace to his entire family. The reasoner, Cléante, makes the point clear, and seems to be speaking for the rest of the sane people. Again and again (as we noted in our Introduction) the play shows the modest values of human decency threatened—and in Orgon rejected—in the name of a piety so extreme that it sees human kindness as worldliness, indifference to the death of all one's nearest and dearest as moral elevation, and consideration for a daughter's happiness as "human weakness." Here as everywhere, the part of Orgon is pivotal; and part of the richness of the play's comic fabric is the fact that it was Molière himself who played it.

TARTUFFE
OR, THE IMPOSTOR

CHARACTERS

MADAME PERNELLE, *mother of Orgon*
ORGON, *husband of Elmire*
ELMIRE, *wife of Orgon*
DAMIS, *son of Orgon*
MARIANE, *daughter of Orgon, in love with Valère*
VALÈRE, *in love with Mariane*
CLÉANTE, *brother-in-law of Orgon*
TARTUFFE, *religious hypocrite*
DORINE, *lady's maid to Mariane*
MONSIEUR LOYAL, *a bailiff*
A GENTLEMAN *of the King's Guard*
FLIPOTE, *maid to Madame Pernelle*

The scene is the salon of Orgon's house in Paris.

A C T I

Scene 1.   MADAME PERNELLE, FLIPOTE, ELMIRE,
   MARIANE, DORINE, DAMIS, CLÉANTE

MADAME PERNELLE. Come on, Flipote, come on, out
   of this place.

ELMIRE. I can't keep up, you set so fast a pace.

MADAME PERNELLE. Daughter-in-law, I'll find my way
    out. Please,
  I have no need for these amenities.

ELMIRE. We merely show you the regard we owe.
  But, Mother, why are you so quick to go?

MADAME PERNELLE. I can't abide the goings-on in
    there,
  And no one in the household seems to care.
  Yes, child, I'm leaving you, unedified,
10 My good advice ignored, if not defied.
  Everyone speaks right out on everything:
  It's like a court in which Misrule is king.

DORINE. If . . .

MADAME PERNELLE. You're a maid, like many of
    your kind,
  Too saucy and too quick to speak your mind.
  Nobody asks you, but you *will* be heard.

DAMIS. But . . .

MADAME PERNELLE. Here is what you are, boy, in
    one word:
  A fool. I am your grandmother. I know.
  A hundred times I've told your father so:
  That you were getting wilder every day,
20 And that you'd bring him nothing but dismay.

MARIANE. I think . . .

MADAME PERNELLE. His sister now! A startled fawn,
  Too sweet to understand what's going on.
  Still waters may run deep; they're rarely pure.
  You can't fool me by acting so demure.

ELMIRE. But, Mother . . .

MADAME PERNELLE.   Daughter-in-law, let me say
  You're doing everything in a bad way.
  Set an example for them to revere,
  As their late mother always did, poor dear.
  You spend too much, and I'm distressed to see
  You dressed the way a princess ought to be.   *30*
  If it's your husband that you seek to please,
  My dear, you don't need all these fineries.

CLÉANTE. But, Madame, may I . . . ?

MADAME PERNELLE   As her brother,
    sir,
  I love you and respect you; but if I were
  My son, her husband, I would make it clear
  That I preferred you anywhere but here.
  You preach a way of life to everyone
  That decent people really ought to shun.
  I guess that's pretty frank, but that's my way:
  When I feel strongly, I must have my say.   *40*

DAMIS. Monsieur Tartuffe is virtuous, no doubt . . .

MADAME PERNELLE. He is a good man; you should
    hear him out;
  And I am irritated through and through
  To hear him criticized by fools like you.

DAMIS. What? Would you have me sit back overawed
  By that despotic, sanctimonious fraud?
  And may we have no fun, no merriment,
  Unless that gentleman deigns to consent?

DORINE. He loves to preach an ethic so sublime
  That anything we do becomes a crime.   *50*
  He frowns on everything and runs it down.

MADAME PERNELLE. And everything he frowns on
    earns his frown.
  He leads the way to Heaven, and my son
  Should make you love him, each and every one.

DAMIS. Not even Father ever could compel
    Me, Grandmother, to wish that fellow well.
    I can't speak otherwise and be sincere:
    I can't abide the things I see and hear.
    I see a showdown coming with that lout,
60   And he and I will have to have it out.

DORINE. I think it's scandalous, a real disgrace,
    To see this stranger seize the master's place.
    When he came here, for shoes, he hadn't any,
    And all his clothes were hardly worth a penny.
    And now this beggar's acting like a king,
    Wanting to be obeyed in everything.

MADAME PERNELLE. Things would go better here, if
    you ask me,
    If you were governed by his piety.

DORINE. You *will* make him a saint, but I submit
70   That he is nothing but a hypocrite.

MADAME PERNELLE. My, what a tongue!

DORINE.   Him and Laurent, his minion
    You can't trust either one, in my opinion.

MADAME PERNELLE. Though for his man I haven't any
    proof,
    I'll guarantee the virtue of Tartuffe.
    The reason you dislike him as you do
    Is that the things he says to you are true.
    Sin is the only thing that makes him burn,
    And Heaven's interest is his sole concern.

DORINE. So be it; but just recently how is it
80   That he opposes any sort of visit?
    Does this so anger Heaven against us
    That he must put up such a dreadful fuss?
    I'll tell you what I think, between us here:
    I think he's jealous of Madame Elmire.

MADAME PERNELLE. Be still, and take some care of
    what you say.
  Others condemn these calls in the same way.
  The consequent commotion and uproar,
  The carriages forever at your door,
  The racket the assembled lackeys make:
  These things keep all the neighborhood awake.   90
  In all of this there may be no real harm;
  But people talk; that's reason for alarm.

CLÉANTE. What then, Madame? Would you forbid
    their chatter?
  I think that it would be no laughing matter
  If in our fear that gossip might ensue
  We had to bid our dearest friends adieu.
  And even if we did this, and stood by it,
  Could we, do you think, keep the whole world
    quiet?
  To gossip seems to be a human need;
  Our best protection is to pay no heed.   100
  Let's live in innocence as best we may,
  And let the gossipmongers have their say.

DORINE. Our neighbor Daphne and her little mate:
  Are they the ones who are so quick to prate?
  Those whose behavior is most asinine
  Are always more than ready to malign;
  They always take the greatest satisfaction
  In spotting the most innocent attraction,
  And joyfully go off to spread the news,
  Twisting it in whatever way they choose.   110
  They paint other men's deeds a darker tone,
  Thinking thereby to justify their own,
  Hoping to blur the contrast, and present
  Their own intrigues as wholly innocent,
  Or else to cast on someone else's name
  Part of the burden of the public blame.

MADAME PERNELLE. All right, criticize Daphne all
    you want;
  But how about the virtuous Orante?
  She thinks of Heaven alone; and her devotion,
  I hear, makes her condemn all your commotion.   120

DORINE. A fine example, quite without a peer!
　　　It's true that now her life is most austere;
　　　Her years have brought her purity; but still
　　　She's only virtuous against her will.
　　　As long as men were at her beck and call,
　　　She took advantage, and enjoyed it all;
　　　But now, her charms not being what they were,
　　　She wants to leave the world, that's leaving her,
　　　And put on virtue as a proud disguise
130　　To hide her faded beauty from our eyes.
　　　These are the tactics of the modern flirt.
　　　She hates to see her gallant swains desert.
　　　Uneasy in her dreary solitude,
　　　She finds her one vocation as a prude,
　　　And people feel this worthy woman's sting.
　　　Forgiving nothing, blaming everything,
　　　She rants against the morals of the age,
　　　Not out of charity, but jealous rage,
　　　Determined for all others to destroy
140　　The pleasures she no longer can enjoy.

MADAME PERNELLE (to ELMIRE). These are the fairy
　　　tales that please your ear.
　　　No one else has a chance to talk in here,
　　　While Madame Chatterbox goes on all day.
　　　But all the same, I mean to have my say.
　　　In taking in that pious man, my son
　　　Did much the wisest thing he's ever done.
　　　I tell you, he is truly heaven-sent,
　　　In your dire need, to make you all repent.
　　　For your salvation, listen to Tartuffe:
150　　Whatever he reproves deserves reproof.
　　　These visits, dances, chats in which you revel
　　　Are nothing but inventions of the Devil.
　　　Here no one speaks of any pious matter;
　　　There's only idle talk and songs and chatter;
　　　The neighbor usually gets his share,
　　　As universal slander fills the air.
　　　Besides, a sober person's head goes round,
　　　At such assemblies, just from all the sound;
　　　For everyone at once must have his say,
160　　And as a preacher said the other day

It really is the Tower of Babylon,
For all the people there just babble on;
And then, to illustrate his point, he spoke . . .
      (CLÉANTE *smiles.*)
Laughing already, sir! Well, what's the joke?
Go find your silly friends and laugh your fill.
Farewell, Elmire; I have said all I will.
I could say more about this house; but then,
You will not catch me in it soon again.
            (*Slapping* FLIPOTE)
Come on, you slut, stop gaping at the moon,   170
Or else I'll slap some sense into you soon.
Come on now.

Scene 2.   CLÉANTE, DORINE

CLÉANTE.   I won't see her to the door
   For fear she may start in on me once more.
   My, that old lady . . . !

DORINE.   Really, it's a shame
   That she can't hear you call her by that name;
   She'd surely tell you that you're quite a wit,
   And that she's not yet old enough for it.

CLÉANTE. What a fuss over nothing! What a blast!
   And what a spell her dear Tartuffe has cast!

DORINE. You think she's bad? Wait till you see her
      son,
   And you'll admit that he's the crazy one.   180
   During our civil wars he showed good sense,
   And served with courage in his king's defense;
   But since he's taken Tartuffe as his hero,
   His sanity has been reduced to zero;
   He calls him brother, holds him far above

Mother, wife, son, or daughter in his love.
There's not a secret he will not confide
To him, as to his spiritual guide.
He pets and spoils him with such tenderness,
190 A mistress would be satisfied with less;
Gives him the place of honor when they dine,
And beams to see him eat enough for nine.*
He saves the choicest bits for that man's part,
And when he belches, he says "Bless your heart!"†
In short, he dotes upon his dear Tartuffe,
Worships his goodness, quotes his words for proof,
Sees miracles of virtue in his ways,
And oracles in every word he says.
Tartuffe, who knows his dupe and means to use
  him,
200 Has countless saintly poses to bemuse him,
Receives good sums, thanks to his pious mask,
And has the nerve to take us all to task.
Even his servant, a presumptuous fool,
Treats us like little children in a school;
He deafens us with wild-eyed homiletics,
And confiscates our ribbons and cosmetics.
Finding a handkerchief a while ago
Inside a *Fleur des Saints*,‡ he tore it—so—
Saying it was a frightful crime to pair
210 A holy object with the devil's snare.

Scene 3.   ELMIRE, MARIANE, DAMIS, CLÉANTE,
                    DORINE

ELMIRE. You're lucky that you did not stay for more

---

*The French reads: "enough for six."
†Here Molière adds this note: "This is a servant speaking."
‡*Flos Sanctorum, o Libro de las vidas de los Santos* (*Flower of
the Saints* . . . , 1599, 2 vols.), a pious work by the Spanish Jesuit
Pedro de Ribadeneira (1526–1611), very popular in French
translation.

And hear the speech she gave us at the door.
But here's my husband. I'll go up and wait
And try to greet him in a proper state.

CLÉANTE. To save his time, I'll merely say hello
To him down here, and then I'll have to go.

DAMIS. One thing. You know my sister wants to
    marry.
Tartuffe seems anxious that her plans miscarry,
And forces Father to procrastinate.
You know my interest in all this is great: 220
Just as love binds my sister and Valère,
As you know, for *his* sister I've my share.
Speak to him . . .

DORINE.   Here he is.

Scene 4.   ORGON, CLÉANTE, DORINE

ORGON.   Brother, good day.

CLÉANTE. I'm glad to see you back; but I can't stay.
I guess you miss the flowers and the trees.

ORGON. Dorine . . . Brother-in-law, one moment,
    please:
Though to be sure I have no cause for fear,
Let me find out what has been happening here.
           (To DORINE*)*
These last two days, how has everything gone?
What are you up to? How is everyone?   230

DORINE. Madame had a bad fever, two days ago,
And a headache that really brought her low.

ORGON. Yes. And Tartuffe?

DORINE.   Tartuffe? Fit as a fiddle:
   Red mouth, pink cheeks, and bulging at the middle.

ORGON. Poor fellow!

DORINE.   Then she had no appetite,
   And therefore couldn't eat a thing that night.
   Her headache still was just too much to bear.

ORGON. Yes. And Tartuffe?

DORINE.   Piously, with her there,
   He ate a brace of partridge like a flash,
240   Then half a leg of mutton in a hash.

ORGON. Poor fellow!

DORINE.   Well, then the whole night went
      by
   Without her managing to close an eye;
   Fever denied her even a wink of sleep;
   It was a nightlong watch we had to keep.

ORGON. Yes. And Tartuffe?

DORINE.   When he had supped, he rose,
   Went to his room, already in a doze,
   Got into his warm bed without delay,
   And slept his carefree fill till the next day.

ORGON. Poor fellow!

DORINE.   When we'd reasoned and we'd pled,
250   She finally consented to be bled,
   And that gave her immediate relief.

ORGON. Yes. And Tartuffe?

DORINE.   He struggled with his grief,
   And, girding up his soul at any cost,
   To make up for the blood Madame had lost,
   He downed at breakfast four great drafts of wine.

ORGON. Poor fellow!

DORINE.   Yes. In short, they both are fine.
    I think I'd better go upstairs and tell
    Madame how glad you are she's getting well.

Scene 5.   ORGON, CLÉANTE

CLÉANTE. She's laughing in your face. Did you see
    her smile?
    Brother, I hestitate to rouse your bile,   260
    But I don't blame her, in this situation.
    Who ever heard of such infatuation?
    And can you really be so hypnotized
    That you've forgotten all you ever prized,
    Given him food, taken him in with you,
    And now you plan . . . ?

ORGON.   No more, sir; that will do.
    You're speaking of a man you do not know.

CLÉANTE. All right, I don't, if you must have it so;
    But if we ever really are to learn . . .

ORGON. Brother, you'd be enchanted in your turn   270
    To know him. I can see it! Oh, I can!
    He's a man . . . who . . . a man . . . in short, a man.
    Follow him: you will be serene, secure,
    And look on everyone as just manure.
    He guides me on new paths in new directions,
    Trains me to mortify all my affections,
    And liberates my soul from every tie.
    My brother, children, mother, wife could die,
    And I could see it without *(snaps his fingers) that*
    much pain.

CLÉANTE. Brother, your sentiments are most humane!   280

ORGON. Ah, if, that day we met, you'd been on hand,
    You'd feel as I do now—you'd understand.
    Each day he came to church, meek as you please,
    And, right across from me, fell on his knees;
    He caught the eye of every person there,
    Such warmth and zeal he put into his prayer;
    His transports were extreme, his sighs profound;
    Each moment he would stoop and kiss the ground;
    And when I left, he always went before
290   To offer me holy water at the door.
    His man, who imitates his every deed,
    Informed me of his background and his need.
    I gave him gifts; but in his modest way,
    He'd give me back a part and humbly say:
    "That is too much, that's twice too much for me;
    I am not worthy of your sympathy";
    And then when I refused to compromise,
    He'd give half to the poor, before my eyes.
    At last Heaven prompted me to take him in;
300   And ever since, how splendid things have been!
    I see him censure everything, and take
    Great interest in my wife, all for my sake;
    He warns me when men ogle her on the sly,
    And acts far jealouser of her than I.
    Upon himself he lays his hardest sentence:
    A trifle, like a sin, demands repentance;
    The merest nothing fills him with dismay.
    He came and blamed himself the other day
    Because while praying he had caught a flea
310   And killed the creature much too angrily.

CLÉANTE. Good Lord! Brother, you're mad, I do
    believe.
    Are you sure you're not laughing up your sleeve?
    Why, this is nonsense! Or do you insist . . . ?

ORGON. Brother, you're talking like an atheist;
    Your soul's been spattered with freethinking
    grime.
    I've warned you more than once, an ugly time
    Awaits you if you will not change your mind.

CLÉANTE. These are the arguments of all your kind:
  Since they can't see, they think that no one ought;
  Whoever does, is tainted with free thought;   320
  Whoever balks at pious affectation
  Fails to hold piety in veneration.
  Come now, for all your talk, I'm not afraid;
  Heaven sees my heart, and I know what I've said;
  Your simulators don't disarm my wits.
  Like courage, piety has its hypocrites.
  Just as we see, where honor beckons most,
  The truly brave are not the ones who boast;
  The truly pious people, even so,
  Are not the ones who make the biggest show.   330
  What? Do you really see no difference
  Between devoutness and devout pretense?
  Do you want to give them both the selfsame place,
  Honor the mask just as you do the face,
  Equate artifice with sincerity,
  And take similitude for verity?
  Isn't there any difference for you
  Between phantoms and men, false coins and true?
  Most men are strangely made; they always stray
  Out of the natural and proper way;   340
  Rejecting reason's bounds as limitations,
  They range about amid their aberrations;
  Even the noblest things they often mar
  By forcing them and pushing them too far.
  I mention this because it's apropos.

ORGON. Oh yes, you are a learned sage, I know;
  The sapience of the world within you lies;
  You alone are enlightened, truly wise,
  An oracle, a Cato through and through;
  All other men are fools compared to you.   350

CLÉANTE. I don't possess the wisdom of the ages,
  And I am not a learned sage of sages;
  My only knowledge and my only art
  Is this: to tell the true and false apart.
  And, as there are no heroes I revere
  More than those whose devoutness is sincere,
  And nothing worthier of veneration

Than genuine religious dedication,
So, nothing seems more odious to me
360   Than the disguise of specious piety,
Than those breast-beaters in the public square
Whose sacrilegious and deceitful air
Turns to its own advantage, with a sneer,
All that men hold most holy and most dear;
Men whom the lust for gain has so possessed
That they turn piety to interest,
And try to purchase honor and high places
By simulated zeal and false grimaces,
Those men, I say, whose vehement devotion
370   By way of Heaven seeks temporal promotion,
Who, while they pray, still manage to extort,
And preach of solitude—but stay at court,
Who know how to make zeal and vices mix;
Vengeful, quick-tempered, faithless, full of tricks;
And, when they want to ruin someone, make
It seem they do it all for Heaven's sake;
Most dangerous in that their bitter hate
Makes use of weapons that we venerate,
And that their zeal, which merits our applause,
380   Seeks to destroy us in a holy cause.
Though far too many fakers meet our eyes,
True piety's not hard to recognize.
Even today, brother, there may be found
Admirable examples all around:
Consider Ariston and Périandre,
Oronte, Alcidas,* Polydore, Clitandre:
No one contests their claim to piety,
Yet they do not parade their sanctity;
Their modest zeal is never out of season,
390   But human and accessible to reason.
They do not lay about in all directions;
They find excessive pride in such corrections,
And leave to others all the lofty speech,
While all they do is practice what they preach.
They do not censure every bagatelle,
But judge with charity and wish men well.

*The name in Molière is "Alcidamas."

They don't promote intrigue or petty strife,
But mainly seek to lead a virtuous life;
Rather than rage against a reprobate,
They think the sin alone deserves their hate,   *400*
And don't espouse, with such intensity,
The cause of Heaven beyond Heaven's own
  decree.
These are the men that win my admiration,
These are the models for our emulation.
You know your man is not at all like these,
And you may vaunt his fervor all you please;
I think appearances lead you astray.

ORGON. Dear brother-in-law, have you had your say?

CLÉANTE. I have.

ORGON.   Your servant.
          (Starts to leave.)

CLÉANTE.   Brother, please don't go.
One more thing. Valère has, as well you know,   *410*
A promise of your daughter's hand from you.

ORGON. Yes.

CLÉANTE.   You had even set a date.

ORGON.   That's true.

CLÉANTE. Why do you put it off, then?

ORGON.   Don't ask me.

CLÉANTE. Have you some other plan in mind?

ORGON.   Maybe.

CLÉANTE. You'd break your promise? Is that what
  you mean?

ORGON. I don't say that.

CLÉANTE.   But what could intervene
To keep you from accomplishing your pledge?

ORGON. Depends.

CLÉANTE.   Why not speak out? Why always
    hedge?
Valère wants me to sound you out again.

ORGON. Praise be to Heaven!

CLÉANTE.   What shall I tell him,
420   then?

ORGON. Why, what you like.

CLÉANTE.   But how can you delay?
He has to know your plans.

ORGON.   I shall obey
The will of Heaven.

CLÉANTE.   Oh yes, so I've heard.
But to the point now: will you keep your word?

ORGON. Farewell.

CLÉANTE.   This looks ominous for Valère.
And I'll go let him know what's in the air.

ACT II

Scene 1. ORGON, MARIANE

ORGON. Mariane.

MARIANE.   Father.

ORGON.   Come over here to me.

MARIANE. What are you looking for?

ORGON *(looking into a small closet).* I want to see
   That no one is around to overhear.
   It's a bad place for privacy, my dear.   *430*
   There, we're all right. Mariane, I've always found
   In you a spirit mild and duty-bound,
   And therefore I have always loved you dearly.

MARIANE. I'm grateful for that, Father, most
   sincerely.

ORGON. Well said, daughter. Now, to deserve it still,
   You must aspire only to do my will.

MARIANE. In that regard I'm proud to do my best.

ORGON. Good. What do you think about Tartuffe,
   our guest?

MARIANE. I, sir?

ORGON.   Answer, but think before you do.

MARIANE. Alas! I'll say whatever you want me to.   *440*

ORGON. That's a good girl. Then say, so I can hear it,
That everything about him tells his merit,
That you are fond of him, and would rejoice
To take him as your husband, by my choice.
Well?

MARIANE *(starts back in surprise)*. What?

ORGON.   What's wrong?

MARIANE.   You mean . . . ?

ORGON.   What?

MARIANE.   Tell me, pray . . .

ORGON. What?

MARIANE.   Father, *who* is it I am to say
I am so fond of that I would rejoice
To take him as my husband by your choice?

ORGON. Tartuffe.

MARIANE.   But that's not so, I swear it. Why
450 Do you want to have me tell you such a lie?

ORGON. But you forget: I want it to be true.
My mind's made up, and that's enough for you.

MARIANE. You mean, Father . . . ?

ORGON.   I mean to bring Tartuffe
Into this family, under this roof.
He is to be your husband; that I swear;
And since you owe . . .

Scene 2.   DORINE, ORGON, MARIANE

ORGON *(to* DORINE*)*.   What are you doing there?
  I gather that you find a fascination
  In trying to overhear our conversation?

DORINE. There is a rumor going around here,
  Chance or conjecture, I have no idea;   *460*
  But when I heard these two were to be wed,
  I just assumed someone was off his head.

ORGON. What? Do you doubt it then?

DORINE.   Indeed I do;
  Yes, even though I've heard it now from you.

ORGON. You will believe it soon, before I'm done.

DORINE. Yes, yes, I know; you like to have your fun.

ORGON. I'm telling you what soon you will attest.

DORINE. Nonsense!

ORGON *(to* MARIANE*)*. I tell you, daughter, it's no jest.

DORINE *(to* MARIANE*)*. Don't mind the games your fa-
      ther plays with you:
  Just jokes.

ORGON.   I say . . .

DORINE.   No matter what you do,   *470*
  They won't believe you.

ORGON.   I am getting mad . . .

DORINE. All right, they will, then; and that *is* too bad.
  What, sir? Can you, who always have appeared

So wise, with your mustache and solemn beard,
Be fool enough to try . . .

ORGON.   Listen to me:
You give yourself a lot of liberty,
My girl. I won't put up with it, I swear.

DORINE. Now, let's not get excited, sir; there, there.
How could you dream up such a silly plot?
480   Your daughter for a bigot? I hope not.
He has to have his mind on other things.
Besides, what do you think this union brings?
And when you are so wealthy, why select
A beggar son-in-law . . . ?

ORGON.   What disrespect!
If he is poor, that is no cause to sneer.
His is a misery we must revere.
He stands above our pomp by his austerity,
Since he has sacrificed his own prosperity
By his disdain for all things transitory
490   And his concern for true, eternal glory.
But my assistance may facilitate
His restoration to his old estate.
In his district he holds important lands,
And he's a gentleman just as he stands.

DORINE. Oh yes, he says so, and that vanity
Does not sit well, sir, with his piety.
If holy living really is his aim,
He should prate less about his birth and name;
And true devoutness seeks a low condition
500   Which will not suffer outbursts of ambition.
So why this pride? . . . But you are looking grim.
Enough about his rank; how about him?
Is he the sort of man you could prefer
To have possession of a girl like her?
And shouldn't you consider what is seemly,
And fear the consequences most extremely?
The danger to a girl's virtue is great
When she is wed to an unwelcome mate;
Her aim to live in modesty and honor

Rests on the type of man you wish upon her,   *510*
And many a man with horns upon his brow
Has made his wife the person she is now.
Fidelity is difficult, in short,
Toward certain husbands of a certain sort.
Marry your daughter where she cannot love,
You'll answer for her sins to Heaven above.
The dangers of your enterprise are grave.

ORGON *(to* MARIANE*).* Now *I* must learn from *her* how
  to behave!

DORINE. Take my advice, and you'd do well enough.

ORGON. Daughter, let's not waste time upon this stuff.   *520*
  I am your father; I know what's best for you.
  I *had* promised you to Valère, that's true;
  But I am told he gambles more than he ought,
  And, worse yet, I suspect him of free thought.
  I don't often see him at church, I know.

DORINE. Should he go running there just when you go,
  Like some who go there only to be seen?

ORGON. I did not ask for your advice, Dorine.
  At all events, Heaven views Tartuffe with pleasure;
  And that is, after all, our greatest treasure.   *530*
  This marriage will be all you could desire,
  Full of sweet joys of which you'll never tire.
  You'll live together, in your faithful loves,
  Just like two children, like two turtledoves;
  No quarrel will take place between you two;
  You'll do with him just as you want to do.

DORINE. She'll make a fool of him; just wait and see.

ORGON. What talk!

DORINE.   He's built for it, believe you me.
  Against the power of his horoscope
  Your daughter's virtue, sir, has little hope.   *540*

ORGON. Stop interrupting me, and just be quiet.
   We're minding our affairs; why don't you try it?

DORINE. I speak of this, sir, only for your sake.

(She interrupts ORGON *every time he turns to speak to his daughter.)*

ORGON. Just hush; spare me the interest you take.

DORINE. If I didn't love you . . .

ORGON.   Just don't love me, pray.

DORINE. I *will* love you, no matter what you say.

ORGON. Oh!

DORINE.
            Your good name fills me with too much pride
   To see you ridiculed on every side.

ORGON. Quiet!

DORINE.   My conscience will not let me rest
550   If I allow this match and don't protest.

ORGON. Quiet, you serpent! Wipe that impudent smile . . .

DORINE. Oh! So much piety, and so much bile!

ORGON. Yes, all this nonsense heats my bile, that's true;
   And I don't want another word from you.

DORINE. All right, but just the same, my thoughts are there.

ORGON. Think, if you like; but better have a care.
   Not a word, or . . . enough.
                          (To MARIANE*)*

                        Now, I have weighed
Everything wisely.

DORINE.   Silence, I'm afraid,
  Will drive me mad.

  (ORGON *turns his head toward her; she is silent.*)

ORGON.   True, he's no pretty boy.
  And yet Tartuffe . . .

DORINE.   That snout! Oh, what a joy! *560*

ORGON. . . . Without his other gifts, would be a catch
  Well worth considering . . .
  (*Turns to* DORINE, *crosses his arms, and watches her.*)

DORINE.   A splendid match!
  If I were she, no man would marry me
  Against my will and with impunity.
  Soon after, I would make him understand
  That women have their vengeance close at hand.

ORGON (*to* DORINE). You disregard my orders, is
  that true?

DORINE. What's your complaint? I'm not speaking
  to you.

ORGON. Who *are* you talking to?

DORINE.   To me; that's all.

ORGON. All right. To punish her colossal gall,   *570*
  I'll have to let her have the back of my hand.

(DORINE *is behind* ORGON, *encouraging* MARIANE *to
  speak up and resist. At this and each of the following
  pauses,* ORGON *turns and sets to slap* DORINE, *who
  each time either freezes, silent and motionless, or
  changes her signal to* MARIANE *into an innocent
  gesture.*)

Daughter, you should approve of what I've
    planned . . .
The man I've chosen . . . for your fiancé . . .
(To DORINE*)* Not talking to yourself?

DORINE.   Nothing to say.

ORGON. Just one more little word.

DORINE.   The word is mum.

ORGON. I'm waiting for you.

DORINE.   I should be so dumb!

ORGON. In short, you must obey the master's voice,
    And show yourself compliant to my choice.

DORINE *(fleeing)*. I wouldn't marry that man on a bet.

        (ORGON *tries to slap her, but misses.*)

580 ORGON. That pest will make me lose my temper yet;
    I'd best dismiss her, to avoid that sin.
    I can't go further in the state I'm in.
    Her insolence has vexed me so, I swear,
    I'd better go and get a breath of air.

Scene 3.   DORINE, MARIANE

DORINE. Well, have you lost your tongue completely,
    Miss?
    And do I have to play your part in this?
    Let him propose a project that absurd,
    And not combat it with a single word!

MARIANE. What can I do? My father is the master.

DORINE. Do anything to block such a disaster. 590

MARIANE. What?

DORINE.   Tell him you can't love just on his whim;
  That you are marrying for yourself, not him.
  This is arranged for *you,* supposedly;
  Then you must love the husband, and not he.
  Tell him that if Tartuffe enchants him so,
  Then he should marry him; we shan't say no.

MARIANE. I know, but Father holds such awful sway,
  There's nothing I can bring myself to say.

DORINE. Come, let's talk sense. You're courted by
    Valère.
  Well, do you love him, now, or don't you care? 600

MARIANE. Oh, come, Dorine, be fairer to my love!
  You ask me that? What are you thinking of?
  I've held back nothing from you, Heaven knows.
  Surely you know how far my ardor goes?

DORINE. How do I know you're saying what you feel,
  And that your passion for Valère is real?

MARIANE. Truly, Dorine, you wrong me by your
    doubt;
  My sentiments have clearly spoken out.

DORINE. In short, you love him?

MARIANE.   I should say I do.

DORINE. Right. And apparently he loves you too? 610

MARIANE. So I believe.

DORINE.   Your hearts are both on fire
  To join in marriage?

MARIANE.   That is our desire.

DORINE. About this other match: what is your plan?

MARIANE. To kill myself, if I must have that man.

DORINE. That's fine! I hadn't thought of that resource.
Just die, and end your problems! Why, of course.
A fine solution! Oh, it drives me wild
To hear you talking like a silly child!

MARIANE. Good Lord! Dorine, don't take it out on
    me!
620 You've no compassion for my misery.

DORINE. I've no compassion left for all this drivel,
When, once the chips are down, you simply shrivel.

MARIANE. But I'm so timid! What am I to do?

DORINE. But love requires a touch of firmness too.

MARIANE. I'm firm in my devotion to Valère.
Surely Father's consent is his affair.

DORINE. But if your father's utterly insane,
Since passion for Tartuffe has rocked his brain,
And breaks his promise that you two should wed,
630 Why place the blame upon your suitor's head?

MARIANE. But if I show defiance to a parent,
Won't my love for Valère be too apparent?
Shall I give up, for all his charm and beauty,
The modesty that is a woman's duty?
And is my love a thing you'd have me flaunt . . . ?

DORINE. I wouldn't have a thing. I see you want
To be Madame Tartuffe. I'd be unkind,
Were I to try to make you change your mind.
Why should I argue, since you want this match?
640 Just in himself, he's certainly a catch.
Monsieur Tartuffe! That's quite a thing to be!
In fact Monsieur Tartuffe, it's plain to see,
Is not a man to eat peas with a knife,

And it would be a joy to be his wife.
He basks in honor and in good repute.
He's noble—back at home—a handsome brute:
With that florid complexion, those red ears,
Think what delight you'll have over the years.

MARIANE. Good Lord! . . .

DORINE.   Your soul will know eternal bliss,
Wedded to such a handsome man as this!   *650*

MARIANE. Oh! Please don't torture me; I just can't
    stand it.
How can we break this match, when Father's
    planned it?
I give up. I'll do anything you say.
DORINE. When Father speaks, his daughter must
    obey,
And even take a monkey for her mate.
You've no complaint; you'll have a lovely fate:
In his small town a coach will take you round.
His uncles and his cousins will abound,
And you will find them a delight to meet.
First you'll be introduced to the elite: *660*
A round of jolly calls will fill your life,
To the bailiff's and the tax collector's wife,
Who'll patronize you with a folding chair.
Then once a year there's dancing at the fair,
With a big orchestra—of two musettes—
Sometimes a monkey act and marionettes,
Though if your husband . . .

MARIANE.   Oh! You're killing me.
I need your help, and not this mockery.

DORINE. Madame, your servant.

MARIANE.   Dorine, I beseech you . . .

DORINE. No, this will have to happen, just to teach
670   you.

MARIANE. Dorine, dear!

DORINE.   No.

MARIANE.   If I declare my will . . .

DORINE. Tartuffe's your man, and you shall have
    your fill.

MARIANE. You know how much I always have
    relied . . .

DORINE. No, you shall be—my word!—Tartuffified.

MARIANE. All right! As long as that is all you care,
    Henceforth leave me alone with my despair;
    In that at least my heart will find a cure;
    I know a remedy that's swift and sure.
                    (She starts to go.)

DORINE. There now, come back. I can't be angry long.
680   Do what you will, my pity is too strong.

MARIANE. If this cruel torture is what lies ahead,
    I'll kill myself; I'd far rather be dead.

DORINE. Come, don't be so upset. This much is plain:
    We'll find a way . . . But here's Valère, your swain.

Scene 4.   VALÈRE, MARIANE, DORINE

VALÈRE. Madame, a piece of news is going about,
    Unknown to me, but very fine, no doubt.

MARIANE. What?

VALÈRE.   That you're marrying Tartuffe.

MARIANE.   Indeed,
  That is just what my father has decreed.

VALÈRE. Madame, your father . . .

MARIANE.   Has just changed his mind,
  And now prefers this other match, I find.   690

VALÈRE. Can he be serious?

MARIANE.   Indeed he can.
  He clearly is determined on this plan.

VALÈRE. And what have you in mind, this being so,
  Madame?

MARIANE.   I do not know.

VALÈRE.   You do not know?
  Delightful!

MARIANE. No.

VALÈRE.   No?

MARIANE.   What do you advise?

VALÈRE. Marry the man. I'm sure that would be wise.

MARIANE. That's your advice?

VALÈRE.   Yes.

MARIANE.   Honestly?

VALÈRE.   Indeed:
  This is a noble choice, which you should heed.

MARIANE. That's your advice, sir? Well, just as you
  say.

700 VALÈRE. I think you'll follow it without dismay.

MARIANE. Just as you offered it, it would appear.

VALÈRE. Madame, I offered what you wished to hear.

MARIANE. And I will do what *you* want *me* to do.

DORINE *(withdrawing to the back of the stage)*. Let's
    see what this affair is coming to.

VALÈRE. So that's your love? And it was make-
    believe
    When you . . .

MARIANE.   No more of that, sir, by your leave.
    You clearly said I must not hestitate
    To take the man presented as my mate.
    All right, I'll do precisely that, I vow,
710 Since that is the advice you give me now.

VALÈRE. Just don't make my intentions your excuse.
    You'd made your plans already; that's no use.
    This pretext that you're seizing is absurd
    To justify the breaking of your word.

MARIANE. Of course. Well said.

VALÈRE.   No doubt; and in your heart
    You've never really loved me from the start.

MARIANE. Alas! You're free to choose this
    explanation.

VALÈRE. Yes, yes, I'm free; but in my indignation,
    I may decide to get ahead of you;
720 And I know other girls who would be true.

MARIANE. Indeed they would; I have no doubt of it.
    Your merit . . .

VALÈRE.   Leave my merit out of it:

I haven't much; your act is a reminder.
But I have hopes of finding someone kinder,
And I know one who'll think it no disgrace
To compensate my loss and take your place.

MARIANE. It's no great loss; you'll easily arrange
To find your consolation for this change.

VALÈRE. As you may well believe, I'll do my best.
To be forgotten puts us to the test: 730
We must forget in turn, even pretend,
If all our efforts don't achieve that end.
To show our love for one who's turned us down
Is to be both a coward and a clown.

MARIANE. Well, that's a noble, lofty sentiment.

VALÈRE. And one to which all men should give
    assent.
What? Would you have me foster in my breast
The love that, when you wanted, you possessed?
Am I to watch you seek another's arms
And not console my heart with other charms?   740

MARIANE. No, that's exactly what I want. Alas!
I wish it had already come to pass.

VALÈRE. You do?

MARIANE.   I do.

VALÈRE.   That's all that I can stand,
Madame; I'll go and do as you command.

(Here and later, he starts to leave, then returns.)

MARIANE. All right.

VALÈRE *(returning)*. At least remember that it's you
Who's driving me to what I'm going to do.

MARIANE. Oh, yes.

VALÈRE.   And that by acting in this way,
　I follow your example.

MARIANE.   As you say.

VALÈRE. Enough: I'll carry out your wishes, then.

MARIANE. That's fine.

750 VALÈRE.   You see me now, but never again.

MARIANE. Of course.

VALÈRE (goes, but turns back at the door). Eh?

MARIANE.   What?

VALÈRE.   Didn't you call?

MARIANE.   Not I.
　You're dreaming.

VALÈRE.   Then, Madame, my last goodbye.
　I'm off.

MARIANE. Goodbye, sir.

DORINE.   Well, if you ask me,
　We've had enough of this tomfoolery.
　I've let you bandy insults to and fro
　To see how far the two of you would go.
　Seigneur Valère! Hey!
　(She goes and holds his arm to stop him, and he makes
　　　　　a great show of resistance.)

VALÈRE.   What is it, Dorine?

DORINE. Come here.

VALÈRE.   No, no, I've got to vent my spleen.
　Don't turn me back from what she has decreed.

DORINE. Stand still.

VALÈRE.   No, don't you see? We've both agreed.   760

DORINE. Oh, my!

MARIANE.   He hates my sight, he wants to leave;
  And I'm the one should go, I do believe.

DORINE (*leaves* VALÈRE *and runs to* MARIANE). Now
    you!
  Where to?

MARIANE.   Let go.

DORINE.   You stay right here.

MARIANE. Dorine, don't try to hold me back, do you
    hear?

VALÈRE. Why, she's in torment at the sight of me.
  I'd better disappear, and set her free.

DORINE (*leaves* MARIANE *and runs to* VALÈRE). You
    again? No, you don't. Confound you two!
  Now stop this nonsense. Come here, both of you.

(*She pulls first at one, then at the other, bringing them
                together.*)

VALÈRE. What are you trying to do?

MARIANE.   Why   all   this
    bother?

DORINE. To bring you back to sense and to each
    other.   770
                (*To* VALÈRE)
  Fighting like that! Are you out of your head?

VALÈRE. Didn't you hear the heartless things she
    said?

DORINE (*to* MARIANE). Aren't *you* a fool, to work up
　　such a passion?

MARIANE. Didn't you see him treat me in that
　　fashion?

DORINE. Nonsense on both sides.
　　　　　　　　　(*To* VALÈRE)
　　　　　　　　　　　　　Why, her only care
　　Is to preserve herself for you, I swear.
　　　　　　　　　(*To* MARIANE)
　　He loves you, and he wants you for his wife,
　　Above all else; on this I'll stake my life.

MARIANE. Why give me such advice? Now, was that
　　right?

780　VALÈRE. Why ask for it at all in such a plight?

DORINE. You're both insane. Now, your hands, both
　　of you.
　　Come on, you.

VALÈRE (*giving* DORINE *his hand*). What's that for?

DORINE.　　　　　　　　　　All right, yours too.

MARIANE (*giving* DORINE *her hand too*). What good
　　will that do?

DORINE.　　　　　　　Heavens! Come on, let's go!
　　You love each other better than you know.

VALÈRE (*after a pause, to* MARIANE). It doesn't hurt
　　that much, you must confess.
　　Look at a fellow without bitterness.

(MARIANE *glances at* VALÈRE *with just a bit of a smile*.)

DORINE. To tell the truth, lovers are all insane!

VALÈRE. But look, haven't I reason to complain?

In all sincerity, weren't you unkind
To enjoy driving me out of my mind?   *790*

MARIANE. If I have ever seen ingratitude . . .

DORINE. Suppose we just postpone this little feud,
And try to block this marriage if we can.

MARIANE. Tell us, what shall we do? What is your
plan?

DORINE. We shall use everything we can invoke.
Your father's mad; this thing is a bad joke;
But you had best indulge his antic bent
By the appearance of a meek consent,
So that you may more easily prolong
The waiting period, should things go wrong.   *800*
Time is the very best of remedies.
At first your reason may be some disease,
Which, coming suddenly, demands delay;
A bad omen will do another day:
You dreamed of muddy water, chanced to pass
A funeral, or broke a looking glass.
And don't forget: however hard they press,
You can't be married without saying yes.
But you'd be foolish, in this situation,
To let yourselves be seen in conversation.   *810*
              (*To* VALÈRE)
Go on, get your friends busy on our side
To make him keep the promise he's denied.
We'll get his son to join us in the strife,
And try to gain assistance from his wife.
Goodbye.

VALÈRE (*to* MARIANE). For all the rest of us may do,
The one I'm really counting on is you.

MARIANE (*to* VALÈRE). I can't be sure what Father
may decide;
But I shall never be another's bride.

VALÈRE. How happy you have made me! Come
what may . . .

820 DORINE. Lovers never run out of things to say!
Come on, be off.

VALÈRE *(takes one step and comes back)*. In short . . .

DORINE.   No time for chat.
You go out this way, and you go out that.
(Pushes them by the shoulder toward opposite exits.)

ACT III

Scene 1.   DAMIS, DORINE

DAMIS. Let lightning right this moment strike me
        down,
    Let me be called a villain and a clown,
    If reverence or power holds me back
    When everything within me cries: Attack!

DORINE. Please moderate your anger if you can:
    Your father's only talked about this plan.
    Not all that men propose becomes a fact,
    Nor does intention always lead to act.   830

DAMIS. I'll block that coxcomb's plans, just wait and
        see;
    It won't be long before he hears from me.

DORINE. Gently! See what your stepmother can do
    To get around him and your father too.
    She seems to have Tartuffe under her sway;
    He treats her in the most obliging way,
    And may well feel a certain fascination . . .
    Would God he did! That *would* be a sensation.
    She has to see him, in your interest,
    Sound him out on this marriage you detest,   840
    Learn where he stands, and make him realize
    What altercations surely will arise
    If he persists in pressing this affair.
    His servant says he's busy now in prayer,
    But shortly will be on his way down here.
    Please go along, and do not interfere.

DAMIS. I have a right to hear this interview.

285

DORINE. No. They must be alone.

DAMIS.   I promise you,
I will not speak.

DORINE.   You can't avoid extremes.
850   You'll throw a fit, and shatter all our schemes.
Go on.

DAMIS.   I want to watch; I won't make trouble.

DORINE. Not much! He's coming. In there, on the
double.

(At DORINE'S *direction* DAMIS *hides in a closet at the
back of the stage.)*

Scene 2.   TARTUFFE, LAURENT *(offstage)*, DORINE

TARTUFFE *(seeing* DORINE; *to* LAURENT *offstage)*. Put
back my scourge and hair shirt in their place,
Laurent, and pray for Heaven's enlightening grace.
If someone asks for me, I may be found
Among the prisoners, giving alms all round.

DORINE. What affectation! What pretentious cheek!

TARTUFFE. What do you want?

DORINE.   To say . . .

TARTUFFE *(taking a handkerchief from his pocket)*.
Good Lord! Don't speak
Until you take this handkerchief.

DORINE.   Who, me?

860   TARTUFFE. Cover that bosom, which I must not see.

Souls can be harmed by objects of that kind;
And they bring sinful thoughts to a man's mind.

DORINE. You must be very weak against temptation
And very prone to fleshly stimulation.
I don't know what can set you so on fire:
For my part, I am slower to desire,
And if I saw you bare from tip to toe,
Your epidermis wouldn't tempt me—so!

TARTUFFE. Unless you speak more modestly, I vow
That I shall have to leave you here and now.   870

DORINE. No, *I'll* leave *you* in peace; I'm on my way;
And I have only these few words to say:
Madame is coming down, and asks of you
The signal favor of an interview.

TARTUFFE. Alas, most happily!

DORINE (*aside*).   Ah, how polite!
My word! I still believe that I am right.

TARTUFFE. Will she be coming soon?

DORINE.   Yes, I believe
I hear her. Here she comes; I'll take my leave.

Scene 3.   ELMIRE, TARTUFFE

TARTUFFE. For you may Heaven's grace ever abound,
Preserve your soul and body safe and sound,   880
And bless your days, according to the love
I humbly offer to the Lord above.

ELMIRE. Your wishes are most pious, I declare.
Thank you. But let's sit down; here is a chair.

TARTUFFE. I trust your recent illness is all past?

ELMIRE. Oh yes, thank you; that fever didn't last.

TARTUFFE. My prayers, I know, would never qualify
To have drawn down such mercy from on high;
But every supplication I have made
890   Has been for your good health, and Heaven's aid.

ELMIRE. Your zeal has been concerned for me too
    much.

TARTUFFE. Madame, my care for your dear health is
    such
That I'd have given my own to make it better.

ELMIRE. Such Christian love goes far beyond the
    letter;
Your kindness leaves me much obliged to you.

TARTUFFE. Alas, it is far less than is your due.

ELMIRE. I want to talk to you in secrecy,
And I am grateful for this privacy.

TARTUFFE. You can't be as delighted as I am
900   To be alone with you this way, Madame:
I've often prayed to Heaven for this boon,
But it has never judged it opportune.

ELMIRE. What I want is a word with you apart,
Where you'll speak frankly with an open heart.

TARTUFFE. No other grace would I so highly prize
As to reveal my soul unto your eyes,
And swear to you that if I've caused alarms
Over the visits prompted by your charms,
There is no hatred in the way I feel,
910   But rather just an overpowering zeal,
A pure desire . . .

ELMIRE.   A pious aspiration
In which your sole concern was my salvation.

TARTUFFE *(squeezing her fingertips)*. Yes, Madame,
   and my fervent hopes betray . . .

ELMIRE. You squeeze too hard.

TARTUFFE.   Zeal carries me away.
   Surely you don't believe I could have planned
   To harm you . . . *(Puts his hand on her knee.)*

ELMIRE.   What are you doing with your
   hand?

TARTUFFE. Feeling your gown: what soft, velvety
   stuff!

ELMIRE. Please don't, I'm very ticklish. That's
   enough.
(She moves her chair away, and TARTUFFE *brings his
   closer.)*

TARTUFFE *(fondling the lace collar of her gown)*. Lord,
   but this needlepoint is marvelous!
   The way they work now is miraculous;   920
   I've never seen the like, upon my word.

ELMIRE. Indeed. But to the point. From what I've
   heard,
   My husband now intends Mariane for you,
   Though he had pledged her elsewhere. Is that true?

TARTUFFE. He's spoken of it; but, since you inquire,
   That's not the rapture to which I aspire;
   And, Madame, it is elsewhere that I turn
   For the felicity for which I yearn.

ELMIRE. That's because you love nothing here below.

TARTUFFE. My heart is not a heart of stone, you know. 930

ELMIRE. Come now, Heaven's the one object of
   your sighs,
   And nothing here on earth delights your eyes.

TARTUFFE. To love eternal beauties far above
  Is not to be immune to other love;
  Our senses may be easily fascinated
  By perfect works that Heaven has created.
  It shows itself in others by reflection,
  But you alone display its true perfection:
  The beauties that upon your face it's lavished
  Dazzle men's eyes and leave their feelings
940   ravished.
  I could not look at you, O perfect creature,
  And not admire the Author of all nature,
  Feeling my heart most fervently impassioned
  For this lovely self-portrait he has fashioned.
  My first reaction was to be afraid
  This ardor was a snare the Devil had laid;
  And I avoided you as a temptation
  That might stand in the way of my salvation.
  But finally I knew, O gracious beauty,
950 That passion need not be at odds with duty,
  That I can reconcile it with propriety;
  And so I yield to it without anxiety.
  I know it is audacious on my part
  To make you this poor offering of my heart;
  But though my efforts are infirm and vain,
  I know that you are gracious and humane;
  On you depends my hope and quietude,
  My wretchedness or my beatitude;
  You must decide what lies ahead of me:
960 Celestial bliss or utter misery.

ELMIRE. That is indeed a gallant declaration,
  But one that quite confounds my expectation.
  You should, I think, have striven for self-control
  And turned this matter over in your soul.
  For one so pious to have such a plan . . .

TARTUFFE. I may be pious, but I'm still a man.
  And at the sight of your celestial charms,
  Reason and heart alike lay down their arms.
  Coming from me, I know these words distress you;
970 But after all, I'm not an angel, bless you;
  And if you think I've put myself to shame,

It's your bewitching charms that are to blame.
For, once I saw their superhuman splendor,
My heart had no recourse but to surrender;
The indescribable sweetness of your eyes
Forced my resistance to demobilize;
It overcame my fasts, my tears, my prayers,
And made your charms the object of my cares.
My eyes, my sighs, a thousand times, no less,
Have told you what my words would now express.   *980*
A bit of sympathy is all I crave
For the distress of your unworthy slave.
If your kindness, Madame, should ever deign
To condescend to me, and end my pain,
Nothing could be as constant and as true
As the devotion I shall have for you.
Your honor will not be in jeopardy,
And will not run a single risk with me.
All those court fops, on whom the ladies dote,
Are far too noisy and too prone to gloat;   *990*
They cannot bear to keep their luck concealed;
Each favor granted is at once revealed;
And by their loose and faithless declaration
They smirch the object of their adoration.
But men like us burn with a hidden fire;
The secrecy we offer is entire:
The care we take to keep our own good name
Guarantees our beloved against shame;
Accept our hearts, and you will find, my dear,
Love without scandal, pleasure without fear.   *1000*

ELMIRE. I've heard you out, and found you eloquent
In giving utterance to your intent.
Aren't you afraid that I may take a notion
To tell my husband of this warm devotion,
And that your passion, if he ever knew,
Might undermine his friendliness for you?

TARTUFFE. I know that you are gracious and benign,
And will forgive this recklessness of mine,
Blame human weakness for the violence
Of this my love, at which you take offense,   *1010*
And, looking in your mirror, keep in mind

That man is flesh and blood, and I'm not blind.

ELMIRE. Others might take this in another fashion,
But my discretion recommends compassion.
I will not tell my husband; well and good.
But in return I want it understood
That you will bring your influence to bear
To join Mariane in marriage with Valère,
Give up your own inequitable plan
1020   To take a girl pledged to another man,
And . . .

Scene 4. DAMIS, ELMIRE, TARTUFFE

DAMIS *(coming out of the closet where he had been
     hiding)*. No, Madame, this has to be revealed.
I heard it all from where I was concealed;
Heaven's goodness must have put me there inside
To let me dash this noxious traitor's pride,
Avenge his odious impertinence,
His rank hypocrisy and insolence,
Open my father's eyes, and bare to view
This scoundrel soul that talks of love to you.

ELMIRE. No, Damis: he shall merely learn his place,
1030   And study to deserve my promised grace.
Don't let it out. I've given him my word.
A scene about it would be quite absurd:
A wife laughs off a lot of what she hears,
And doesn't din it in her husband's ears.

DAMIS. You have your reasons for this compromise,
But I have mine for doing otherwise.
To want to spare this bigot is all wrong;
His insolence has lorded it too long
Over my righteous anger, and has tried
1040   To spread dissension here on every side.
Too long he's held my father in his spell,

And crossed my sister's love, and mine as well.
His deceit must be bared to Father's glance,
And Heaven offers me a perfect chance.
It has my deepest gratitude for this,
And the occasion is too good to miss.
I would deserve to have it snatched away
If I did not use it without delay.

ELMIRE. Damis . . .

DAMIS.   No, please, I'll do as I think right.
My soul is overflowing with delight;   *1050*
There's no use telling me to be discreet;
An overdue revenge is doubly sweet.
It's time all this was settled, anyhow;
And, sure enough, here comes my father now.

Scene 5.   ORGON, DAMIS, TARTUFFE, ELMIRE

DAMIS. Father, here's a development that's new
And may well come as a surprise to you.
You're well repaid for your beneficence;
Monsieur has his own kind of recompense.
And it's his zeal on your behalf, I guess,
That leads him to dishonor you, no less.   *1060*
I've just caught him, in the most shameful fashion,
Asking Madame to share his guilty passion.
Discreet and over mild, she did not choose
To have you inconvenienced by the news;
But I cannot condone such impudence
Or hide it without giving you offense.

ELMIRE. I think we should not vex a husband's mind
With incidents of such a foolish kind;
That honor does not rest on points like these:
Enough to check familiarities.   *1070*
Those are my feelings; and if you, Damis,

Had heeded them, you would have held your
peace.

Scene 6.   ORGON, DAMIS, TARTUFFE

ORGON. What have I heard? Heavens! Can this be
true?

TARTUFFE. Yes, brother, I am evil through and
through,
Guilty, full of iniquity and sin,
The greatest scoundrel that has ever been;
Each moment of my life is black with grime;
It is a mass of filthiness and crime;
And I am sure that this mortification
1080   Is just a sign of Heaven's indignation.
Whatever sin they charge against my name,
I won't defend myself, such is my shame.
Believe their stories, everything they say,
And like a criminal send me away:
Whatever ignominy lies in store,
I know that I have merited far more.

ORGON (to his son). Oh! Traitor! Would you dare to
stigmatize
His perfect virtue with this pack of lies?

DAMIS. What? Because this impostor beats his chest,
You give the lie . . . ?

1090 ORGON.   Silence, accursed pest.

TARTUFFE. You're wrong to blame him so. Don't cut
him short.
Really, you should believe his whole report.
Why favor me, in this case, as you do?
Do you really think you know me through and
through?

Brother, how can you trust my semblance so,
And think me better for my outward show?
Appearances are leading you astray,
And I am anything but what men say.
Alas! Everyone views me with respect,
But in truth I am utterly abject.   1100
                    (To DAMIS*)*
Dear son, go on; tell me my crimes are great;
Call me thief, killer, traitor, reprobate;
Load me with epithets still more abhorred:
I won't say no; they are my just reward;
After my life of crime, in expiation,
I'll kneel and suffer that humiliation.

ORGON *(to* TARTUFFE*)*. Dear brother, that's too much.
                    (To his son)
                              Have you no heart,
    Traitor?

DAMIS.   How's this? You still will take his part?

ORGON. Be quiet, scoundrel.
                    (To TARTUFFE*)*
                              Brother, pray you, rise.
                    (To his son)
    Wretch!

DAMIS.   He can . . .

ORGON.   Hush!

DAMIS.   I don't believe my eyes. *1110*

ORGON. If you say one word more, I swear I'll
    break . . .

TARTUFFE. Brother, control your wrath, for Heav-
    en's sake.
    I'd rather suffer pain, in any amount,
    Than have him get a scratch on my account.

ORGON *(to his son)*. Ingrate!

TARTUFFE.   Leave him alone. Upon
   my knees
I ask you to forgive him.

ORGON *(also on his knees, embracing* TARTUFFE *as he
    addresses him).*   Stop it, please!
             (To his son)
That good man!

DAMIS.   So . . .

ORGON.   Hush!

DAMIS.   What! I . . .

ORGON.   Hush, do you hear?
I know what lies behind this wicked smear:
You all hate him. Why, just today I've seen
1120   My wife, children, and servants vent their spleen.
I'm shocked to see how brazenly you plan
To separate me from this pious man.
The more you try to drive Tartuffe away,
The harder I shall strive to make him stay;
And soon he'll have my daughter as his bride,
Just to confound my family and its pride.

DAMIS. You'd force your daughter to accept that cad?

ORGON. Yes, and this evening, just to make you mad.
Oh! You may try your best to interfere:
1130   You must obey; I am the master here.
Take it back, rascal; and for your conceit,
Get down and ask his pardon at his feet.

DAMIS. Who, me! From that dissembling pietist . . . ?

ORGON. So! You insult him, wretch, and still resist?
    (To TARTUFFE, *who remains motionless)*
Give me a stick! A stick! Don't hold me back.
    (To his son)
Go on, out of this house; no time to pack,
And never have the nerve to show your face . . .

DAMIS. All right, I'll go; but . . .

ORGON.   Quick, out of this place.
  I disinherit you; and, what is worse,
  You scoundrel, all I leave you is my curse.   *1140*

Scene 7.   ORGON, TARTUFFE

ORGON. To offend a holy man in such a way!

TARTUFFE. May Heaven forgive him for my pain, I
    pray!
                    (To ORGON*)*
  If you knew how it hurts when someone tries
  To blacken me before my brother's eyes . . .

ORGON. Alas!

TARTUFFE.   The thought of this ingratitude
  Inflicts a torment of such magnitude . . .
  My heart is torn . . . I'm simply horrified . . .
  I cannot speak . . . 'Twere better that I died.

ORGON *(in tears, runs to the door through which he
    drove out his son)*. Villain! I spared your life!
  Now I repent.
  I should have struck you down before you went.   *1150*
               (To TARTUFFE*)*
  Forgive him, brother; set your mind at peace.

TARTUFFE. I can't endure these scenes; they've got
    to cease.
  And since I bring dissension, I believe
  That it is time, brother, for me to leave.

ORGON. What? Are you joking?

TARTUFFE.   No, they hate me
    here,
  And try to make you think I'm not sincere.

ORGON. So? Do you really think I hear them out?

TARTUFFE. They will keep persecuting me, no doubt;
  And these same stories, which you now reject—
1160 You'll listen to them some day, I expect.

ORGON. No, brother, never.

TARTUFFE.   Oh, brother, a wife
  Affects her husband's soul, his very life.

ORGON. No, no.

TARTUFFE.   Let me go soon, without a fuss,
  And leave them no excuse to hound me thus.

ORGON. No, you shall stay; my very life's at stake.

TARTUFFE. I'll mortify myself, then, for your sake.
  But if you wanted . . .

ORGON.   Ah!

TARTUFFE.   All right. That's that.
  But henceforth I must be a diplomat.
  Honor is touchy; and to be your friend,
1170 I must bring all these rumors to an end.
  I shall avoid your wife, and thus forestall . . .

ORGON. No, you shall see her; I defy them all.
  To drive them crazy is my main delight,
  And you shall be with her in all men's sight.
  Nor is that all; to spite them through and through,
  I want to have no other heir than you;
  And legally—I don't intend to wait—
  I'll see that you inherit my estate.
  A good true friend, my son-in-law-to-be,
1180 Is dearer than my son, wife, kin to me.
  Won't you accept this offer I suggest?

TARTUFFE. Let Heaven's will be done as it is best.

ORGON. Poor fellow! Let's just get this drawn up right,
  And then let envy burst its seams for spite!

ACT IV

Scene 1.   CLÉANTE, TARTUFFE

CLÉANTE. Yes, it is common gossip, and the story,
Believe me, will add little to your glory;
I'm glad I found you, sir; it's overdue;
Briefly, I want to speak my mind to you.
I'm not examining the accusation;
But even if it is without foundation,   1190
Even supposing Damis is to blame
And that he's falsely slandered your good name,
Shouldn't a Christian pardon the offense
And rid his heart of all malevolence?
For all your quarrel, should you stand aloof
And see a son denied his father's roof?
I tell you once again that what you've done,
Frankly, seems scandalous to everyone;
If you'll take my advice, you'll work for peace,
And stop carrying on against Damis.   1200
No, sacrifice your wrath to God above,
And help the son regain the father's love.

TARTUFFE. Alas! I would, sir, and with all my heart;
I harbor no resentment, for my part;
He has my full forgiveness, not my blame;
To help him out would be my dearest aim.
But Heaven's interest will not have it so;
And if he comes back in here, I must go.
Since he has charged me with a crime so base,
We can't associate without disgrace.   1210
God knows what everyone's first thoughts would
   be!
They'd chalk it up to sheer expediency,
And say that, to disguise the guilt I feel,
I'm putting on a charitable zeal,

299

And trying, out of crass self-interest,
To get my accuser to let matters rest.

CLÉANTE. This is a specious case, sir, that you plead,
And your arguments are far-fetched indeed.
Why treat the will of Heaven as your own?
1220   Can't Heaven mete out discipline alone?
Our role is not to punish or reward,
But to forgive. Leave vengeance to the Lord.
And whether men speak of you well or ill,
Don't worry; merely follow Heaven's will.
What? Shall your fear to be misunderstood
Make you pass up a chance for doing good?
No, no; let's do what Heaven has assigned,
And not let other things disturb our mind.

TARTUFFE. My heart forgives him, as you've heard
        me say;
1230   And thus, when Heaven orders, I obey;
But Heaven has not ordered me, I know,
To live with him, when he has hurt me so.

CLÉANTE. And does it order you to listen rather,
Sir, to the sheer caprice of the boy's father,
And to accept his making you his heir,
When equity rejects this as unfair?

TARTUFFE. All those who know me will believe, I'm
        sure,
That all my motives in this case are pure.
I do not care for this world's goods, you see:
1240   Their specious luster does not dazzle me;
And if I am prevailed upon to take
This present that Orgon has willed to make,
I do so because honestly I dread
That it may fall in wicked hands instead,
In those of men who, playing fast and loose,
May put these riches to some evil use,
And not employ them, as I surely would,
For Heaven's glory and my neighbor's good.

CLÉANTE. Oh! Sir, give up this conscientious care

That may cause lawsuits by the rightful heir;   *1250*
Leave him, with less concern about his fate,
To all the risks of owning his estate.
He may not use it so one may applaud him,
But better thus than that you should defraud him.
When Orgon spoke to you of his intent,
How could you hear without embarrassment?
Must genuine devotion be so prone
To rob an heir of all that is his own?
And if it's true that Heaven won't allow
You and Damis to live together now,   *1260*
Why not make your departure in good season,
And not stand by while, contrary to reason,
A father undertakes, in your behoof,
To drive his son from underneath his roof?
This is a strange example, believe me,
Of virtue, sir . . .

TARTUFFE.   Sir, it is half-past three:
·I have devotions at this time of day,
And you'll excuse me if I do not stay.

CLÉANTE. Oh!

Scene 2.   ELMIRE, MARIANE, DORINE, CLÉANTE

DORINE.   Sir, please help us out, for Heaven's sake:
She's suffering so, I fear her heart will break;   *1270*
Her father's plan to marry her tonight
Has put her in a really desperate plight.
He's coming now. Together, if you will,
Let's try to undermine, by strength or skill,
This wretched match that we deplore and fear.

Scene 3.   ORGON, ELMIRE, MARIANE, CLÉANTE,
DORINE

ORGON. I'm glad to see you all together here.
            (To MARIANE)
Here is the contract that assures your bliss,
Mariane, and you know what I mean by this.

MARIANE (on her knees). Father, by Heaven, which
            knows the pain I feel,
1280   And by whatever else hears my appeal,
Waive some of your paternal rights, I pray,
And in this, do not force me to obey;
Don't use your power to constrain me so
That I begrudge the duty that I owe;
And do not make this life, which I possess,
Alas, from you, one long unhappiness.
If I must be denied my dearest prayer,
Of marrying the man I love, Valère,
At least be kind, and spare me, I implore,
1290   A marriage to a person I abhor;
And do not drive me into desperation
By using all the powers of your station.

ORGON (touched). Be firm, my heart! No human
            weakness now!

MARIANE. Pamper him all you like, no matter how:
I am not jealous of the things you do;
Give him your property, and add mine too;
For all this you shall have my full consent.
But as regards my person, please relent,
And let me drag my sad steps toward the tomb
1300   Within a convent's consecrated gloom.

ORGON. Oh, that's a daughter for you! Every one,
When once her love is crossed, must be a nun!
Get up! The more you think you cannot bear it,
The more by your acceptance you will merit.

So, by this marriage, mortify your senses,
And spare me all your feminine defenses.

DORINE. But what . . . ?

ORGON.   Shut up, you! Talk to your
    own kind:
    From now on I won't let you speak your mind.

CLÉANTE. Might I put in a word of counsel, though?

ORGON. Your counsel, brother, I have cause to know, *1310*
    Is wonderful; I care a lot about it;
    But please don't mind if I just do without it.

ELMIRE *(to her husband)*. Words fail me when I see
    the things I see,
    And your persistent blindness baffles me.
    You must be quite bewitched by him, I'd say,
    To doubt our word on what went on today.

ORGON. I trust evidence more than anyone.
    I know you dote upon my rascal son,
    And that you were afraid to disavow
    His little plot against Tartuffe just now.   *1320*
    You were too calm for me to be impressed;
    In fact, you didn't seem the least distressed.

ELMIRE. If someone simply tells us of his passion,
    Must our honor take arms in martial fashion?
    And where it is involved, must we reply
    Only with scornful lip and blazing eye?
    I take such propositions with a smile,
    And do not find explosiveness worthwhile;
    I like to see our virtue free of spite,
    And do not think those pious prudes are right   *1330*
    Whose honor arms itself with teeth and claws
    To scratch men's eyes out for the slightest cause:
    Heaven keep me from a virtue such as that!
    I just want to be decent, not a cat.
    And I believe that it is quite enough
    To check a suitor with a cool rebuff.

ORGON. I know what's what, and I won't be put off.

ELMIRE. I marvel at your readiness to scoff.
How would your incredulity react
1340   If you should see that what we say is fact?

ORGON. See it?

ELMIRE.   Yes.

ORGON.   Nonsense.

ELMIRE.   If I found a way
To show it to you in the light of day?

ORGON. Fairy tales.

ELMIRE.   Answer me; don't be absurd.
I am not asking you to take our word.
But if you hid so you could see and hear
Everything that went on, perfectly clear,
What would you say if you saw your idol fall?

ORGON. In that case, I would say . . . nothing at all.
It can't be true.

ELMIRE.   You've been too long deceived,
1350 And I am tired of not being believed.
For our contentment, without more ado,
You shall observe all we've been telling you.

ORGON. All right. I'll take you up on that, you know.
We'll just see what it is you have to show.

ELMIRE *(to* DORINE*)*. Have him come here.

DORINE.   He is a
hypocrite,
And may not be so easy to outwit.

ELMIRE. Oh, no! A lover is not hard to cheat,
And self-deception springs from self-conceit.

Have him come down.
                    (*To* CLÉANTE *and* MARIANE)
                              Go along, *s'il vous plaît*.

Scene 4.   ELMIRE, ORGON

ELMIRE. Bring up this table. Get under, right away.   *1360*

ORGON. How's that?

ELMIRE.   You must be out of sight, you
    see.

ORGON. Why under there?

ELMIRE.   Good Lord! Listen to me:
    I have my plan; you'll judge this whole affair.
    Get underneath, I say; and when you're there,
    Make sure that you are neither seen nor heard.

ORGON. I'm being very patient, 'pon my word.
    But just go right ahead; I'll see it through.

ELMIRE. And you may come to thank me if you do.
(*To her husband, who is now under the table*)
    These are strange matters that I shall discuss,
    And you must listen and not make a fuss.   *1370*
    Whatever I say, it must be understood:
    It's to convince you, as I said I would.
    By sweet enticements it will be my task
    To lure this hypocrite to drop his mask,
    Flatter his passion and his shameless lust,
    And countenance his boldness, as I must.
    Since it is for your sake, and for his shame
    That I shall seem responsive to his flame,
    As soon as you're convinced, just let me know,
    And that will be as far as things will go.   *1380*
    It's up to you to check his wild desire

When matters are as clear as you require,
To spare your wife, and not expose her to
More than you need to disillusion you.
Your interest is at stake; you are the judge,
And . . . Here he comes. Keep quiet, and don't
    budge.

Scene 5.   TARTUFFE, ELMIRE, ORGON

TARTUFFE. They told me that you wished to see me
    here.

ELMIRE. Yes. I have secrets for your private ear.
    But shut that door, before I say a word,
1390 And look and see that we're not overheard.
    (TARTUFFE *closes the door, looks in the closet, and*
                                comes back.)
    A mishap like that one just now, indeed,
    Is certainly the last thing that we need.
    I really can't remember such a fright;
    Damis had me in terror at your plight,
    And you could see I did my very best
    To calm his fury, in your interest.
    True, I was so confused I never thought
    To contradict his story as I ought;
    But even that, thank Heaven, worked out well,
1400 And things are that much safer, I can tell.
    Your reputation makes it all auspicious;
    My husband simply cannot be suspicious.
    So as to show the gossips they are wrong,
    He wants us two together all day long;
    And that's what makes it possible for me
    To see you freely in such privacy
    And to lay bare to you, in such a fashion,
    A heart perhaps too heedful of your passion.

TARTUFFE. I do not understand. A little while
1410 Ago, Madame, you used a different style.

ELMIRE. Oh! If such a refusal makes you smart,
How little do you know a woman's heart,
And what it is endeavoring to convey
When it resists in such a feeble way!
Our modesty combats the stimulus
Of the sweet feelings you arouse in us.
However strong and justified our flame,
We never can admit it without shame.
Even our first resistance is too tender
Not to give notice of our heart's surrender.   1420
Though honor makes our lips combat temptation,
Such a refusal is an invitation.
I know that this avowal is too free
And too unsparing of my modesty;
But since I have resolved to speak my piece,
Would I have struggled to restrain Damis,
Would I have sat so long, composed and mute,
I ask you, while I listened to your suit?
Would I have taken things in such a fashion
If I'd been unresponsive to your passion?   1430
And when I urged you not to carry through
The marriage that my husband planned for you,
What could such great insistency suggest,
If not my overwhelming interest;
And fear that soon I could not call my own
A heart I want to have as mine alone?

TARTUFFE. Of course, Madame, it's very sweet to hear
Such words as these spoken by lips so dear:
Their honeyed flavor floods my every sense.
Such bliss I never did experience.   1440
To please you is my one solicitude,
And your love is my heart's beatitude;
But please allow that heart the liberty
To dare to doubt its own felicity.
These words might be a scheme, and nothing more,
To have me break a marriage that's in store;
To be quite candid, as I fear I must,
Sweet words are not enough to win my trust,
Unless some of your favors, which I burn for,
Should give the reassurance that I yearn for,   1450
And fill my soul with lasting confidence

In all the charming bounties you dispense.

ELMIRE *(coughs to warn her husband).* How fast you
    move against a woman's heart!
Must you exhaust our kindness from the start?
She immolates herself to offer you
A sweet avowal, but that will not do,
And you will not be satisfied unless
At once she grants her utmost tenderness.

TARTUFFE. The less we merit, the less we dare expect,
1460   And words alone don't have enough effect.
Such perfect bliss arouses our suspicion,
And our belief awaits its full fruition.
I'm so aware of my indignity,
I cannot credit my felicity,
And I shall not—that is, Madame, until
Your acts attest your genuine good will.

ELMIRE. My, but your love is the despotic kind,
And puts me in a troubled state of mind!
It presses for a dictatorial sway,
1470   And violently wants to have its way!
Must you pursue at such a frantic pace?
And am I not allowed a breathing space?
Is it becoming to employ such rigor,
To urge your points with such relentless vigor,
And, when our weakness puts us in your hands,
Press your advantage with such strong demands?

TARTUFFE. But if you countenance this suit of mine,
Why do you then refuse me such a sign?

ELMIRE. But thus I would offend, beyond a doubt,
1480   That Heaven that you love to talk about.

TARTUFFE. If Heaven is all that leads you to resist,
Such obstacles are easily dismissed;
Do as I ask, and set your mind at ease.

ELMIRE. But they frighten us so with Heaven's
    decrees!

TARTUFFE. These foolish fears, Madame, I can dispel,
    And all your scruples won't be hard to quell.
    It's true, there are some pleasures Heaven denies;*
    But there are ways to reach a compromise.
    Yes, now there is a science that succeeds
    In stretching consciences to meet our needs,   *1490*
    And can correct, by a sublime invention,
    An evil deed just by a pure intention.
    To all this there are keys I can provide you;
    All you need do, Madame, is let me guide you.
    Content my longings, free yourself of dread:
    If there is sin, I'll take it on my head.
    You've a bad cough, Madame.

ELMIRE.   I'm tortured by it.

TARTUFFE. I have a bit of licorice; won't you try it?

ELMIRE. It's a persistent cold, and I can tell
    That all your licorice won't make it well.   *1500*

TARTUFFE. That is a shame.

ELMIRE.   Yes, more than words can say.

TARTUFFE. Your scruple, then, is easy to allay:
    Our secret will be safe with us alone,
    And there's no evil if the thing's not known.
    The one offense lies in the public shame,
    And secret sin is sin only in name.

ELMIRE *(coughs again)*. I see I'll have to yield to
    your behest
    And grant you everything that you request;
    Since nothing else will do, I guess I must,
    To make you happy and to win your trust.   *1510*
    I wish you were not so demanding, though;
    You press me further than I want to go;
    But since you so insist on nothing less,

*Here a note of Molière's adds: "It's a scoundrel speaking."

And doubt my word unless I acquiesce,
Since full conviction is what you require,
I must give in, and do as you desire.
If this is bad, if I am wrong to do it,
So much the worse for you, who drive me to it;
And I am not to blame, assuredly.

1520 TARTUFFE. I'll take the full responsibility.

ELMIRE. Open the door, will you, and take a glance;
See if my husband's there by any chance.

TARTUFFE. Why bother with precautions such as
      those?
He is a man to lead round by the nose;
And he's so glad I have these talks with you,
He'd see the worst and swear it wasn't true.

ELMIRE. No matter; for a moment, please go out
And have a very careful look about.

Scene 6.   ORGON, ELMIRE

ORGON (coming out from under the table). Yes, he's
      an evil man, I do admit!
1530   I'm really stunned; I can't get over it.

ELMIRE. What? Coming out so soon? Don't be
      absurd.
It's not yet time; get back, and not a word;
Don't trust conjecture; don't be premature,
But wait until the end, to be quite sure.

ORGON. No, nothing worse ever came out of hell.

ELMIRE. You can't believe the things that people tell.
Don't yield till you're convinced; I'll get along.
And take your time, for fear you might be wrong.

(As TARTUFFE returns, she has her husband hide be-
            hind her.)

Scene 7.   TARTUFFE, ELMIRE, ORGON

TARTUFFE. Madame, my satisfaction is complete:
  I've had a look around the entire suite.   *1540*
  No one is there; and now I am delighted . . .

ORGON *(stopping him)*. Hold on, lover, you're getting
    too excited:
  You mustn't let your passions run so free.
  You holy man, you'd make a fool of me!
  Oh, how you let temptations rule your life!
  Marry my daughter, and seduce my wife!
  I kept on doubting what I might have known,
  And kept looking for you to change your tone;
  But now my fears are verified indeed:
  I am convinced, and that is all I need.   *1550*

ELMIRE *(to* TARTUFFE*)*. I do not like the part I've had
    to play,
  But I was forced to treat you in this way.

TARTUFFE. What? You believe . . . ?

ORGON.   That's enough
    out of you.
  Get out of here without further ado.

TARTUFFE. My aim . . .

ORGON.   There's nothing more for me
    to hear:
  Come on, right now, I want you out of here.

TARTUFFE. You are the one to leave, despite your
    tone:
  This house is mine, and I will make it known,
  And show you that you have recourse in vain
  To these low tricks, thinking to cause me pain,   *1560*
  That to insult me thus is most unwise,

That I can both expose and punish lies,
Avenge offended Heaven, and bring low
Anyone here who wants to make me go.

Scene 8.   ELMIRE, ORGON

ELMIRE. What does he mean? And what is all this
     chatter?

ORGON. Faith, I'm dismayed. This is no laughing
     matter.

ELMIRE. What?

ORGON.   From his talk I see I've been mistaken;
     And that donation has me rather shaken.

ELMIRE. Donation?

ORGON.   Yes, the thing's already signed.
1570 But that is not what most disturbs my mind.

ELMIRE. What else?

ORGON.   I'll tell you. First let's go and see
     If that strongbox is where it ought to be.

ACT V

Scene 1.   ORGON, CLÉANTE

CLÉANTE. Where are you off to?

ORGON.   Alas! I couldn't say.

CLÉANTE. I think we should confer about a way
  To try to cope with this unhappy turn.

ORGON. That strongbox is by far my main concern;
  More than all else it drives me to despair.

CLÉANTE. Then it conceals some ominous affair?

ORGON. It was Argas, a friend whose plight
    commands
  My sympathy, who placed it in my hands: 1580
  He picked me out to keep it when he fled;
  And these are documents, from what he said,
  On which his property and life depend.

CLÉANTE. And you gave these to your supposed
    friend?

ORGON. A conscientious scruple made me err.
  I went straight to my traitor to confer;
  And his persuasion led me to agree
  To put the strongbox in his custody,
  So that in case of an investigation
  I could fall back upon prevarication,   1590
  With a clear conscience stifle all I knew,
  And take an oath denying what was true.

CLÉANTE. I must confess your prospects do look dim;

313

The deed of gift, your confidence in him
Were both, to speak more frankly than politely,
Dangerous steps, and taken rather lightly.
Holding such weapons, he can lead you far.
Since his advantages are what they are,
To push him to extremes was a mistake,
1600   And you could not afford an open break.

ORGON. What? Can it be that such a pious face
Conceals a heart so false, a soul so base?
I took him in without a cent, and then . . .
That does it; I renounce all worthy men:
Henceforth I put them all under my curse,
And I shall be a devil to them, or worse.

CLÉANTE. So! There you go, in your exasperation!
You never are content with moderation;
The path of reason's not for you, it seems,
1610   And you fly back and forth between extremes.
You've seen your error now, and fully know
That you were cozened by a pious show;
But to correct yourself, why must you make,
In reason's name, an even worse mistake,
And lump the character of all good men
With that of this repulsive specimen?
Because one rogue has hoodwinked you for fair
By his impressive act and fervent air,
You now think everyone behaves that way,
1620   And that no pious man exists today?
Leave such conclusions to the libertines;
Strip off the mask and learn what virtue means,
And, carefully avoiding each extreme,
Be slower in conferring your esteem.
Refuse to honor falsity as real,
But meanwhile, don't attack authentic zeal;
And if you must fall into one excess,
Err on the side of trusting more, not less.

Scene 2.   DAMIS, ORGON, CLÉANTE

AMIS. What! Father, can it possibly be true
That that ungrateful scoundrel's threatening you,   *1630*
And that his cowardly and brazen pride
Uses your bounties to support his side?

RGON. It's true, son, and it brings me close to tears.

AMIS. Leave it to me; I'll cut off both his ears.
His insolence demands to be brought low;
I'll rid you of him with a single blow;
Just let me strike him down, and you'll be freed.

LÉANTE. That's spoken like a young man, yes
    indeed.
Please simmer down; try not to sound insane:
We're living in a time and in a reign   *1640*
Where violence is never the way out.

Scene 3.   MADAME PERNELLE, MARIANE, ELMIRE,
           DORINE, DAMIS, ORGON, CLÉANTE

MADAME PERNELLE. What are these mysteries I've
    heard about?

RGON. These are strange things, observed with my
    own eyes;
You've seen my kindnesses, now see the prize.
I raise a man out of his misery,
And like a brother take him in with me,
Load him with favors that should carry weight,
Give him my daughter and my whole estate;
And that vile wretch, that blight upon my life,
Undertakes foully to seduce my wife;   *1650*
Nor is that all; he's not contented yet,

But dares to hold against me as a threat
The favors I have armed him with too long,
Tries to make use of them to do me wrong,
Take away all I do (or did) possess,
And leave me where I found him, in distress.

DORINE. Poor fellow!

MADAME PERNELLE. Son, it cannot be a fact
That he meant to commit so base an act.

ORGON. What?

MADAME PERNELLE. Worthy men are prone to be
    maligned.

ORGON. What do you mean, Mother? What's on
1660   your mind?

MADAME PERNELLE. People live strangely here, as I
        have stated,
And anyone can see how much he's hated.

ORGON. Is that related to the case at all?

MADAME PERNELLE. I've told you a hundred times
        when you were small:
Virtue is always harassed here below;
The envious will die, but envy, no.

ORGON. And therefore I suppose he's not to blame?

MADAME PERNELLE. They've made up tales to blacken
        his good name.

ORGON. I've seen the whole thing; that's why I'm
        indignant.

MADAME PERNELLE. Slanderous people can be quite
1670   malignant.

ORGON. Mother, you'll have me damned. Listen to
me:
With my own eyes I saw this, can't you see?

MADAME PERNELLE. Venom is what their tongues will
never lack,
And nothing here below escapes attack.

ORGON. This is sheer nonsense. Can't you realize,
I say I saw this, saw with my own eyes,
I mean I *saw!* Now must I spell it out
A hundred times, and stamp my feet and shout?

MADAME PERNELLE. Good Lord, appearances can be
deceiving,
And seeing mustn't always be believing.   1680

ORGON. I shall go mad.

MADAME PERNELLE.   Beware of false suspicions.
Good can seem evil under some conditions.

ORGON. And when he tries to make love to my wife,
I am to call this charity?

MADAME PERNELLE.   In life,
No accusation should be premature;
You should have waited till you were quite sure.

ORGON. The devil! You'd have had me get more
proof?
I should have sat and watched, then, while
Tartuffe . . . ?
You make it hard for me to be genteel.

MADAME PERNELLE. His soul is ravished with too pure
a zeal;   1690
I simply can't accept it as a fact
That he could be involved in such an act.

ORGON. If you were not my mother, I don't know
What I might say, you aggravate me so.

DORINE. In all of this, sir, there's a kind of justice:
    She won't trust you, but then, you wouldn't trust
    us.

CLÉANTE. We're wasting precious time on idle
    chatter;
    We need a plan of action in this matter.
    His is no empty threat, yet here we are.

1700 DAMIS. What? Would he carry insolence so far?

ELMIRE. For my part, I don't think it's possible;
    His thanklessness would be too visible.

CLÉANTE. Don't be too sure; no doubt he can pull
    strings
    And give the color that he wants to things;
    And a cabal has often, for much less,
    Entangled people in a nasty mess.
    I repeat: with such arms at his command,
    You never should have dared to force his hand.

ORGON. True, but what could I do? That traitor's
    pride
1710   Was more than my resentment could abide.

CLÉANTE. I wish with all my heart we could renew
    Some semblance of a peace between you two.

ELMIRE. If I had known what he held over us,
    I wouldn't have occasioned such a fuss,
    And my . . .
        (MONSIEUR LOYAL *appears at the door.*)

ORGON (*to* DORINE). That man, what does he want?
    What is it?
    I'm in a fine state to receive a visit!

Scene 4.   MONSIEUR LOYAL, MADAME PERNELLE,
        ORGON, DAMIS, MARIANE, DORINE, ELMIRE,
                    CLÉANTE

MONSIEUR LOYAL. Good day, dear sister; kindly let
    me see
    The master of the house.

DORINE.   He isn't free.
    Sorry, but this a bad time to get him.

MONSIEUR LOYAL. My presence isn't likely to upset
    him.   1720
    I'm sure he will be not dissatisfied
    At seeing me, but even gratified.

DORINE. Your name?

MONSIEUR LOYAL.   Give him this message, if you
        would:
    Monsieur Tartuffe has sent me, for his good.

DORINE (to ORGON). Sir, it's a pleasant-seeming man
        out there,
    Sent by Monsieur Tartuffe on an affair
    Which, he declares, will please you.

CLÉANTE.   You must see
    What this man wants, and just who he can be.

ORGON. Perhaps he's come to offer me some pact:
    If so, how do you think I'd better act?   1730

CLÉANTE. Don't let resentment carry you away;
    And if he talks peace, let him have his say.

MONSIEUR LOYAL. Good day, sir. Heaven smite your
        enemies,
    And, I hope, bring you everything you please!

ORGON *(to* CLÉANTE*)*. This mild opening confirms
    my expectation,
    And seems to promise some accommodation.

MONSIEUR LOYAL. Your family, sir, I cherish and
    admire;
    And once I used to serve your honored sire.

ORGON. I beg your pardon, sir, but to my shame,
1740   I cannot place you or recall your name.

MONSIEUR LOYAL. My name is Loyal, I'm from
    Normandy,
    A bailiff with a wand, as you can see.
    For forty years, thank Heaven, I've enjoyed
    Being thus well and honorably employed;
    And I am here, sir, if you will permit,
    To serve you duly with a certain writ.

ORGON. What? You are here . . . ?

MONSIEUR LOYAL.   Sir, there's no
    need to shout:
    It's nothing but a summons to move out,
    Yourself, your furniture, and all your kin,
1750   And clear the place so others may move in,
    Without delay and with all proper speed . . .

ORGON. I? Leave this house?

MONSIEUR LOYAL.   Yes, please, sir; yes indeed.
    For now the rightful owner, need I mention?
    Is good Monsieur Tartuffe, beyond contention.
    His ownership of all your goods is clear
    By virtue of a contract I have here;
    It's in due form, and there is no defense.

DAMIS. My word, I marvel at this impudence.

MONSIEUR LOYAL. Sir, you are not involved in this
    affair,
1760   As is this gentleman; he's mild and fair,

And knows the role a worthy man must play
Too well to flout justice in any way.

ORGON. But . . .

MONSIEUR LOYAL. Nothing would induce you to rebel,
  Sir, not a million francs, I know full well;
  And like a gentleman, you will allow
  Me to enforce my orders here and now.

DAMIS. Sir Bailiff-with-a-wand, a stick may fall
  On that black jacket of yours after all.

MONSIEUR LOYAL. Sir, make your son be silent or
    withdraw.
  I'd rather not report you to the law   1770
  And have your name on record with the court.

DAMIS. This Mister Loyal's a disloyal sort!

MONSIEUR LOYAL. For all good men my tenderness
    is large;
  And thus I took this matter in my charge
  Only to see the thing was nicely done
  And keep them from assigning anyone
  Who would not share my love and admiration
  And would proceed with less consideration.

ORGON. Could you do worse than order such a seizure
  And drive us from our home?

MONSIEUR LOYAL.   But you have leisure; 1780
  And I shall even grant you one more day
  Before you do, sir, what the orders say.
  I'll merely bring ten of my men with me
  To spend the night, without publicity.
  Before you go to bed, though, if you please,
  For form's sake, you must let me have your keys.
  I shall take care not to disturb your rest,
  And allow only what is for the best.
  You must remove tomorrow, when you wake,
  Any belongings that you want to take;   1790

My men will give you—and I picked them stout—
A helping hand to get everything out.
No one could act more gently than I do;
And since that is the way I'm treating you,
I ask you, sir, for your cooperation
In checking any further aggravation.

ORGON. If I still have a hundred louis d'or,
I'd give them happily, and many more,
If I could just land one resounding clout,
1800   My very best, upon that ugly snout.

CLÉANTE. Hold on, don't ruin matters.

DAMIS.   What a nerve!
I itch to give him what such men deserve.

DORINE. You have a handsome back, sir; I can tell
That a few cudgel blows would suit you well.

MONSIEUR LOYAL. You could get into trouble, with
    your jaw,
My girl; women are not above the law.

CLÉANTE. Enough; let's have no more, sir; pray you,
    cease.
Please serve your paper and leave us in peace.

MONSIEUR LOYAL. Au revoir, one and all. May
Heaven content you!

ORGON. May it confound you, and the man who
1810   sent you!

Scene 5.   ORGON, CLÉANTE, MARIANE, ELMIRE,
        MADAME PERNELLE, DORINE, DAMIS

ORGON. Well, Mother, now you know about our
    guest,
And from this summons you can judge the rest,
Is his treachery clear to you at last?

MADAME PERNELLE. Where have I been? I'm utterly
    aghast!

DORINE. You're wrong to blame the poor man, and
    complain;
  And this makes all his pious purpose plain:
  He loves his fellow man more than himself;
  And, knowing the corrupting power of pelf,
  In charity he frees you from temptation
  Toward any obstacle to your salvation.   1820

ORGON. Shut up! For the last time I'm telling you.

CLÉANTE. Let us consider what you'd better do.

ELMIRE. Expose the brazen ingrate's ugly story.
  This action makes the contract nugatory;
  And his black treachery will be too plain
  To yield him the success he hopes to gain.

Scene 6.   VALÈRE, ORGON, CLÉANTE, ELMIRE,
MARIANE, MADAME PERNELLE, DORINE, DAMIS

VALÈRE. Sir, though I hate to bring unpleasant news,
  Such is your danger that I cannot choose.
  A dear old friend of mine, who knows how strong
  Has been my interest in you all along,   1830
  On my behalf has dared to violate
  The secrecy owed to affairs of state,
  And writes to say that in your present plight
  The only course for you is instant flight.
  The scoundrel who imposed upon you so
  Denounced you to the King an hour ago,
  And put into his hands, to bring you down,
  The strongbox of an enemy of the crown,
  Claiming your failure to reveal it shows
  You slight the duty that a subject owes.   1840
  I lack details about the charges pressed,

But there's an order out for your arrest.
Tartuffe himself was told to come along
To lend a hand and see nothing goes wrong.

CLÉANTE. It's at your property the traitor aims,
And he has weapons to enforce his claims.

ORGON. That man is certainly a wicked beast!

VALÈRE. Delay is fatal, sir, even the least.
There is my carriage waiting at the door;
1850 And you may need this thousand louis d'or.
Let's waste no time: this is a lightning blow,
Which you can parry only as you go.
Please let me guide you to a safer site
And keep you company throughout your flight.

ORGON. Alas! How vastly I am in your debt!
Even the time to thank you is not yet;
Some day, Heaven give me opportunity
To recognize your generosity.
Farewell; be careful, all . . .

CLÉANTE.   Come on, now, run.
1860 Brother, we'll see that everything is done.

Scene 7.   The GENTLEMAN of the King's Guard,
TARTUFFE, VALÈRE, ORGON, ELMIRE, MARI-
ANE, MADAME PERNELLE, DORINE, CLÉANTE,
DAMIS

TARTUFFE. Hold on, hold on there, sir, stay where
     you are:
Your new abode is not so very far,
And we arrest you now in the King's name.

ORGON. Traitor, you've brought me to this final
     shame!

This is the stroke, scoundrel, that lays me low,
And all your treachery is in this blow.

TARTUFFE. Your insults have no power to rouse my
    gall,
And for the sake of Heaven I'll suffer all.

CLÉANTE. That is great moderation, I must say.

DAMIS. To prate of Heaven in such a shameless way! *1870*

TARTUFFE. You cannot anger me, with all your spite;
    And all I want to do is what is right.

MARIANE. I trust this is a source of proud enjoyment.
    You've surely picked an honorable employment!

TARTUFFE. Any employment is a source of pride
    When the King's interests are on our side.

ORGON. Did you remember that my charity
    Rescued you, ingrate, out of poverty?

TARTUFFE. I know about your help and everything;
    But my first duty is to serve my King;   *1880*
    The power of that sacred obligation
    Annihilates my own appreciation,
    And to it I would sacrifice my wife,
    My friend, my relatives, my very life.

ELMIRE. Impostor!

DORINE.   What a master of pretense!
    He cloaks himself in all we reverence!

CLÉANTE. But if this pressing zeal that you display
    Is quite as perfect as you always say,
    Why was it so reluctant to appear
    Until he caught you trying to tempt Elmire?   *1890*
    Why did you not denounce him, but hold back,
    Until his honor forced him to attack?
    I do not mention—it did not dissuade you—

The gift of all his goods that he had made you;
But since you treat him like a culprit now,
What made you take his presents anyhow?

TARTUFFE *(to the* GENTLEMAN*)*. Deliver me from
every bleeding heart.
You have your orders, sir, pray do your part.

GENTLEMAN. Yes, I've been waiting overlong to do it,
1900 And it is fitting that you urge me to it.
Here it is: follow me without delay
Into the prison where you are to stay.

TARTUFFE. Who? I, sir?

GENTLEMAN.   You, indeed.

TARTUFFE.   To prison? Why?

GENTLEMAN. You're not the one I mean to satisfy.
                    (To ORGON*)*
Sir, your escape was narrow, but complete.
We live under a king who hates deceit,
A king whose eyes see into every heart
And can't be fooled by an impostor's art.
The keen discernment that his greatness brings
1910 Gives him a piercing insight into things;
Nothing can disconcert his readiness,
And his firm reason always shuns excess.
He honors all the best of humankind;
But zeal for virtue never makes him blind:
The love that for the truly good he fosters
Does not prevent his hatred for impostors.
This fellow could not catch him unawares,
And he has thwarted many craftier snares.
His insight penetrated from the start
1920 The twisted treason of that scoundrel's heart.
Accusing you, Tartuffe revealed his state,
And by an equitable stroke of fate
Led the King to recall his shady fame
For crimes committed under another name.
His record is a long and ugly one

That would fill volumes and still not be done.
Revolted by the black disloyalty
Of that ungrateful wretch, his Majesty
Added this horror to the list at hand
And sent me here, as if at his command,   *1930*
Only to see how far his gall extends
And bring him here to make you full amends.
Yes, all your papers, which he claims to own,
I shall restore into your hands alone.
The King now chooses to invalidate
The deed of gift that cost you your estate,
And finally he pardons your offense
In shielding even a friend at his expense;
And thus the courage that you once displayed
Against his enemies, shall be repaid,   *1940*
To show how suddenly, in case of need,
The King can recompense a noble deed,
That merit has no reason for alarm,
Since he remembers help better than harm.

DORINE. Heaven be praised!

MADAME PERNELLE.   Now I can breathe anew!

ELMIRE. How fortunate!

MARIANE.   Can you believe it's true?

ORGON (*to* TARTUFFE). Well, traitor, there you are . . .

CLÉANTE.   Stop, brother, please,
And do not stoop to such indignities;
Leave the poor wretch to his unhappy course,
And do not add your bit to his remorse;   *1950*
But rather hope his heart, after today,
May happily return to virtue's way,
That he'll correct his life, detest his crime,
And soften the King's justice in due time,
While you go on your knees before the King
And thank his clemency for everything.

ORGON. Well said: let's go and kneel before the throne,
And praise him for the bounties he has shown.
Then, once this first duty is gladly done,
1960 We must start thinking of another one,
And by the marriage of the loving pair,
Reward the deep devotion of Valère.

Don Juan

DON JUAN

A prose comedy in five acts, first performed February 15, 1665, at the Palais-Royal by Molière's Troupe de Monsieur. Molière played Sganarelle; other roles were probably these: Don Juan, La Grange; Don Louis, Béjart; M. Dimanche, Du Croisy; Pierrot, Hubert; La Ramée, de Brie; Elvire, Mlle. du Parc; Charlotte, Mlle. Molière; Mathurine, Mlle. de Brie. The play was both a success and a scandal. In the face of violent attacks, Molière let it drop, and never either published it or revived it. After his death, his widow sold the rights to Thomas Corneille, whose expurgated version in verse was the only form of the play known for almost two centuries. Only in the last twenty years, with the productions and performances of Louis Jouvet, Maria Casarès, and Jean Vilar, has it been generally accepted as one of Molière's great plays.

In order to live and to keep his troupe alive, Molière needed a new play; the subject was in the air and on many stages. Earlier versions offered few problems: for the Spaniard Tirso de Molina, the Italians Cicognini and Giliberto, and the Frenchmen Dorimon and Villiers, Don Juan was a wicked seducer punished by God—and little more. Molière's play is full of problems, at which many critics have thrown up their hands; it is vigorous, thronged with characters who come and go, indifferent to the unities and the usual principles of plausibility.

To try to understand it we must look to its main lines and especially to what is new. Virtually new in Molière's version is the complexity of Sganarelle and his relation to Don Juan, as well as Don Juan's good qualities: a gentleman's pride and courage, a kind of generosity. But even in these qualities Don Juan is so completely self-centered that for him no one else exists in his own right; all must admire him and do his will. Contrasted to him, sometimes weakly opposed to him, are all sorts of people, but mainly his cowardly, bumbling valet Sganarelle. If Sganarelle is supposed to stand for right-mindedness—as he claims and often seems to—it suggests that this is apt to be weak and infused with superstition.

At least this much seems clear: that *Don Juan*, like *Tartuffe* (which was obviously on Molière's mind when he wrote it), shows us what a terrible thing a wicked hypocrite is to the people he encounters. No human can check him; as it takes a near-miracle to make the world safe from Tartuffe, so it takes a miracle, and his destruction, to make the world safe from Don Juan. The good qualities Molière gives him serve mainly to make him more human than the usual villain of melodrama and thus more real, more appealing at times, and more dangerous; while his special vices, such as atheistic religious hypocrisy, show his relation in Molière's mind to the assailants of *Tartuffe*.

Thus once again Molière's deep earnestness involves him in an ugly subject resistant to the comic form he gives it. He lavishes his devices to keep it comic: the patois and naïveté of the peasants, the virtuosity of Don Juan in satisfying Charlotte and Mathurine and later in putting off the unforgettable M. Dimanche, and most of all the cowardice and inept reasoning of Sganarelle. He lavishes his characters—seventeen in all, if we count the Specter but not the retinues—mainly, it would appear, to show Don Juan in as many confrontations and lights as possible. If the resulting portraits, of Don Juan and Sganarelle, are, like the entire play, puzzling to the tidy-minded, they are vigorously alive, especially on stage, where after all they were meant to live. Of all Molière's plays, *Don Juan* is probably the one that most needs to be not merely read but seen.

It is also the one that to the present translator seems most to defy effective translation into English.

DON JUAN
OR, THE STONE GUEST*

CHARACTERS

DON JUAN, *son of Don Louis*
SGANARELLE, *valet to Don Juan*
ELVIRE, *wife of Don Juan*
GUSMAN, *squire to Elvire*
DON CARLOS } *brothers of Elvire*
DON ALONSE }
DON LOUIS, *father of Don Juan*
THE POOR MAN†
CHARLOTTE } *peasant girls*
MATHURINE }
PIERROT, *a peasant*
THE STATUE OF THE COMMANDER
LA VIOLETTE } *lackeys of Don Juan*
RAGOTIN }
MONSIEUR DIMANCHE, *a tradesman*
LA RAMÉE, *a ruffian*
ATTENDANTS TO DON JUAN
ATTENDANTS TO THE BROTHERS DON CARLOS AND DON ALONSE
A SPECTER

The scene is in Sicily.

---

*Dom Juan, ou le Festin de Pierre (Don Juan, or the Stone Banquet). Molière apparently borrowed his title from a popular French play whose title seems to be an adaptation of the subtitle of Spanish and Italian plays about "the stone guest."
†Molière designated him thus in the text. In the cast of characters he gave him a name, Francisque, which is presumably that of the actor who played the part.

333

ACT I
(A palace)

Scene 1.   SGANARELLE, GUSMAN

SGANARELLE *(holding a snuffbox)*. Whatever Aristotle, and Philosophy itself, may say, there's nothing like tobacco: it's the passion of all gentlemen, and he who lives without tobacco is unworthy to live. Not only does it delight and clear the human brain, but also it trains the soul for virtue, and with it one learns how to become a gentleman. Don't you always see, as soon as a man takes it, how obliging his manner becomes with everyone, and how delighted he is to offer it right and left, wherever he may be? He doesn't even wait to be asked, but anticipates people's wishes; so true it is that tobacco inspires sentiments of honor and virtue in all those who take it.

But enough of that; let's get back to what we were talking about. So then, my dear Gusman, your mistress, Doña Elvire, surprised at our leaving, is in full career after us; and her heart, which my master succeeded in touching all too deeply, could not live, you say, without coming to seek him here. Shall I tell you what I think, between you and me? I'm afraid that she's ill repaid for her love, that her journey to this city will bear little fruit, and that you would have gained just as much by not stirring from home.

GUSMAN. And what's your reason? Tell me, please, Sganarelle, what it is that can inspire in you such an ominous fear. Has your master opened his heart to you about it, and has he told you that he felt some coldness toward us that obliged him to leave?

SGANARELLE. No, no; but from one look around, I know

pretty well how things are going; and without his having said anything to me yet, I would almost bet that that's where this affair is heading. I might possibly be wrong; but after all, on such matters, experience has given me some light.

GUSMAN. What? Could this unexpected departure be an infidelity of Don Juan's? Could he wrong the chaste love of Doña Elvire in this way?

SGANARELLE. No, it's just that he's still young, and hasn't the courage to . . .

GUSMAN. Could a man of his quality do such a cowardly deed?

SGANARELLE. Oh, yes, his quality! That's a fine reason, and that's what would put a stop to things!

GUSMAN. But he is bound by the holy ties of marriage.

SGANARELLE. Oh! Poor old Gusman, my friend, you don't know yet, believe me, what sort of a man Don Juan is.

GUSMAN. Indeed I don't know what sort of a man he can be if he has really treated us with such perfidy; and I do not understand how, after showing so much love and so much impatience, so much urgent homage, so many vows, sighs, and tears, so many passionate letters, ardent protestations, and repeated oaths, in short so many transports and outbursts as he displayed, until in his passion he even forced the sacred obstacle of a convent to place Doña Elvire within his power—I do not understand, I say, how, after all that, he could have the heart to go back on his word.

SGANARELLE. *I* don't have much trouble understanding it; and if you knew his character, you'd find the matter pretty easy for him. I don't say that he has changed his feelings about Doña Elvire, I have no certainty about that yet: you know that by his orders I left before him, and he hasn't talked with me since he arrived. But let me inform you by way of precaution, *inter nos,* that in my master Don Juan you see the greatest villain that the earth ever bore, a madman, a dog, a devil, a Turk, a heretic, who doesn't believe in Heaven, Hell, or were-wolf, who spends his life like a real brute beast, one of Epicurus' swine, a regular Sardanapalus, who closes his ears to every remonstrance you can make, and treats everything we believe in as nonsense. You tell me he married your mistress; believe me, he would have done more than that for his passion, and besides her he would have married you, his dog, and his cat as well. A marriage costs him nothing to contract; he uses no other snares to catch beauties, and he's a marrier for all comers. Grown lady, young lady, bourgeoise, peasant girl, he finds nothing too hot or too cold for him; and if I told you the names of all the women he has married in various places, it would be a chapter to last us until evening.

You are surprised, and you change color at what I say; that's only a mere sketch of the personage, and to complete his portrait would require far broader brush strokes. Enough to say that the wrath of Heaven must crush him some day; that I'd be much better off belonging to the Devil than to him; and that he makes me witness so many horrors that I wish he was already—I don't know where. But a great lord who is a wicked man is a terrible thing. I have to be faithful to him in spite of myself; fear fulfills the function of zeal in me, curbs my feelings, and very often reduces me to ap-plauding what my soul detests.

Here he comes now to take a walk in this palace. Let's part. But listen: I've confided this to you in frank-ness, and it came out of my mouth pretty fast; but if any of it had to come to his ears, I would declare boldly that you had lied.

Scene 2.   DON JUAN, SGANARELLE

DON JUAN. Who was that man talking with you? It seems to me he looks a lot like Doña Elvire's good old Gusman.

SGANARELLE. Indeed, it's something about like that.

DON JUAN. What? Is that who it was?

SGANARELLE. Himself.

DON JUAN. And how long has he been in this town?

SGANARELLE. Since yesterday evening.

DON JUAN. And what brings him here?

SGANARELLE. I think you have a pretty good idea of what may be worrying him.

DON JUAN. Our departure, no doubt?

SGANARELLE. The poor man is quite mortified about it, and was asking me the reason.

DON JUAN. And what answer did you give him?

SGANARELLE. That you had said nothing to me about it.

DON JUAN. But still, what do you think about it? What do you imagine this is all about?

SGANARELLE. I? I think—no offense to you—that you have some new love in mind.

DON JUAN. You think so?

SGANARELLE. Yes.

DON JUAN. My word! You're not a bit mistaken, and I must admit to you that another object has driven Elvire out of my mind.

SGANARELLE. Oh! My Lord! I have my Don Juan at my fingertips, and I know that your heart is the greatest lady-chaser in the world. It loves to ramble from bond to bond, and doesn't much like to stay put.

DON JUAN. And tell me, don't you think I'm right to act this way?

SGANARELLE. Oh! Sir.

DON JUAN. What? Speak up.

SGANARELLE. Certainly you're right, if that's the way you want it; there's no going against that. But if you didn't want it that way, perhaps it would be another matter.

DON JUAN. Well! I give you leave to speak out and tell me what you feel about it.

SGANARELLE. In that case, sir, I'll tell you frankly that I don't approve of your way at all, and I think it's very bad to make love right and left the way you do.

DON JUAN. What? Do you want us to bind ourselves for good to the first object that captivates us, give up the world for her, and have no more eyes for anyone else? That's a fine thing, to want to pride ourselves on some false honor of fidelity, to bury ourselves forever in one passion, and to be dead from our youth on to all the other beauties that may strike our eyes! No, no: constancy is good only for nincompoops. Every beautiful woman has the right to charm us, and the advantage of having been the first one we met must not rob the others of the just claims they all have on our hearts. As for me, beauty entrances me wherever I find it, and I easily yield to the sweet violence with which it sweeps us along. I may be bound; but the love I have for one beautiful woman does not bind my soul to do injustice to the others; I still have eyes to see the merit of them all, and I pay to each one the homage and tribute that nature requires of us. Whatever my situation, I cannot refuse my heart to anyone I see to be lovable; and as soon as a fair face asks me for it, if I had ten thousand hearts I'd give them all. After all, budding inclinations have unaccountable charms, and the whole pleasure of love lies in change. We savor an infinite sweetness in overcoming a young beauty's heart by a thousand acts of homage, in seeing day by day the little steps by which we progress, in combating by our transports, tears, and sighs, the innocent modesty of a soul loath to surrender its arms, in forcing, step by step, the little obstacles with which she resists, in conquering the scruples in which she takes honor, and bringing her gently to the point where we want to bring her. But once we are the master, there's nothing more to say and nothing more to wish for; all the beauty of the passion is finished, and in the tranquillity of such a love we fall asleep, unless some new object comes to awaken our desires and offer our heart the alluring charms of a conquest to be made. In short, there's nothing so sweet as to triumph over the resistance of a beauty; and in this matter I have the ambition of the conquerors who perpetually fly from victory to victory and cannot bring themselves to limit their aspirations. There is nothing that can arrest the impetuosity of my desires: I feel a heart in me fit to love the whole world; and like Alexander, I could wish there were other worlds, so that I might extend my amorous conquests there.

SGANARELLE. Mercy me, how you rattle it off! It seems as though you've learned it by heart, and you talk just like a book.

DON JUAN. What do you have to say about it?

SGANARELLE. My word! I have to say . . . I don't know what to say; for you turn things in such a manner that you seem to be right; and yet the truth is that you're not. I had the best ideas in the world, and your talk has muddled the whole thing up. Give me a chance: another time I'll put my reasonings in writing, to argue with you.

DON JUAN. Well you may.

SGANARELLE. But, sir, would it be within the permission you have given me if I told you that I am just a bit scandalized at the life you lead?

DON JUAN. How's that? What kind of life do I lead?

SGANARELLE. A very good one. But, for example, to see you getting married every month the way you do . . .

DON JUAN. Is there anything pleasanter?

SGANARELLE. That's true, I suppose it *is* very pleasant and very diverting, and I'd like it well enough myself, if there weren't any harm in it; but, sir, to make sport of a holy sacrament that way, and . . .

DON JUAN. Come, come, that's a matter between Heaven and me, and we'll settle it together well enough without your worrying about it.

SGANARELLE. My word, sir! I've always heard that to mock Heaven is wicked mockery, and that libertines never come to a good end.

DON JUAN. Hold it! Master fool, you know I've told you that I don't like expostulators.

SGANARELLE. I know, and I'm not speaking to you, God forbid. Now *you* know what you're doing; and if you don't believe in anything, you have your reasons. But there are some impertinent little people in the world who are libertines without knowing why, who set up as freethinkers because they think it's becoming to them; and if I had a master like that, I would look him in the face and say to him very plainly: "Do you really dare to set yourself up against Heaven in this way, and doesn't it make you tremble to make fun of the holiest things as you do? Is it really for you, little earthworm, little ant (I'm speaking to the master I mentioned), is it really for you to want to make a joke of what everyone reveres? Do you think that because you are a gentleman and wear a well-curled blond wig, feathers in your hat, a coat well trimmed with gold lace, and flame-colored ribbons (I'm not talking to you, but to the other one)—do you think, I say, that you're an abler man for all that, that you're free to do anything you like, and that no one will dare to tell you the truth about yourself? Take it from me, though I'm your servant, that sooner or later Heaven punishes the impious, that an evil life brings on an evil death, and that . . ."

DON JUAN. Enough!

SGANARELLE. You have some business?

DON JUAN. My business is to tell you that I have my heart set on a certain beauty, and that, led on by her charms, I have followed her all the way to this town.

SGANARELLE. And have you nothing to fear, sir, here, from the death of that Commander you killed six months ago?

DON JUAN. And why fear? Didn't I kill him properly?

SGANARELLE. Very properly, very well indeed, and he has no grounds for complaint.

DON JUAN. I got my pardon for that affair.

SGANARELLE. Yes, but maybe that pardon doesn't extinguish the resentment of relatives and friends; and . . .

DON JUAN. Oh! Let's not go thinking about the harm that may happen to us, and let's think about only what can give us pleasure. The person I'm telling you about is a young engaged girl, lovely as can be, who was brought here by the very man she is coming to marry; and it was by chance that I saw this couple of sweethearts three

or four days before their trip. Never have I seen two
people so happy with each other and displaying more
love. The visible tenderness of their mutual passion
stirred me; I was struck to the heart by it, and my love
began in jealousy. Yes, from the first, I couldn't bear
seeing them so happy together; vexation alerted my desires, and I imagined an extreme pleasure in being able
to disturb their understanding and break this attachment at which the delicacy of my heart considered itself
offended; but up to now all my efforts have been useless, and I am having recourse to the final remedy.
Today this would-be husband is to treat his mistress to
a boat ride on the sea. Without my telling you anything
about it, everything is prepared for me to satisfy my
love, and I have some men and a small boat, with which
I expect to carry off my beauty very easily.

SGANARELLE. Oh! Sir . . .

DON JUAN. Eh?

SGANARELLE. Good for you, you're behaving as you
should. There's nothing in this world like having your
way.

DON JUAN. Then get ready to come with me, and be sure
yourself to bring along all my weapons, so that . . . Oh!
Ill met! Traitor, you didn't tell me that she herself
was here.

SGANARELLE. Sir, you didn't ask me.

DON JUAN. Is she out of her mind, not to have changed her
dress, and to come to this place in her country clothes?

Scene 3.   DOÑA ELVIRE, DON JUAN, SGANARELLE

DOÑA ELVIRE. Will you do me the kindness, Don Juan, to
be willing to recognize me? And may I at least hope
that you will deign to turn your face this way?

DON JUAN. Madame, I confess I am surprised, and I wasn't expecting you here.

DOÑA ELVIRE. Yes, I can see very well that you weren't expecting me here; and you are surprised indeed, but quite otherwise than I hoped; and the way you show it fully convinces me of what I was refusing to believe. I marvel at my simplicity and weakheartedness in doubting a betrayal which so much evidence confirmed. I was fond enough, I confess, or rather stupid enough, to try to deceive myself, and to struggle to give the lie to my eyes and judgment. I sought reasons to excuse to my heart the weakened affection it observed in you; and I deliberately made up to myself a hundred legitimate reasons for such a precipitate departure, to justify you for a crime of which my reason accused you. My just suspicions spoke to me each day in vain; I rejected their voice, which would have made you criminal in my eyes, and listened with pleasure to a thousand ridiculous fancies which represented you to my heart as innocent. But now at last this reception leaves me no room for doubt, and your look when you first saw me tells me far more things than I could wish to know. However, I should like very much to hear from your own lips the reasons why you left. Speak, Don Juan, I pray you, and let's see with what countenance you will justify yourself!

DON JUAN. Madame, here is Sganarelle who knows why I left.

SGANARELLE. I, sir? If you please, I don't know anything about it.

DOÑA ELVIRE. Well, Sganarelle, speak. It doesn't matter from whose lips I hear these reasons.

DON JUAN (beckoning SGANARELLE to approach). Come on, then, speak to Madame.

SGANARELLE. What do you want me to say?

DOÑA ELVIRE. Come here, since it is so willed, and tell me something about the reasons for such a sudden departure.

DON JUAN. Aren't you going to answer?

SGANARELLE. I have nothing to answer. You're making sport of your servant.

DON JUAN. Will you answer, I tell you?

SGANARELLE. Madame . . .

DOÑA ELVIRE. What?

SGANARELLE (turning back toward his master). Sir . . .

DON JUAN. If . . .

SGANARELLE. Madame, the reasons for our departure are conquerors, Alexander, and other worlds. There, sir, that's all I can say.

DOÑA ELVIRE. Will you be kind enough, Don Juan, to enlighten us about these fine mysteries?

DON JUAN. Madame, to tell you the truth . . .

DOÑA ELVIRE. Oh! How poorly you know how to defend yourself for a courtier, who must be accustomed to this sort of thing! I pity you, to see the confusion you're in. Why don't you arm your brow with noble effrontery? Why don't you swear to me that you still have the same feelings for me, that you still love me with unequaled ardor, and that nothing but death is capable of tearing you from me? Why don't you tell me that business of the utmost importance forced you to leave without letting me know; that in spite of yourself you have to remain here for some time, and that I have only to go back to where I came from, assured that you will follow in my footsteps as soon as you possibly can; that it is certain that you burn to be with me again, and that apart from me you suffer what a body suffers separated from its soul? That's how you should defend yourself, and not just be speechless, as you are.

DON JUAN. I admit, Madame, that I do not have the talent to dissimulate, and that I have a sincere heart. I will not tell you that I still have the same feelings for you and that I burn to be with you again, since after all it is established that I left only to flee you; not for the reasons that you may imagine, but from a purely conscientious motive, and because I did not believe that I could live with you any longer without sin. Scruples came to me, Madame, and I opened the eyes of my soul upon what I was doing. I reflected that in order to marry you I stole you from the enclosure of a convent, that you broke vows that bound you elsewhere, and that Heaven is very jealous of this kind of thing. Repentance seized me, and I dreaded the divine wrath; I came to believe that our marriage was nothing but a disguised adultery, that it would bring upon us some retribution from on high, and that in short I should strive to forget you and give you a way to go back to your first bonds. Madame, would you oppose so pious a thought, and would you have me go bringing Heaven down upon me, by . . . ?

DOÑA ELVIRE. Oh! You villain, now I know you through and through; and to my misfortune, I know you when it is too late, and when such knowledge can no longer help me except to drive me to despair. But know that your crime shall not remain unpunished, and that the same Heaven you mock will be able to avenge me for your perfidy!

DON JUAN. Sganarelle, Heaven!

SGANARELLE. Yes indeed, a lot we care about that, we do!

DON JUAN. Madame . . .

DOÑA ELVIRE. That's enough. I don't want to hear any more, and I even blame myself for having heard too much. It is despicable to have one's shame explained too clearly; and on such subjects a noble heart should choose its course at once. Don't expect me to break out here in reproaches and insults; no, no, my wrath is not one to spend itself in empty words, and its full heat is reserved for its vengeance. I tell you once more, Heaven will punish you, traitor, for the wrong you are doing me; and if Heaven has nothing you can fear, fear at least the anger of an outraged woman. *(Exit.)*

SGANARELLE. If only remorse could seize him!

DON JUAN *(after a moment's reflection)*. All right, let's think about carrying out our amorous enterprise.

SGANARELLE. Oh! What an abominable master I am forced to serve!

ACT II
(In the country by the seashore)

Scene 1.   CHARLOTTE, PIERROT

CHARLOTTE. Land's sakes, Pierrot, you sure were there in the nick of time.

PIERROT. By golly, it woulda took less than a hair's breadth and they'd a' been drownded, the two of 'em.

CHARLOTTE. Then it was that gale blew up sudden this morning that tipped 'em over in the sea?

PIERROT. Look, Charlotte, here you go, I'm gonna tell you right from the start how it happened; 'cause like the fella says, I spotted 'em first, spotted 'em first I did. So anyway, I'm on the seashore, see, me and fat Lucas, an' we're horsin' around an' tossin' chunks of earth at each other's head; 'cause you know dang well, fat Lucas he likes to horse around, an' me, sometimes I horse around too. So while we're horsin' around, since horsin' around is what we're doin', well, I spotted somethin' way out there kinda wrigglin' around in the water, an' now an' then it seemed like it was comin' toward us. I could see it, it was visuable all right, an' then, sudden like, I could see that I couldn't see nothin' no more. "Hey, Lucas!" I says to him, "reckon that's some men swimmin' out there."—"Honest," he says to me, "you must a' seen a cat die, you're seein' things."*—"By jingo," says I, "I ain't seein' things; them's men."—"Not on your life," he says to me, "you ain't seein' straight."—"Wanna bet," says I, "that I *am* seein' straight," says I, "an' that that there's two men," says

---

A peasant superstition in Molière's day.

347

I, "an' swimmin' right this way?" says I. "By gum," he
says to me, "I bet it ain't."—"Oh, so!" says I, "wanna
bet ten sous on it?"—"All right with me," he says to
me; "and just to show you, there's my money down,"
he says to me. Me, I weren't no fool nor no half-wit; so
brave as can be, I up an' plunk down five sous in large
coins, minted coins, an' the rest in small, thirty double
deniers; I done it, by jiminy, as bold as if I been swal
lowin' down a glass of wine; 'cause I'll take a chance,
will, an' I don't stop for nothin'. I knew what I wa
doin', all the same. That Lucas, what a clown! So any
way, I hadn't no sooner bet when I seen them two men
plain as day, an' they're makin' signs to go fetch 'em
an' me, first I picks up the stakes. "C'mon, Lucas," I
says, "you can see how they're callin' us; quick, let's go
help 'em."—"Naw," he says to me, "they made me
lose." Oh! Well then, what with one thing an' another
finally, to make it short, I preached him so much tha
we got ourselves in a boat an' then we tugged 'em an
hauled 'em an' all like that an' we got 'em outa the
water, an' then we took 'em back home next to the fire
an' then they got stripped all naked so's to dry out, an
then along came two more of 'em out of the same
bunch, an' they'd got out all by themselves, an' then
Mathurine came in, an' one of 'em made eyes at her
An' that's it, Charlotte, that's just how it all happened

CHARLOTTE. Didn't you tell me, Pierrot, that there's one
of 'em is much better lookin' than the others?

PIERROT. Yes, that's the master. He must be some big, big
gentleman, 'cause he's got gold all over his coat all the
way from top to bottom; an' the people who serve him
they're gentlemen too, themselves; but that don't mat
ter, big gentleman or no, by jeepers, he'd be drownded
if I hadn't been there.

CHARLOTTE. Well, will you listen to that!

PIERROT. Oh! by golly, without us, he'd a' had his all right

CHARLOTTE. Is he still at your house all naked, Pierrot?

PIERROT. No, not him; they got him dressed again right in front of us. By gum, I never had seen one of 'em being dressed! What a lot of contraptions an' doohickeys those courtier fellows do put on themselves! I'd get lost in all o' that, I would, an' I had my jaw hangin' down watchin' it. Look, Charlotte, they got hair that don't stay on their heads; an' they slap that on after all the rest like some big flax bonnet. They got shirts that got sleeves that we could get inside of, you an' me, just the way we are. 'Stead o' breeches they got 'em a great big apron as wide as from here to Easter; 'stead of a doublet, a little old waistcoat that don't even come down to their sole aplexus; 'stead o' neckbands, a great big lace neckerchief with four big linen tassels that hangs down over their stomach. Then they got other little neckbands at the end o' their arms, like, an' then great funnels o' lace on their legs, an' then on top o' all that such a lot o' ribbons, *such* a lot o' ribbons, it really makes you sorry for 'em. Why, they ain't even the shoes that ain't all loaded with 'em, right from one end to the other; an' the way they're fixed up, I'd sure as heck break my neck.

CHARLOTTE. Gracious sakes, Pierrot, I gotta go have a look at that.

PIERROT. Oh! Listen here to me for just a bit first, Charlotte: me, I got somethin' else to tell you.

CHARLOTTE. Well! Tell me, what is it?

PIERROT. You see, Charlotte, like the fella says, I gotta uncork my heart. I love you, an' you know it, an' we're fixin' to get married together; but my gosh, I just ain't satisfied with you.

CHARLOTTE. How do you mean? What's the matter, then?

PIERROT. The matter is, well, that you vex my mind, frankly.

CHARLOTTE. And how do you mean, then?

PIERROT. Doggone it all, you don't love me.

CHARLOTTE *(laughing)*. Ha, ha! An' that's all?

PIERROT. Yeah, that's all, an' it's plenty, too.

CHARLOTTE. Lord's sakes, Pierrot, you're always comin' tellin' me the same thing.

PIERROT. I'm always tellin' you the same thing, 'cause it always is the same thing, an' if it weren't always the same thing, I wouldn't always be tellin' you the same thing.

CHARLOTTE. But what's ailin' you? What do you want?

PIERROT. Gosh darn it! I want you to love me.

CHARLOTTE. Why, don't I love you?

PIERROT. No, you don't love me; and still I do everything I can to make you: I buy you—no offense—ribbons from all the peddlers that come by; I break my neck goin' an' gettin' blackbirds out of their nests for you; I get the fiddlers to play for you when it's your birthday; and all that, just like I was battin' my head against a wall. Look now, it ain't neither nice nor decent not to love the folks as love us.

CHARLOTTE. But land's sakes, I love you too.

PIERROT. Oh yes, that's a fine way you love me!

CHARLOTTE. Then how do you want a person to do?

PIERROT. I want you to do the way people do when they love the way they should.

CHARLOTTE. And don't I love you the way I should?

PIERROT. No: when it is that way, you can tell; and people play a thousand little monkey tricks on people when they love them really, from the heart. Look at fat Thomasse, how daft she is about young Robin: she's always around him and annoyin' him, an' never lets him alone; she's always playin' some trick on him an' givin' him a clout when she goes by; an' the other day when he's sittin' on a stool she goes an' yanks it out from under him an' down he goes full length on the ground. Tarnation! That's how you can tell folk that are in love; but you, you never say a word to me, you're always there like a bump on a log; an' I could go by in front of you twenty times an' you'd never stir a stump to give me the least little blow or say the least little thing to me. Gee whillikins! After all, that's not right, and you're too cold to people.

CHARLOTTE. And what do you want me to do about that? That's my temperment, and I can't change that.

PIERROT. Temperment or no, when a person feels friendly like toward a person, they always do some little something to show it.

CHARLOTTE. Anyway, I love you every bit I can, and if that don't suit you, you can just go love someone else.

PIERROT. See, there you are! That's what I get. Goshamighty! If you loved me, would you say that to me?

CHARLOTTE. Then why do you go gettin' me all in a fluster?

PIERROT. Jeepers! What harm am I doin' you? All I ask you for is a little bit of friendship.

CHARLOTTE. Well then! You go easy too, and don't press me so. Maybe it'll come all of a sudden without thinkin' about it.

PIERROT. Shake on it, then, Charlotte.

CHARLOTTE. All right! There.

PIERROT. Then promise me you'll try to love me more.

CHARLOTTE. I'll do all I·can, but it'll have to come by itself. Pierrot, is that the gentleman?

PIERROT. Yep, there he is.

CHARLOTTE. Oh! Mercy me, isn't he nice, and wouldn't it
have been a pity if he'd a' been drownded!

PIERROT. I'll be back in a minute; I'm gonna have myself
a pint to set me up just a bit from gettin' so tired.

Scene 2.   DON JUAN, SGANARELLE, CHARLOTTE

DON JUAN. We've missed our chance, Sganarelle, and that
unexpected squall upset not only our boat but the plans
we had made; but to tell you the truth, the peasant girl
I've just left makes up for that mishap, and I could see
charms in her that wipe out of my mind all the chagrin
I felt at the ill success of our enterprise. This heart must
not escape me, and I have already worked to dispose it
so that it will not endure my sighing long in vain.

SGANARELLE. Sir, I confess, you astound me. Hardly have
we escaped a deadly peril, and you, instead of giving
thanks to Heaven for the pity it deigned to take on us,
you are starting to work all afresh to draw down its
wrath by your usual fancies and your loves, that are
really crim—(seeing DON JUAN look angry; to himself)
Peace, rascal that you are. You don't know what you're
saying, and Monsieur knows what he's doing. Get along
with you!

DON JUAN (noticing CHARLOTTE). Aha! Where has this
other peasant girl come from, Sganarelle? Did you ever
see anything prettier? And tell me, don't you think this
one is well worth the other?

SGANARELLE. Oh, yes indeed. *(Aside)* Here we go again.

DON JUAN. To what do I owe, my beauty, such a delightful meeting? What? In these rustic surroundings, amid these trees and rocks, there are persons as lovely as you to be found?

CHARLOTTE. As you see, sir.

DON JUAN. Are you from this village?

CHARLOTTE. Yes, sir.

DON JUAN. And you live here?

CHARLOTTE. Yes, sir.

DON JUAN. Your name is . . . ?

CHARLOTTE. Charlotte, at your service.

DON JUAN. Oh, what a beautiful girl, and what piercing eyes!

CHARLOTTE. Sir, you're making me all ashamed.

DON JUAN. Ah! Don't be ashamed at hearing the truth about you. What do you say, Sganarelle? Did you ever see anything more charming? Turn around a little, if you please. Oh! what a pretty figure! Lift your head a little, pray. Oh, what a cute face! Open your eyes all the way. Oh, how beautiful they are! Let me have just a look at your teeth, I beg you. Oh, how loving they are! And those appetizing lips! As for me, I'm enchanted, and I've never seen such a charming person.

CHARLOTTE. Sir, you're pleased to say so, and I don't know whether you're making fun of me or not.

DON JUAN. I, make fun of you? God forbid! I love you too much for that, and I'm speaking from the bottom of my heart.

CHARLOTTE. I'm much obliged to you, if that's so.

DON JUAN. Not at all! You're under no obligation to me for anything I'm saying, and you owe it only to your beauty.

CHARLOTTE. Sir, all that is too well said for me, and I have no wit to answer you with.

DON JUAN. Sganarelle, just look at her hands.

CHARLOTTE. Fie, sir! They're as black as I don't know what.

DON JUAN. Oh, what are you saying? They're the loveliest in the world. Allow me to kiss them, pray.

CHARLOTTE. Sir, that's too much honor you're paying me, and if I'd known that earlier, I wouldn't have failed to wash them in bran.

DON JUAN. Now tell me just one thing, my fair Charlotte: you're not married, I trust?

CHARLOTTE. No, sir, but I am to be soon, to Pierrot, the son of our neighbor Simonette.

DON JUAN. What? A person like you should become the wife of a mere peasant? No, no: that would be a profanation of so much beauty, and you weren't born to live your life in a village. There's no question you deserve a better lot; and Heaven, which knows this well, has brought me here on purpose to prevent this marriage and do justice to your charms. For in short, my fair Charlotte, I love you with all my heart, and if you just say the word I'll take you out of this wretched place and set you up in the position you deserve. No doubt this love is very sudden; but what can I do? It's an effect of your great beauty, Charlotte; and a man comes to love you as much in a quarter of an hour as he might someone else in six months.

CHARLOTTE. Honest, sir, I just don't know what to do when you talk like that. What you say makes me feel good, and I'd like nothing better than to believe it; but I've always heard tell that you must never believe what the gentlemen say, and that you court folk are cajolers and only out to take advantage of the girls.

DON JUAN. I am not one of those people.

SGANARELLE *(aside)*. Not much.

CHARLOTTE. You see, sir, there's no pleasure in being taken advantage of. I'm a poor peasant girl; but I care about honor, and I'd rather see myself dead than dishonored.

DON JUAN. And would I have such a wicked soul as to take advantage of a girl like you? I should be base enough to dishonor you? No, no; I have too much of a conscience for that. I love you, Charlotte, in all faith and honor; and to show you that I'm telling you the truth, let me tell you that I have no other intentions than to marry you. Do you want greater proof? I'm ready whenever you wish; and I call on this man here to witness my pledge.

SGANARELLE. No, no, have no fear: he'll marry you as much as you like.

DON JUAN. Ah, Charlotte! I see very well that you don't know me yet. You do me great wrong to judge me by others; and if there are scoundrels in the world, men who seek only to take advantage of girls, you must count me out of their number and not cast doubt on the sincerity of my word. And then, your beauty makes you perfectly safe. Anyone who looks like you is necessarily protected against all fears of that sort. Believe me, you don't look the part of a girl that could be taken advantage of; and for my part, I confess, I'd pierce my heart with a thousand stabs if I had had the slightest thought of betraying you.

CHARLOTTE. My goodness! I don't know whether you're telling me the truth or not, but you make a person believe you.

DON JUAN. In believing me you will certainly only do me justice, and I repeat once more the promise I made you. Don't you accept it, and won't you consent to be my wife?

CHARLOTTE. Yes, providing my aunt is willing.

DON JUAN. Shake hands on it then, Charlotte, since for your part you are willing.

CHARLOTTE. But remember, sir, don't go and deceive me, I beg you; that would be bad of you, and you see how I'm going about this in good faith.

DON JUAN. What? You still seem to doubt my sincerity! Do you want me to swear some dreadful oaths? May Heaven . . . !

CHARLOTTE. My goodness, don't swear; I believe you.

DON JUAN. Then give me one little kiss as a pledge of your word.

CHARLOTTE. Oh, sir! Wait till I'm married and all, please; after that, I'll kiss you all you want.

DON JUAN. Very well, fair Charlotte, I want whatever you do; but just allow me your hand, and let me express to it, by a thousand kisses, the ecstasy I feel . . .

Scene 3. DON JUAN, SGANARELLE, PIERROT,
CHARLOTTE

PIERROT (coming between them and pushing DON JUAN). Easy there, sir, hands off, if you please. You're getting too het up, and you could catch a pleurisy.

DON JUAN *(pushing* PIERROT *back roughly).* How did this meddler get here?

PIERROT. I tell you, hands off, and you don't go caressing our fi-an-cees.

DON JUAN *(still pushing him back).* Oh, what a lot of fuss!

PIERROT. Tarnation! That's no way to go pushin' folk.

CHARLOTTE *(taking* PIERROT *by the arm).* Well, you leave him be too, Pierrot.

PIERROT. How's that? I should leave him be? Well, me, I don't want to.

DON JUAN. Ah!

PIERROT. Doggone it! 'Cause you're a genneman, you'll come and caress our wives right to our face? Go on out of here and caress your own wives.

DON JUAN. So?

PIERROT. So. (DON JUAN *slaps him.*) Gosh sakes! Don't hit me. *(Another slap)* Oh, doggone it! *(Another slap)* Jeepers! *(Another slap)* Dad bust it! Tarnation! It's not right to go beatin' folk, and that's no way to reward me, nohow, for savin' you from gettin' drownded.

CHARLOTTE. Pierrot, don't get mad.

PIERROT. I will too get mad; and you, you're a bad girl, to let him wheedle you.

CHARLOTTE. Oh, Pierrot! It's not the way you think. This gentleman wants to marry me, and you got no call to get angry.

PIERROT. How's that? Dad rat it! You're promised to me.

CHARLOTTE. That makes no never-mind, Pierrot. If you

love me, shouldn't you be mighty pleased to see me
become a real lady?

PIERROT. Dang bust it, no! I'd rather see you croaked than
see you belong to somebody else.

CHARLOTTE. Come on, Pierrot, come on, don't get all
upset. If I get to be a lady, I'll see that you earn something, and you'll bring us our butter and cheese to the
house.

PIERROT. By jiminy! I won't bring you none, never, even
if you paid me twice as much. So that's the way you
listen to the things he tells you, is it? By golly! If I'd a'
known that just now, I sure wouldn't never a' pulled
him out of the water, and I'd a' given him a good knock
on the head with the oar.

DON JUAN (*coming up to* PIERROT *to hit him*). What's that
you're saying?

PIERROT (*getting behind* CHARLOTTE). Consarn it! I ain't
scared of nobody.

DON JUAN (*coming around after* PIERROT). Hold on a bit!
Wait for me.

PIERROT (*dodging around* CHARLOTTE). I don't give a rap
what you do.

DON JUAN (*running after* PIERROT). Let's see about that.

PIERROT (*again hiding behind* CHARLOTTE). I seen folk
like you by the dozens.

DON JUAN. Well!

SGANARELLE. Oh, sir! Let the poor wretch alone. It's a
shame to beat him. (*To* PIERROT) Listen to me, my poor
chap, go on away and don't say anything to him.

PIERROT (*passes in front of* SGANARELLE *and speaks*

proudly to DON JUAN). I will say something to him, I will.

DON JUAN (*raises his hand to slap* PIERROT). Ah! I'll teach you.

(PIERROT *ducks, and* SGANARELLE *gets the slap.*)

SGANARELLE (*looking at* PIERROT, *who is still ducking*). A plague on the oaf!

DON JUAN. That's what you get for your charity.

PIERROT. Dang it! I'm going to tell her aunt about all these carryings-on.

DON JUAN. At last I'm going to be the happiest of men, and I wouldn't exchange my good fortune for anything in the world. What pleasures there will be when you're my wife! And how . . .

Scene 4.   DON JUAN, SGANARELLE, CHARLOTTE, MATHURINE

SGANARELLE (*seeing* MATHURINE). Oh oh!

MATHURINE (*to* DON JUAN). Why, sir, what are you doing here with Charlotte? Are you talking love-talk to her too?

DON JUAN (*to* MATHURINE). No, on the contrary, it was she who was indicating her desire to be my wife, and I was telling her in reply that I was contracted to you.

CHARLOTTE. Why, what in the world does Mathurine want with you?

DON JUAN (*aside, to* CHARLOTTE). She's jealous at seeing

me talking to you, and would like me to marry her; but I tell her it's you I want.

MATHURINE. What? Charlotte . . .

DON JUAN (*aside, to* MATHURINE). Anything you tell her will be useless; she's got this into her head.

CHARLOTTE. How's that again? Mathurine . . .

DON JUAN (*aside, to* CHARLOTTE). There's no point in your talking to her; you'll never rid her of that fancy.

MATHURINE. Do you mean . . . ?

DON JUAN (*aside, to* MATHURINE). There's no way to make her listen to reason.

CHARLOTTE. I'd like . . .

DON JUAN (*aside, to* CHARLOTTE). She's as obstinate as the devil.

MATHURINE. Really . . .

DON JUAN (*aside, to* MATHURINE). Don't say anything to her, she's mad.

CHARLOTTE. I think . . .

DON JUAN (*aside, to* CHARLOTTE). Let her alone, she's not quite all there.

MATHURINE. No, no, I must speak to her.

CHARLOTTE. I want to get some idea of her reasons.

MATHURINE. What . . . ?

DON JUAN (*aside, to* MATHURINE). I'll bet she'll tell you I've promised to marry her.

CHARLOTTE. I . . .

DON JUAN *(aside, to* CHARLOTTE*)*. Let's bet she'll maintain that I've given her my word to make her my wife.

MATHURINE. Say, Charlotte, it's not right to cut in on other folk's arrangements.

CHARLOTTE. It's not nice, Mathurine, to be jealous because the gentleman is speaking to me.

MATHURINE. I'm the one the gentleman saw first.

CHARLOTTE. If he saw you first, he saw me second, and promised to marry me.

DON JUAN *(aside, to* MATHURINE*)*. Well? What did I tell you?

MATHURINE. I kiss your hands; it was me, not you, he promised to marry.

DON JUAN *(aside, to* CHARLOTTE*)*. Wasn't I right?

CHARLOTTE. Tell that to somebody else, please; it was me, I tell you.

MATHURINE. You're kidding; it was me, I tell you again.

CHARLOTTE. Here's the man to tell you if I'm wrong.

MATHURINE. Here's the man to give me the lie if I'm not telling the truth.

CHARLOTTE. Sir, did you promise to marry her?

DON JUAN *(aside, to* CHARLOTTE*)*. You're making sport of me.

MATHURINE. Is it true, sir, that you gave her your word to be her husband?

DON JUAN *(aside, to* MATHURINE*)*. Can you believe such a thing?

CHARLOTTE. You see that's what she's claiming.

DON JUAN *(aside, to* CHARLOTTE*)*. Let her do as she likes.

MATHURINE. You're a witness to how she persists.

DON JUAN *(aside, to* MATHURINE*)*. Let her talk.

CHARLOTTE. No, no, we have to know the truth.

MATHURINE. This has got to be decided.

CHARLOTTE. Yes, Mathurine, I want Monsieur to show you how naïve you are.

MATHURINE. Yes, Charlotte, I want Monsieur to take you down a peg.

CHARLOTTE. Sir, settle the quarrel, please.

MATHURINE. Clear us up, sir.

CHARLOTTE *(to* MATHURINE*)*. You'll see.

MATHURINE *(to* CHARLOTTE*)*. You'll see yourself.

CHARLOTTE *(to* DON JUAN*)*. Tell her.

MATHURINE *(to* DON JUAN*)*. Speak up.

DON JUAN *(embarrassed, speaking to them both)*. What do you want me to say? You both alike maintain that I promised to take you for my wives. Doesn't each of you know what the truth is, without my needing to explain myself further? Why make me repeat myself on this? Hasn't the one I really gave my promise to enough self-assurance to laugh at the other one's claims, and should she be worried, provided I fulfill my promise? All this talk doesn't get us anywhere; we must do, not say, and actions speak louder than words. So that's the only way I mean to clear you up, and when I get married you'll see which of the two has possession of my heart. *(Aside, to* MATHURINE*)* Let her think what she likes. *(Aside, to* CHARLOTTE*)* Let her flatter herself with her fancies. *(Aside, to* MATHURINE*)* I adore you. *(Aside, to* CHARLOTTE*)* I am wholly yours. *(Aside, to* MATHURINE*)* All faces are ugly beside yours. *(Aside, to* CHARLOTTE*)* Anyone who has seen you can't bear others. *(To both)* I have a little order to give; I'll be back to see you in a quarter of an hour.

CHARLOTTE *(to* MATHURINE*)*. Anyway, I'm the one he loves.

MATHURINE *(to* CHARLOTTE*)*. I'm the one he'll marry.

SGANARELLE. Oh, you poor girls! I pity your innocence, and I can't bear to see you rushing to your ruin. Believe me, both of you: don't listen to all the stories you're told, and stay in your village.

DON JUAN *(coming back)*. I'd certainly like to know why Sganarelle isn't following me.

SGANARELLE. My master is a cheat; his only intention is to take advantage of you, and he has taken advantage of plenty of others; he's the marrying kind—of the whole human race—and . . . *(He sees* DON JUAN.*)* That's not true; and if anyone tells you that, you are to tell him he's a liar. My master is not the marrying kind— of the whole human race—he's not a cheat, he has no intention of deceiving you, and he hasn't taken advantage of plenty of others. Oh, look! Here he is; ask *him*.

DON JUAN. Yes.

SGANARELLE. Sir, since the world is full of slanderers, I'm forestalling them; and I was telling the girls that if anyone was to come to them and speak ill of you, they should take good care not to believe him, and should not fail to tell him he's a liar.

DON JUAN. Sganarelle.

SGANARELLE. Yes, Monsieur is a man of honor, I vouch for him myself.

DON JUAN. Hm!

SGANARELLE. Such people are impertinent rascals.

Scene 5.   DON JUAN, LA RAMÉE, CHARLOTTE,
                  MATHURINE, SGANARELLE

LA RAMÉE. Sir, I've come to warn you that it's not healthy for you here.

DON JUAN. How's that?

LA RAMÉE. Twelve horsemen are hunting for you, and should be here any moment. I don't know how they were able to follow you; but I learned the news from a peasant whom they questioned, and they gave him your description. The matter is urgent, and the sooner you get out of here the better.

DON JUAN (to CHARLOTTE and MATHURINE). Urgent business obliges me to leave; but I beg you to remember the promise I gave you, and to believe that you will hear from me before tomorrow evening. (Exeunt CHARLOTTE and MATHURINE.) Since I'm outnumbered, I must resort to a stratagem, and adroitly elude the misfortune that pursues me. I want Sganarelle to put on my clothes, and I . . .

SGANARELLE. Sir, you're joking. Expose me to being killed in your clothes, and . . . ?

DON JUAN. Come on, quick, I'm doing you too much

honor, and happy is the valet who can have the glory of dying for his master.

SGANARELLE. Thanks a lot for such an honor! *(Alone)* O Heaven, since it's a matter of life and death, grant me not to be taken for someone else!

ACT III
(A forest)

Scene 1. DON JUAN *(in country clothes)*, SGANARELLE *(dressed as a doctor)*

SGANARELLE. My word, sir, you must admit that I was
  right, and that here are the two of us wonderfully disguised. Your first plan wasn't the thing at all, and this
  hides us much better than what you wanted to do.

DON JUAN. It's true that you're well rigged out, and I don't
  know where you dug up that ridiculous outfit.

SGANARELLE. Am I? It's the costume of some old doctor,
  that was left in pawn at the place where I got it, and it
  cost me money to have it. But do you know, sir, already
  this gown gives me consideration, I'm greeted by the
  people I meet, and some are coming to consult me just
  as they would an able man?

DON JUAN. How's that?

SGANARELLE. Five or six country people, seeing me go by,
  have come to ask me my opinion about various
  maladies.

DON JUAN. And you answered that you didn't know a
  thing about it?

SGANARELLE. I? Not at all. I wanted to maintain the honor
  of my gown. I theorized about the illness, and I gave
  them each a prescription.

DON JUAN. And what remedies did you prescribe for
  them, then?

SGANARELLE. My word, sir, I took them where I could find them; I gave my prescriptions at random; and it would be a funny thing if the patients got well and came to thank me for it.

DON JUAN. And why not? Just why shouldn't you have the same privileges as all the other doctors? They have nothing more to do with curing their patients than you, and their whole art is pure pretense. All they do is take the credit for the fortunate results, and you can profit as they do from the patient's good luck, and see attributed to your remedies all that may come from the favors of chance and the forces of nature.

SGANARELLE. What, sir, you're impious in medicine too?

DON JUAN. It's one of the great errors of mankind.

SGANARELLE. What? You don't believe in senna, or cassia, or emetic wine?

DON JUAN. And why would you have me believe in them?

SGANARELLE. You have the soul of a real unbeliever. However, you have seen that for some time emetic wine has been making quite a stir. Its miracles have converted the most incredulous minds, and not three weeks ago I saw, me, just as I'm speaking to you, a marvelous effect from it.

DON JUAN. And what was that?

SGANARELLE. There was a man who had been in agony for six days; they didn't know what to prescribe for him any more, and all the remedies weren't doing anything; finally they thought of giving him emetic wine.

DON JUAN. He got well, did he?

SGANARELLE. No, he died.

DON JUAN. That was an admirable result.

SGANARELLE. What? For six whole days he hadn't been able to die, and that made him die right away. Could you ask for anything more efficient than that?

DON JUAN. You're right.

SGANARELLE. But let's leave medicine, which you don't believe in, and talk about other things; for this costume gives me wit, and I feel in the mood to argue with you. You allow me to argue with you, you know, and all you forbid me is remonstrances.

DON JUAN. Well then?

SGANARELLE. I'd just like to get to the bottom of what you think. Is it possible that you don't believe in Heaven at all?

DON JUAN. Let that question alone.

SGANARELLE. In other words, no. And in Hell?

DON JUAN. Eh?

SGANARELLE. Same thing. And in the Devil, may I ask?

DON JUAN. Yes, yes.

SGANARELLE. Just as little. Don't you believe in the after-life at all?

DON JUAN. Oh! oh! oh!

SGANARELLE. Here's a man I'm going to have a lot of trouble converting. Tell me now: the Bogeyman,* what do you believe about him, eh?

DON JUAN. A plague on the fool!

*This is *le Moine bourru* (the crazy monk), a sprite who runs about the streets at Christmas and predicts trouble. This bit (the next few lines) is omitted in many editions.

SGANARELLE. And that's what I can't stand; for there is nothing truer than the Bogeyman, and I'd let myself be hanged for him. But still, you have to believe something in this world: now what *do* you believe?

DON JUAN. What do I believe?

SGANARELLE. Yes.

DON JUAN. I believe that two and two makes four, Sganarelle, and that four and four makes eight.

SGANARELLE. That's a fine belief, and those are fine articles of faith! So your religion, as far as I can see, is arithmetic? You have to admit, men do get strange follies into their heads, and most of the time people are less wise the more they've studied. For my part, sir, I haven't studied like you, thank God, and no one can boast of ever having taught me anything; but with my own wee common sense, my own wee judgment, I see things better than all the books, and I understand very well that this world that we see is not some sort of mushroom that came here of itself in one night. I'd like to ask you who made these trees, these rocks, this earth, and that sky you see up there, and whether all that built itself. Now here are you, for example, you are here: did you make yourself, all alone, and didn't your father have to get your mother pregnant in order to make you? Can you see all the contrivances that the machine called Man is composed of without wondering at the way one part is fitted into another: these sinews, these bones, these veins, these arteries, these ... this lung, this heart, this liver, and all these other ingredients that are there, and that ... ? Oh, good Lord, please interrupt me if you wish; I can't argue unless I'm interrupted. You're keeping quiet on purpose and letting me talk on out of sheer malice.

DON JUAN. I'm waiting for your argument to be finished.

SGANARELLE. My argument is that there is something admirable in man, no matter what you say, that all the

scholars could never explain. Isn't it wonderful that
here I am, and that I have something in my head that
thinks a hundred different things in one moment, and
does whatever it likes with my body? I want to clap my
hands, lift my arm, raise my eyes to Heaven, bow my
head, move my feet, go to the right, to the left, forward,
backward, turn . . . *(As he turns, he falls.)*

DON JUAN. Fine! Now your argument has a broken nose.

SGANARELLE. Good Lord! I'm pretty stupid to waste my
time arguing with you. Believe what you like: a lot I
care whether you're damned!

DON JUAN. But while we've been arguing, I think we've
lost our way. Go call that man I see over there and ask
him for directions.

SGANARELLE. Hello there, man! Hey, brother! Hey,
friend! A word with you, please.

Scene 2.   DON JUAN, SGANARELLE, THE POOR MAN

SGANARELLE. Tell us which is the way to town, will you?

POOR MAN. You have only to follow this road, gentlemen,
and turn off to the right when you come to the end of
the forest. But I warn you that you must be on your
guard, and that for some time now there have been robbers hereabouts.

DON JUAN. I'm much obliged to you, my friend, and I
thank you with all my heart.

POOR MAN. If you would be good enough, sir, to help me
out with a bit of alms?

DON JUAN. Aha! Your warning is self-serving, I see.

POOR MAN. I'm a poor man, sir, retired all alone in this wood for ten years, and I shall not fail to pray to Heaven to give you all sorts of good things.

DON JUAN. Well! Pray it to give you a suit of clothes, and don't worry about other people's affairs.

SGANARELLE. You don't know Monsieur, my good man; he doesn't believe in anything except two and two makes four and four and four makes eight.

DON JUAN. What is your occupation here among the trees?

POOR MAN. Praying to Heaven all day long for the prosperity of the worthy people who give me something.

DON JUAN. Then it couldn't be that you're not very well off?

POOR MAN. Alas, sir! I am in the greatest possible need.

DON JUAN. You must be joking. A man who prays to Heaven all day long cannot fail to be in comfortable circumstances.

POOR MAN. I assure you, sir, that most of the time I haven't even a piece of bread to get my teeth into.*

DON JUAN. That *is* strange, and you are ill rewarded for your pains. Aha! I'll give you a louis d'or right now as long as you're willing to swear.

POOR MAN. Oh, sir! Would you want me to commit such a sin?

*The next eight speeches are not given by some editors (including Despois and Mesnard), since Molière may have suppressed them and changed the ensuing speech by Don Juan to read as follows:
"I want to give you a louis d'or, and I give it to you for love of humanity. (Looking off in the forest) But what's this I see over there? One man attacked by three others? The odds are too unequal, and I must not tolerate this cowardice. (He runs to the scene of the combat.)"

DON JUAN. All you need to do is see whether you want to earn a louis d'or or not. Here's one I'll give you if you'll swear. Here, you must swear.

POOR MAN. Sir . . .

DON JUAN. Unless you do, you won't get it.

SGANARELLE. Come on, come on, swear a bit, there's no harm in it.

DON JUAN. Here it is, take it; take it, I tell you; but go on and swear.

POOR MAN. No, sir, I'd rather die of hunger.

DON JUAN. Come, come, I'll give it to you for love of humanity. *(Looking off in the forest)* But what's this I see over there? One man attacked by three others? The odds are too unequal, and I must not tolerate this cowardice. *(He runs to the scene of the combat.)*

Scene 3.   DON JUAN, DON CARLOS, SGANARELLE

SGANARELLE. My master is a real madman to go to meet a danger that isn't looking for him; but, my word! His help has worked, and the two have put the three to flight.

DON CARLOS *(sword in hand)*. From the flight of these robbers, we see the full power of your arm to help. Allow me, sir, to offer my thanks for such a generous action, and to . . .

DON JUAN *(returning, sword in hand)*. I have done nothing, sir, that you wouldn't have done in my place. Our own honor is involved in such adventures, and the action of those scoundrels was so cowardly that not to oppose it would have amounted to taking part in it. But how did you happen to fall into their hands?

DON CARLOS. I had been separated by accident from my brother and all our retinue; and as I was trying to get back to them, I met up with these robbers, who first killed my horse, and, but for your valor, would have done as much to me.

DON JUAN. Are you planning to travel in the direction of town?

DON CARLOS. Yes, but I don't want to go inside the town. We find ourselves obliged, my brother and I, to keep to the fields, on account of one of these unpleasant affairs that oblige gentlemen to sacrifice themselves, and their families, to the rigorousness of their honor, since after all the happiest result of it all is still disastrous, and since, if we don't quit life itself, we are constrained to quit the kingdom. And it's in this respect that I consider a gentleman's condition unhappy, that he cannot be secure in all the prudence and all the decency of his own conduct, that he is subjected by the laws of honor to the lawlessness of other people's conduct, and that his life, his repose, and his property depend on the fancy of the first rash fool who decides to offer him one of those affronts for which a man of quality must be ready to die.

DON JUAN. We have this satisfaction, that we make them run the same risk and also spend their time badly, those who take it into their head to come and offer us an offense just for the fun of it. But would it be an indiscretion to ask you what this affair of yours may be?

DON CARLOS. The state of the matter is such that there's no point in making a secret of it any longer; and once the insult has been made public, our honor does not aim to try to hide our shame, but to make public our vengeance and even our plan for it. Thus, sir, I shall not hesitate to tell you that the offense we are seeking to avenge is the seduction of a sister who was carried off from a convent, and that the author of this offense is one Don Juan Tenorio, son of Don Louis Tenorio. We have been looking for him for some days, and we followed him this morning on the report of a valet who told us that he was riding out on horseback in company with four or five men, and that he had set out along this coast; but all our pains have been useless, and we haven't been able to find out what has become of him.

DON JUAN. Do you know him, sir, this Don Juan that you are speaking of?

DON CARLOS. For my part, no. I have never seen him, and I have only heard him described by my brother; but his reputation is hardly of the best, and he's a man whose life . . .

DON JUAN. Stop, sir, if you please. He's something of a friend of mine, and it would be a kind of cowardice on my part to hear him ill spoken of.

DON CARLOS. For your sake, sir, I'll say nothing about him, and certainly that's the least thing I owe you, after you have saved my life, to be silent in your presence about a person whom you know, when I cannot talk about him without speaking ill of him. But however much you may be a friend of his, I dare to hope that you will not approve of his action and will not find it strange that we are trying to take vengeance for it.

DON JUAN. On the contrary, I want to help you in this, and spare you useless pains. I am a friend of Don Juan, I can't help that; but it is not reasonable that he should offend gentlemen with impunity, and I promise to have him give you satisfaction.

DON CARLOS. And what satisfaction can be given for this sort of offense?

DON JUAN. All that your honor can desire; and, without your giving yourself the trouble to seek Don Juan any further, I'll bind myself to have him meet you where you want, and when you like.

DON CARLOS. That hope, sir, is very sweet to offended hearts; but after what I owe you, it would be too great a pain to me for you to be a participant.

DON JUAN. I am so attached to Don Juan that he could not fight without my fighting too; but anyway, I'll answer for him as for myself, and you have only to say when you want him to appear and give you satisfaction.

DON CARLOS. How cruel is my destiny! Must I owe you my life, and must Don Juan be a friend of yours?

Scene 4.   DON ALONSE and three ATTENDANTS, DON
           CARLOS, DON JUAN, SGANARELLE

DON ALONSE. Have my horses watered there, and bring them after us; I want to walk a bit. *(Seeing both men)* Heavens! What do I see here! What! Brother, here you are with our mortal enemy?

DON CARLOS. Our mortal enemy?

DON JUAN *(taking three steps backward and putting his hand proudly on his sword hilt)*. Yes, I myself am Don Juan, and your advantage in numbers will not make me try to disguise my name.

DON ALONSE. Ah, traitor! You shall perish, and . . .

DON CARLOS. Ah, brother, stop! I owe him my life; and without the help of his arm, I would have been killed by some robbers I met with.

DON ALONSE. And do you mean to let this consideration hinder our vengeance? All the services an enemy's

hand may do for us do not deserve to bind our soul at
all; and if we must measure the obligation against the
offense, your gratitude in this case, brother, is ridiculous; and since honor is infinitely more precious than
life, to owe our life to someone who has stolen our
honor is really to owe nothing at all.

DON CARLOS. Brother, I know the difference a gentleman
must always make between the two things, and recognition of my obligation does not wipe out my resentment
at the offense. But allow me to return to him here what
he has lent me, to pay back on the spot, by putting off
our vengeance, the life I owe him, and to leave him
the freedom to enjoy, for a few days, the fruits of his
good deed.

DON ALONSE. No, no, it is risking our vengeance to delay
it, and the chance to get it may never come again.
Heaven offers it to us here and now, it's up to us to
take advantage of it. When honor is mortally wounded,
we must not think of any restraints; and if you find it
repugnant to lend your arm to this action, you have
only to withdraw and leave me the glory of such a
sacrifice.

DON CARLOS. I beg you, brother . . .

DON ALONSE. All this talk is superfluous: he must die.

DON CARLOS. Stop, brother, I tell you. I will absolutely not
allow an attack on his days, and I swear to Heaven that
I will defend him here against anyone whatever, and
I'll make a rampart for him of this same life that he
saved; and to aim your blows at him, you'll have to
pierce me.

DON ALONSE. What? You're taking our enemy's side
against me; and far from being seized, at the sight of
him, with the same transports as I, you show for him
feelings of mildness?

DON CARLOS. Brother, let's show moderation in a legitimate action, and let's not avenge our honor with the frenzy that you display. Let's have a courage that we are masters of, a valor that has nothing savage about it, and that moves to act by a pure deliberation of our reason and not on an impulse of blind fury. Brother, I do not want to remain indebted to my enemy, and I have an obligation to him that I must acquit before anything else. Our vengeance will be none the less signal for being deferred; on the contrary, it will gain by it; and this chance we had of taking it will make it appear the more just in everyone's eyes.

DON ALONSE. Oh! What a strange weakness, and dreadful blindness, to risk the interests of our honor thus for the ridiculous notion of an imaginary obligation!

DON CARLOS. No, brother, don't worry. If I am making a mistake, I shall be able to make amends for it, and I'll take the care of our honor all upon myself. I know what it requires of us, and this one-day postponement, which my gratitude asks of it, will only increase my ardor to satisfy it. Don Juan, you see that I am at pains to return the good I have received from you, and from that you must judge the rest, and believe that I repay whatever I owe with the same warmth, and that I shall be no less exact in paying you for the affront than for the benefit. I do not want to oblige you here and now to explain your feelings, and I give you your freedom to consider at leisure what you must resolve. You know well enough how great an offense you have done us, and I leave you to judge for yourself what reparations it demands. There are gentle ways to satisfy us; there are violent and bloody ones; but anyway, whichever you choose, you have given me your word to have Don Juan give me satisfaction. Keep that in mind, I beg you, and remember that from this point on I have no further obligation except to my honor.

DON JUAN. I have required nothing of you, and I shall keep the promise I have given.

DON CARLOS. Come, brother; a moment's mildness gives no offense to the rigorousness of our duty.

Scene 5. DON JUAN, SGANARELLE

DON JUAN. Hey! Hello! Sganarelle!

SGANARELLE (*coming out from where he was hiding*). Sir?

DON JUAN. What, you rogue, you run away when I'm attacked?

SGANARELLE. Pardon me, sir; I've just come from right near by. I think this costume is purgative, and that wearing it amounts to taking medicine.

DON JUAN. A plague on your insolence! At least cover your cravenness with a more decent veil. Do you know who it was whose life I saved?

SGANARELLE. Me? No.

DON JUAN. It was a brother of Elvire's.

SGANARELLE. A . . .

DON JUAN. He's a rather decent chap, he behaved well, and I'm sorry to have a quarrel with him.

SGANARELLE. It would be easy for you to make everything peaceful.

DON JUAN. Yes; but my passion for Doña Elvire is spent, and it doesn't suit my mood to be tied down. I like freedom in love, as you know, and I could never bring myself to enclose my heart within four walls. I've told you twenty times I have a natural inclination to let myself go toward whatever attracts me. My heart belongs to all beautiful women, and it's up to them to take it in turn and keep it as long as they can. But what is the splendid building that I see among these trees?

SGANARELLE. You don't know?

DON JUAN. No, really.

SGANARELLE. Why, that's the tomb that the Commander was having built when you killed him.

DON JUAN. Ah! You're right. I didn't know it was out this way. Everyone has told me wonderful things about it and about the statue of the Commander as well, and I'd like to go and see it.

SGANARELLE. Sir, don't go there.

DON JUAN. Why not?

SGANARELLE. It's not civil to go and call on a man you've killed.

DON JUAN. On the contrary, I mean this visit as a civility to him, and he should receive it with good grace if he's a gentleman. Come on, let's go in.

(The tomb opens, and reveals a superb mausoleum and THE STATUE OF THE COMMANDER.*)*

SGANARELLE. Oh! How beautiful it is! Beautiful statues! Beautiful marble! Beautiful pillars! Oh! How beautiful it is! What do you think of it, sir?

DON JUAN. That a dead man's ambition could hardly go further; and what I consider remarkable is that a man who during his life got along with a rather simple abode should want to have such a magnificent one for the time when he has no further use for it.

SGANARELLE. Here's the statue of the Commander.

DON JUAN. My heavens! He's really decked out with his Roman emperor costume!

SGANARELLE. My word, sir, that's a fine piece of work! It seems as if he's alive and just about to speak. He looks at us in a way that would frighten me if I were all alone, and I think he is not pleased to see us.

DON JUAN. He would be wrong, and that would be a poor way to receive the honor I am paying him. Ask him if he will come to supper with me.

SGANARELLE. That's something he doesn't need, I think.

DON JUAN. Ask him, I tell you.

SGANARELLE. Are you joking? It would be crazy to go talking to a statue.

DON JUAN. Do what I tell you.

SGANARELLE. How absurd! My lord Commander . . . *(Aside)* I'm laughing at my stupidity, but it's my master who makes me do this. *(Aloud)* My lord Commander, my master Don Juan asks you if you will do him the honor to come to supper with him. (THE STATUE *nods its head.*) Ah!

DON JUAN. What is it? What's the matter with you? Speak up, will you?

SGANARELLE *(nodding just as* THE STATUE *did).* The statue . . .

DON JUAN. Well! What are you trying to say, traitor?

SGANARELLE. I tell you, the statue . . .

DON JUAN. Well? The statue? I'll brain you if you don't speak.

SGANARELLE. The statue signaled to me.

DON JUAN. A plague on the rascal!

SGANARELLE. It signaled to me, I tell you: that's the absolute truth. Go on and talk to him yourself and see. Maybe . . .

DON JUAN. Come on, you rogue, come on, I want to rub your nose in your own cowardice. Now watch. Would the lord Commander like to come to supper with me? (THE STATUE *nods its head again.*)

SGANARELLE. I wouldn't have missed that for ten pistoles. Well, sir?

DON JUAN. Come on, let's get out of here.

SGANARELLE. There are your freethinkers for you, who won't believe anything!

ACT IV
(Don Juan's lodgings)

Scene 1. DON JUAN, SGANARELLE

DON JUAN. Whatever it may have been, let's drop the subject; it's a trifle, and we may have been fooled by a bad light, or affected by some sort of dizziness that troubled our sight.

SGANARELLE. Oh, sir! Don't try to deny what we saw with these very eyes. Nothing could be more absolutely true than that nod of the head; and I have no doubt that Heaven, scandalized by your life, has produced this miracle to convince you and draw you back from . . .

DON JUAN. Listen. If you pester me any more with your stupid moralizing, if you say the least little word more to me about it, I'm going to call someone to fetch a bull's pizzle, have you held by three or four men, and give you a thousand lashes. Do you understand me?

SGANARELLE. Very well, sir, perfectly. You explain yourself clearly. That's what's good about you: you don't go beating about the bush; you say things with wonderful precision.

DON JUAN. Come, have my supper served as soon as possible. Boy! A chair!

Scene 2.   DON JUAN, SGANARELLE, LA VIOLETTE

LA VIOLETTE. Sir, here's your furnisher, Monsieur Dimanche, asking to speak to you.

SGANARELLE. Fine! That's just what we need, a greeting from a creditor! What does he think he's doing coming and asking us for money? And why didn't you tell him that Monsieur is out?

LA VIOLETTE. I've been telling him that for three quarters of an hour; but he won't believe it, and he sat down inside to wait.

SGANARELLE. Let him wait as long as he likes.

DON JUAN. No, on the contrary, show him in. It's very bad policy to go into hiding from your creditors. It's good to give them some satisfaction, and I have the secret for sending them away happy without paying them a penny.

Scene 3.   DON JUAN, MONSIEUR DIMANCHE,
SGANARELLE, ATTENDANTS

DON JUAN *(with a great show of politeness)*. Ah, Monsieur Dimanche,* do come here. How delighted I am to see you, and how angry I am with my servants for not showing you in right away! I *had* given orders to admit no

---

*The salutation "Monsieur Dimanche," rather than simply "Monsieur," is familiar and here contemptuous. Don Juan uses it repeatedly and, with the same effect, asks about "Madame Dimanche." Meanwhile of course Monsieur Dimanche consistently, and politely, addresses Don Juan as "Monsieur."

visitors; but those orders are not for you, and you have a right never to find my door closed to you.

MONSIEUR DIMANCHE. Sir, I am very much obliged to you.

DON JUAN *(to his lackeys)*. Good heavens, you rascals! I'll teach you to leave Monsieur Dimanche in an antechamber, and I'll see that you learn who's who.

MONSIEUR DIMANCHE. Sir, that's nothing.

DON JUAN. What? To tell you I'm not there? You, Monsieur Dimanche, my best friend?

MONSIEUR DIMANCHE. Sir, I'm your servant. I came . . .

DON JUAN. Come, quick, a seat for Monsieur Dimanche.

MONSIEUR DIMANCHE. Sir, I'm fine like this.

DON JUAN. No, no, I want you to sit beside me.

MONSIEUR DIMANCHE. That's not necessary.

DON JUAN. Take away that folding chair and bring a comfortable one.

MONSIEUR DIMANCHE. Sir, you're joking, and . . .

DON JUAN. No, no, I know what I owe you, and I don't want any distinction shown between the two of us.

MONSIEUR DIMANCHE. Sir . . .

DON JUAN. Come, sit down.

MONSIEUR DIMANCHE. There's no need, sir, and I have only one word to say. I came . . .

DON JUAN. Sit there, I tell you.

MONSIEUR DIMANCHE. No, sir, I'm fine. I'm coming to . . .

DON JUAN. No, I won't listen to you unless you sit.

MONSIEUR DIMANCHE. I will, sir, since you insist. I . . .

DON JUAN. My heavens, Monsieur Dimanche! You're looking well.

MONSIEUR DIMANCHE. Yes, sir, at your service. I came . . .

DON JUAN. You look wonderful, the picture of health, red lips, ruddy complexion, sparkling eyes.

MONSIEUR DIMANCHE. I would like . . .

DON JUAN. How is Madame Dimanche, your wife?

MONSIEUR DIMANCHE. Very well, sir, thank Heaven.

DON JUAN. She's a good woman.

MONSIEUR DIMANCHE. She is your servant, sir. I was coming . . .

DON JUAN. And your little girl Claudine, how is she?

MONSIEUR DIMANCHE. She couldn't be better.

DON JUAN. What a pretty little girl she is! I love her with all my heart.

MONSIEUR DIMANCHE. You do her too much honor, sir. I . . .

DON JUAN. And little Colin, is he still making as much noise as ever with his drum?

MONSIEUR DIMANCHE. As much as ever, sir. I . . .

DON JUAN. And your little dog Brusquet? Does he still growl as loud as ever, and does he still bite at the legs of the people who come to your house?

MONSIEUR DIMANCHE. More than ever, sir, and we can't break him of it.

DON JUAN. Don't be surprised if I ask for news of the whole family, for I take a great interest in them.

MONSIEUR DIMANCHE. We are infinitely obliged to you, sir. I . . .

DON JUAN (offering him his hand). Then shake hands on it,* Monsieur Dimanche. Are you really a friend of mine?

MONSIEUR DIMANCHE. Sir, I am your servant.

DON JUAN. By heavens! I'm yours with all my heart.

MONSIEUR DIMANCHE. You do me too much honor. I . . .

DON JUAN. There is nothing I wouldn't do for you.

MONSIEUR DIMANCHE. Sir, you are too kind to me.

DON JUAN. And that without self-interest, please believe me.

MONSIEUR DIMANCHE. I certainly have not deserved this favor. But, sir . . .

DON JUAN. Oh, come, Monsieur Dimanche, don't stand on ceremony. Will you have supper with me?

MONSIEUR DIMANCHE. No, sir, I have to go right back. I . . .

DON JUAN (rising). Come, quick, a torch to guide Monsieur Dimanche! And four or five of my men, take muskets to escort him.

MONSIEUR DIMANCHE (also rising). Sir, that's not necessary, and I'll go back perfectly well alone. But . . .

*In Molière's time, a rather formal offer of friendship.

(SGANARELLE *promptly removes the chairs.*)

DON JUAN. What? I want you to be escorted, and I take too much interest in your personal welfare not to. I am your servant, and what's more, your debtor.

MONSIEUR DIMANCHE. Oh! sir . . .

DON JUAN. That's a thing I don't hide, and I tell it to everybody.

MONSIEUR DIMANCHE. If . . .

DON JUAN. Would you like to have me show you out?

MONSIEUR DIMANCHE. Oh, sir! You're joking. Sir . . .

DON JUAN. Then embrace me, please. Once again, I beg you to believe that I am entirely at your disposal, and that there is nothing in the world that I wouldn't do to serve you.

(Exit.)

SGANARELLE. You must admit that in Monsieur you have a man who is very fond of you.

MONSIEUR DIMANCHE. That's true; he pays me so many civilities and so many compliments that I never could possibly ask him for money.

SGANARELLE. I assure you that his entire household would die for you; and I wish something would happen to you, someone would take a notion to give you a drubbing; you'd see just how . . .

MONSIEUR DIMANCHE. I believe it; but Sganarelle, I beg you to put in a word to him about my money.

SGANARELLE. Oh! Don't worry, he'll pay you to your heart's content.

MONSIEUR DIMANCHE. But you, Sganarelle, you owe me something on your own account.

SGANARELLE. Fie! Don't speak of it.

MONSIEUR DIMANCHE. What? I . . .

SGANARELLE. Don't I know very well that I owe you money?

MONSIEUR DIMANCHE. Yes, but . . .

SGANARELLE. Come, Monsieur Dimanche, I'm going to light your way.

MONSIEUR DIMANCHE. But my money . . .

SGANARELLE (taking MONSIEUR DIMANCHE by the arm). Are you joking?

MONSIEUR DIMANCHE. I want . . .

SGANARELLE (pulling him). Come.

MONSIEUR DIMANCHE. I mean . . .

SGANARELLE (pushing him). Nonsense!

MONSIEUR DIMANCHE. But . . .

SGANARELLE (pushing him). Fie!

MONSIEUR DIMANCHE. I . . .

SGANARELLE (pushing him all the way off stage). Fie, I say.

Scene 4.   DON LOUIS, DON JUAN, LA VIOLETTE,
                        SGANARELLE

LA VIOLETTE. Sir, here is your father.

DON JUAN. Ah, that's just fine! This visit is just what I needed to drive me insane.

DON LOUIS. I see very well that I'm embarrassing you and that you would very gladly dispense with my presence. The truth is it's remarkable how we rub each other the wrong way; and if you're tired of seeing me, I too am very tired of your behavior. Alas! How little we know what we're doing when we do not leave to Heaven the responsibility for the things we need, when we try to be wiser than it is, and when we come to pester it with our blind wishes and our thoughtless requests! I wished for a son with unequaled ardor, I prayed for one unremittingly with incredible fervor; and this son, whom I obtain by wearying Heaven with my entreaties, is the grief and the torment of this very life of which I thought he was to be the joy and consolation. How do you suppose I can regard that mass of unworthy actions, whose evil appearance can hardly be toned down in the eyes of the world, that unending series of wicked affairs, which constantly reduce us to wearying the King's indulgence, and which have exhausted in his eyes the merit of my services and the credit of my friends? Ah! To what baseness you have sunk! Don't you blush to be so little worthy of your birth? Tell me, have you a right to take any pride in it? And what have you done in the world to be a gentleman? Do you think it is enough to bear the name and the arms of one, and that it is a reason for glory for us to have sprung from a noble family when we live like scoundrels? No, no, birth is nothing where there is no virtue. Moreover, we have a share in our ancestors' glory only insofar as we strive to resemble them; and the luster which their actions cast over us places on us an obligation to do them the same honor, to follow in their footsteps, and not to degenerate from their virtues, if we want to be considered their true descendants. Thus it is in vain that you descend from the ancestors from whom you spring; they disown you as not being of their blood, and all the illustrious things they have done give you no advantage whatever; on the contrary, their luster reflects on you only to your dishonor, and their glory is a torch that lights up the shame of your actions for everyone's eyes. In short, know that a gentleman who lives badly is a monstrosity in nature, that virtue is the first title of nobility, that I am much less concerned with the name a man signs than with the deeds he does, and that I would set more store by the son of a porter who was a decent man than by a king's son who lived as you do.

DON JUAN. Sir, if you sat down, you would be more comfortable for talking.

DON LOUIS. No, insolent wretch, I will not sit down, or talk any longer, and I see very well that all my words make no impression on your soul. But know, unworthy son, that a father's tenderness is exasperated by your actions, that I shall contrive sooner than you think to set a limit to your transgressions, forestall Heaven's wrath upon you, and wash away, by your punishment, the shame of having given you life.

Scene 5.   DON JUAN, SGANARELLE

DON JUAN. Oh! Die as soon as you can, that's the best thing you can do. Each man must have his turn, and it makes me furious to see fathers who live as long as their sons. *(He sits down.)*

SGANARELLE. Ah, sir! You're wrong.

DON JUAN. I'm wrong?

SGANARELLE. Sir . . .

DON JUAN *(gets up from his chair)*. I'm wrong?

SGANARELLE. Yes, sir, you're wrong to have endured what
he said to you, and you should have taken him by the
shoulders and put him out. Could anything be more impertinent? For a father to come and make remonstrances to his son, and tell him to mend his ways,
remember his birth, lead the life of a decent man, and
a hundred other foolish things of the same sort! Can
this be endured by a man like you, who know how life
should be lived? I marvel at your patience; and if I had
been in your place, I would have sent him packing.
(Aside) O cursed complaisance! How low will you
bring me?

DON JUAN. Will my supper be on soon?

Scene 6.   DON JUAN, DOÑA ELVIRE, RAGOTIN, SGANARELLE

RAGOTIN. Sir, here is a veiled lady come to speak to you.

DON JUAN. Who could it be?

SGANARELLE. We must see.

DOÑA ELVIRE. Don't be surprised, Don Juan, to see me at
this hour and in this costume. It is an urgent motive
that forces me to this visit, and what I have to say to
you will brook no delay. I have not come here full of
the wrath that burst from me a while ago, and you see
me very changed from what I was this morning. I am
no longer that Doña Elvire who was praying against
you and whose irritated soul uttered nothing but threats
and breathed nothing but vengeance. Heaven has banished from my soul all that unworthy ardor I felt for

you, all those tumultuous transports of a criminal attachment, all those shameful outbursts of a gross earthly love; and it has left in my heart for you only a flame purified of all sensual matters, a wholly sacred tenderness, a love detached from everything, which does not act at all for itself, and is worried only on your behalf.

DON JUAN (*to* SGANARELLE). I do believe you're crying.

SGANARELLE. Forgive me.

DOÑA ELVIRE. It is this pure and perfect love that brings me here for your good, to convey to you a warning from Heaven, and try to bring you back from the precipice toward which you are rushing. Yes, Don Juan, I know all the transgressions of your life, and that same Heaven, which has touched my heart and turned my gaze upon the lapses of my own conduct, inspired me to come and find you, and tell you in its name that your offenses have exhausted its mercy, that its dread anger is ready to fall upon you, that it lies within you to avoid it by a prompt repentance, and that you may perhaps not have a chance for one more day to escape the greatest of all misfortunes. As for me, I am no longer attached to you by any worldly bond; I have recovered, thanks to Heaven, from all my insane thoughts; my retirement from the world is settled, and all I ask is life enough to be able to expiate my fault and to earn, by austere penance, my pardon for the blindness into which I was plunged by the transports of a guilty passion. But in that retirement, it would be an extreme grief to me for a person whom I have tenderly cherished to become a dire example of Heaven's justice; and it will be an incredible joy to me if I can bring you to ward off from above your head the frightful blow that threatens you. I beseech you, Don Juan, as a final favor, grant me this sweet consolation; do not deny me your own salvation, which I ask of you in tears; and if you are not touched by your own interest, at least be touched by my prayers, and spare me the cruel misery of seeing you condemned to eternal torments.

SGANARELLE *(aside)*. Poor woman!

DOÑA ELVIRE. I have loved you with extreme tenderness; nothing in the world has been so dear to me as you; I have forgotten my duty for you, I have done everything for you; and all the return I ask of you is to reform your life, and to forestall your destruction. Save yourself, I pray you, either for love of yourself or for love of me. Once again, Don Juan, I ask you this in tears; and if the tears of a person you have loved are not enough, I beseech you by whatever is most capable of touching you.

SGANARELLE *(aside, watching DON JUAN)*. Oh, tiger heart!

DOÑA ELVIRE. After these words I'm leaving; and that's all I had to tell you.

DON JUAN. Madame, it's late, stay here: we'll put you up as well as we can.

DOÑA ELVIRE. No, Don Juan, don't detain me any further.

DON JUAN. Madame, you will give me pleasure by staying, I assure you.

DOÑA ELVIRE. No, I tell you, let's not waste time in pointless talk. Let me go quickly, don't insist on seeing me out, and simply think about profiting by my warning.

Scene 7.   DON JUAN, SGANARELLE, LA VIOLETTE, RAGOTIN

DON JUAN. Do you know that I still had a little feeling for her, that I found a certain charm in this bizarre new style, and that her careless dress, her languishing manner, and her tears, reawakened in me some little embers of a dead fire?

SGANARELLE. That is to say, her words had no effect on you.

DON JUAN. Quick, my supper.

SGANARELLE. Very well.

DON JUAN (*sitting down to table*). Just the same, Sganarelle, we must think about reforming.

SGANARELLE. Oh, yes!

DON JUAN. Yes, my word, we must reform; another twenty or thirty years of this life, and then we'll think of our souls.

SGANARELLE. Oh!

DON JUAN. What do you say to that?

SGANARELLE. Nothing. Here's the supper. (*He takes a piece from one of the dishes that are brought and puts it into his mouth.*)

DON JUAN. It seems to me your cheek is swollen; what's the matter? Speak up, what's wrong with you?

SGANARELLE. Nothing.

DON JUAN. Let's just see. Gad! It's an inflammation on his cheek. Quick, a lancet to open it! The poor boy can't go on, and this abscess might choke him. Wait: see how ripe it was. Oh! what a rogue you are!

SGANARELLE. On my word, sir! I wanted to see if your cook hadn't put on too much salt or pepper.

DON JUAN. Come on, sit over there and eat. I'll need you when I've had supper. You're hungry, I see.

SGANARELLE (*sits down at table*). I should think so, sir; I haven't eaten since this morning. Try this, it couldn't be better.

(A lackey takes away SGANARELLE's *plates as soon as there is anything to eat on them.)*

My plate, my plate! Easy there, please! Good Lord, little friend, what a gift you have for giving us clean plates! And you, little La Violette, what timing you have for serving wine!

(While one lackey serves SGANARELLE *with drink, the other lackey again takes away his plate.)*

DON JUAN. Who can be knocking like that?

SGANARELLE. Who the devil is coming to disturb our meal?

DON JUAN. I want at least to eat supper in peace, and not have anyone let in.

SGANARELLE. Let me handle it, I'll go and see myself.

DON JUAN. Well, what is it? What's the matter?

SGANARELLE *(nodding his head as* THE STATUE *did)*. The . . . is there!

DON JUAN. Let's go see, and show that nothing can shake me.

SGANARELLE. Oh, poor Sganarelle! Where are you going to hide?

Scene 8.   DON JUAN, THE STATUE OF THE COMMANDER,
            SGANARELLE, LA VIOLETTE, RAGOTIN

DON JUAN. A chair and a place, quickly now. *(DON JUAN and* THE STATUE *sit down at the table; to* SGANARELLE) Come on, sit down to table.

SGANARELLE. Sir, I'm not hungry any more.

DON JUAN. Sit down there, I tell you. Bring us drinks. To the health of the Commander! I drink it with you, Sganarelle. Give him some wine.

SGANARELLE. Sir, I'm not thirsty.

DON JUAN. Drink up, and sing your song, to entertain the Commander.

SGANARELLE. I have a cold, sir.

DON JUAN. No matter. Come on. The rest of you, come here, accompany his voice.

THE STATUE. Don Juan, that's enough. I invite you to come to supper with me tomorrow. Will you have the courage to?

DON JUAN. Yes, I'll come, with only Sganarelle for company.

SGANARELLE. Thanks just the same, tomorrow is a fast day for me.

DON JUAN *(to* SGANARELLE). Take this torch.

THE STATUE. We need no light when we are guided by Heaven.

(A countryside near the town; then the Tomb of the
COMMANDER)

Scene 1.   DON LOUIS, DON JUAN, SGANARELLE

DON LOUIS. What, my son? Could it be that Heaven's
kindness has granted my prayers? Is what you tell me
really true? Aren't you deluding me with a false hope,
and can I put some confidence in the surprising novelty
of such a conversion?

DON JUAN *(playing the hypocrite)*. Yes, you see me returned from all my errors; I am no longer the same as
last night, and Heaven has suddenly produced in me a
change that is going to surprise everyone. It has
touched my heart and opened my eyes, and I view with
horror the long blindness I have lived in, and the criminal disorders of the life I have led. I go over all my
abominations in my mind, and I am amazed that
Heaven could tolerate them so long, and has not
brought down on my head twenty times the blows of its
dread justice. I see the mercies that its kindness has
done me by not punishing me for my crimes; and I
mean to profit by this as I should, reveal a sudden
change of life to the eyes of the world, make amends
in that way for the scandal of my past actions, and strive
to obtain from Heaven a full pardon for them. That's
what I'm going to work for; and I beg you, sir, to be
willing to contribute to this plan, and help me yourself
to choose some person to serve me as a guide, under
whose direction I may walk securely on the path I am
about to enter.

DON LOUIS. Ah, my son! How easily a father's tenderness
is recalled, and how quickly a son's offenses vanish at

397

the slightest word of repentance! Already I no longer remember all the griefs you have caused me, and everything is wiped out by the words you have just let me hear. I am beside myself, I admit; I am shedding tears of joy; all my wishes are granted, and henceforth I have nothing more to ask of Heaven. Embrace me, my son, and, I conjure you, persist in this praiseworthy plan. For my part, I am going right this moment and bring the happy news to your mother, share with her the sweet transports of the ecstasy I feel, and give thanks to Heaven for the holy resolutions that it has deigned to inspire in you.

Scene 2.   DON JUAN, SGANARELLE

SGANARELLE. Ah, sir, what joy I have in seeing you converted! I'd been waiting for that a long time, and now, thank Heaven, all my wishes are fulfilled.

DON JUAN. A plague on the nitwit!

SGANARELLE. How's that, the nitwit?

DON JUAN. What? You're taking what I've just said at face value, and you think my lips were in agreement with my heart?

SGANARELLE. What? It's not . . . You don't . . . Your . . . (Aside) Oh! What a man! What a man! What a man!

DON JUAN. No, no, I'm not changed a bit, and my sentiments are still the same.

SGANARELLE. You don't surrender to the amazing marvel of that moving and talking statue?

DON JUAN. There certainly is something in that which I don't understand; but whatever it may be, it is not capable of either convincing my mind or shaking my soul; and if I said I wanted to reform my conduct and enter upon an exemplary way of life, that was a plan I formed out of pure politics, a useful stratagem, a necessary pose that I want to hold myself to, in order to keep on the good side of a father whom I need, and to protect myself against a hundred unpleasant adventures that might come my way from the direction of men in general. I'm willing to confide this in you, Sganarelle, and I'm very glad to have a witness of my inmost soul and of the real motives that oblige me to do things.

SGANARELLE. What? You don't believe in anything, and yet you want to set yourself up as a good man?

DON JUAN. And why not? There are so many others like me who ply that trade, and use the same mask to take advantage of people!

SGANARELLE. Oh! What a man! What a man!

DON JUAN. There's no shame in that any more nowadays: hypocrisy is a fashionable vice, and all fashionable vices pass for virtues. The role of a good man is the best of all the roles a person can play today, and there are wonderful advantages to the hypocrite's profession. It's an art whose imposture is always respected; and even when it's uncovered, no one dares to say anything against it. All the other vices of men are exposed to censure, and everyone is free to attack them boldly; but hypocrisy is a privileged vice, whose hand closes everyone's mouth and which peacefully enjoys a sovereign impunity. By dint of dissimulations, one forms a close association with all the other members of the party. If anyone attacks one of them, he has them all on his hands; and even those who we know act in good faith in these matters, and who everyone knows are genuinely stirred, those people, I say, are always dupes of the others; they fall completely for the game of the masqueraders and blindly support these men who merely ape their own actions. Imagine how many of them I know who, by this stratagem, have adroitly reclothed the disorders of their youth, have made themselves a shield of the cloak of religion, and, under this respected garment, are free to be the wickedest men in the world? It doesn't matter that some people, aware of their intrigues, know them for what they are; this doesn't keep them from being held in esteem among men; and a bowed head, a mortified sign, and eyes rolling to Heaven, making up in society for anything they may do.

It's under this favorable shelter that I mean to seek protection, and place my affairs in security. I shall not abandon my pleasant habits; but I shall take care to conceal myself and shall divert myself in a quiet way. And if it happens that I am discovered, without my lifting a finger I'll see the whole cabal espouse my interests and defend me in spite of and against anyone. In short, this is the real way to do anything I want with impunity. I shall set myself up as a censor of the actions of others, judge everyone harshly, and have a good opinion of no one but myself. If once anyone has offended me the least little bit, I shall never forgive, and shall very quietly retain an irreconcilable hatred. I shall play the avenger of Heaven's interests, and, on that convenient pretext, harass my enemies, accuse them of impiety, and contrive to turn loose against them some undiscerning zealots who, without knowing what it's all about, will raise a public outcry against them, load them with insults, and damn them loudly by their own private authority. That's the way to take advantage of men's weaknesses, and for an intelligent mind to adapt itself to the vices of his day.

SGANARELLE. O Heaven! What do I hear now? All you needed was to be a hypocrite to make you really complete; and that's the worst of abominations. Sir, this last one is too much for me, and I can't help speaking out. Do what you please to me, beat me, shower me with blows, kill me, if you want: I must get this off my chest, and as a faithful valet I must tell you what I ought. Learn, sir, that if the pitcher goes to the well too often, it'll finally get broken; and as that author says so well— whom I don't know—man is in this world like a bird on a branch; the branch is attached to the tree; whoever attaches himself to the tree, follows good precepts; good precepts are better than fine words; fine words are found at court; at court are the courtiers; courtiers follow the fashion; fashion comes from fancy; fancy is a faculty of the soul; the soul is what gives us life; life ends in death; death makes us think of Heaven; Heaven is above the earth; the earth is not the sea; the sea is subject to storms; storms toss ships; ships need a good pilot; a good pilot has prudence; prudence is not in young people; young people owe obedience to the old; the old love riches; riches make people rich; the rich are not poor; the poor have necessities; necessity knows no laws; whoever knows no laws lives like a brute beast; and consequently, you will be damned to all the devils in Hell.

DON JUAN. Oh, what fine reasoning!

SGANARELLE. After that, if you don't give up, too bad for you.

Scene 3.   DON CARLOS, DON JUAN, SGANARELLE

DON CARLOS. Don Juan, you are well met, and I'm very glad to speak to you here rather than at your place, to ask you what you have decided. You know that this responsibility concerns me, and that in your presence I have taken this matter upon myself. For my part, I don't hide it, I very much hope that things will go peacefully; and there is nothing I would not do to persuade you to adopt this course, and to see you publicly acknowledge my sister as your wife.

DON JUAN *(in a hypocritical tone)*. Alas! With all my heart I would like to give you the satisfaction that you desire; but Heaven is directly opposed to it; it has inspired in my soul the plan to change my life, and I now have no other thoughts than to abandon all worldly attachments

entirely, to strip myself as soon as possible of every kind
of vanity, and henceforth to correct, by austere conduct,
all the criminal transgressions that I was led to by the
fire of blind youth.

DON CARLOS. This plan, Don Juan, does not conflict with
what I say; and the company of a lawful wife is fully
compatible with the laudable ideas that Heaven inspires in you.

DON JUAN. Alas! Not at all. It's a plan that your sister herself has adopted: she has resolved to retire from the
world, and we were both touched at the same time.

DON CARLOS. Her retirement cannot satisfy us, since it
may be imputed to a disdain of yours for her and our
family; and our honor demands that she live with you.

DON JUAN. I assure you that that cannot be. For my part,
I wanted that more than anything, and even today I
again asked for advice about this from Heaven; but
when I consulted it, I heard a voice that told me that I
must not think of your sister, and that with her I would
certainly not gain salvation.

DON CARLOS. Don Juan, do you think to dazzle us by these
fair excuses?

DON JUAN. I obey the voice of Heaven.

DON CARLOS. What? You expect me to be satisfied with
such talk?

DON JUAN. It is Heaven that so wills it.

DON CARLOS. You will have taken my sister out of a convent and then left her?

DON JUAN. That is the way Heaven ordains.

DON CARLOS. We are to stand for this stain on our family?

DON JUAN. Blame Heaven for it.

DON CARLOS. What? Always Heaven?

DON JUAN. Heaven so desires it.

DON CARLOS. Enough, Don Juan, I understand you. I don't intend to deal with you here, this place does not permit it; but before long I'll find you.

DON JUAN. You will do what you wish. You know that I do not lack heart, and can use my sword when necessary. I'll go right out to that little out-of-the-way street that leads to the big convent. But for my part, I tell you that I'm not the one who wants to fight; Heaven forbids me such a thought; and if you attack me, we shall see what will happen.

DON CARLOS. We shall see, indeed, we shall see.

Scene 4.   DON JUAN, SGANARELLE

SGANARELLE. Sir, what devilish style are you adopting now? This is much worse than the rest, and I would like you much better even as you were before. I was still hoping for your salvation; but now is the time when I despair of it; and I believe that Heaven, which has endured you up to now, will not possibly be able to endure this final horror.

DON JUAN. Go on, go on, Heaven is not as exacting as you think; and if every time that men . . .

Scene 5.   DON JUAN, A SPECTER *(as a veiled woman)*,
                    SGANARELLE

SGANARELLE *(seeing the* SPECTER*)*. Oh, sir! This is Heaven
   speaking to you, and this is a warning it's giving you.

DON JUAN. If Heaven is giving me a warning, it will have
   to speak a little more clearly if it wants me to hear it.

SPECTER. Don Juan has but a moment left to take advantage of Heaven's mercy, and if he does not repent now,
   his doom is sealed.

SGANARELLE. Do you hear, sir?

DON JUAN. Who dares to utter these words? I think I know
   that voice.

SGANARELLE. Oh, sir! It's a specter; I recognize it by its
   walk.

DON JUAN. Specter, phantom, or devil, I mean to see what
   it is.

(The SPECTER *changes its shape and represents Time,
                  scythe in hand.)*

SGANARELLE. O Heaven! Sir, do you see how the shape
   has changed?

DON JUAN. No, no, nothing can terrify me, and I mean to
   test with my sword whether it's a body or a spirit.

(The SPECTER *flies away as Don Juan is about to strike it.)*

SGANARELLE. Oh, sir! Yield to all these proofs, and, quick, take the plunge of repentance.

DON JUAN. No, no, it shall not be said, come what may, that I am capable of repenting. Come on, follow me.

Scene 6.   THE STATUE, DON JUAN, SGANARELLE

THE STATUE. Stop, Don Juan; you gave me your word yesterday to come and eat with me.

DON JUAN. Yes. Where do we go?

THE STATUE. Give me your hand.

DON JUAN. Here it is.

THE STATUE. Don Juan, obduracy in sin brings on a dreadful death, and Heaven's mercy rejected opens the way to its lightning.

DON JUAN. O Heaven! What's this I feel? An invisible fire is burning me, I can bear no more, and my whole body is turning into a fiery furnace. Ah!

(The thunder falls on DON JUAN *with a loud crash and brilliant flashes; the earth opens and swallows him up; and great flames issue from the pit into which he has fallen.)*

SGANARELLE. Oh! My wages! My wages! There, everybody is satisfied by his death. Offended Heaven, violated laws, seduced girls, dishonored families, outraged parents, wives led astray, exasperated husbands, everyone is happy. I'm the only unhappy one, I who, after so many years of service, have no compensation but to see my master's impiety punished before my eyes by the most frightful chastisement in the world. My wages! My wages! My wages!*

---

*The initial "Oh! My wages! My wages!" and the final "My wages! My wages! My wages!" are omitted in the Despois and Mesnard edition and in some of the most authoritative older editions, on which theirs is based. In other editions, the last three "My wages!" replace the three preceding lines, from "I who," to "in the world."

Afterword

Why Molière Now?

As a theater director whose identity and career is defined by productions of Molière's work, I am often asked why theaters should continue to mount productions of this seemingly dated playwright. Unfortunately, this question seems to most often arise when a recent production has emphasized the foppery and silliness of the text. These productions frequently fill the stage with flying canapés and outrageous buffoonery. The depth of character is often paper thin, with the production seeking to push the behavior past anything recognizable as human. The only objective seems to be to get the easy laugh. The text becomes an excuse for outrageous "bits," whether in design, character behavior, or verbal gymnastics.

While many of these elements certainly can be employed to create great productions of Molière, there is a singular lack of depth in the emotional truths contained therein. Thanks to the Molière mentorship that I received from the late Garland Wright at the Guthrie Theater, I have a deeply held belief that these plays contain life-and-death emotional stakes that create what I would call Dangerous Comedy.

How does a director find such stakes? Certainly, Molière's own life is rife with such necessity, as it was defined by great ascendance and equal degradation. Drawing on his own experience, he wrote works that shook the very foundations of power and propriety. In the historical era of scientific discoveries by Copernicus, Galileo, and others, Molière challenged the very conception of the supremacy of the Sun King as the center of the universe. His personal life, his questioning of religious authority, and his audacious wit all defined a life of true risk taking. I don't have space in this Afterword to go in to more dramaturgical depth on Molière the man, and therefore can only offer this most cursory overview. Suffice it to say, a rigorous examination of this playwright's life can generate powerful answers to the questions: Why did Molière *have* to write this play? What burning need made him take pen to paper?

Then, taking that deeply human necessity as its foundation, how might a team of artists create a production of a Molière play that feels equally dangerous? This interpretive act—taking the original necessity of a text and "translating" it so as to resonate with a contemporary audience—is, I believe, the job of any director of classic material. And I believe that Molière's texts offer unique opportunities for such a dynamic creative process.

To some specifics:

In the spring of 2013, the Chicago theater community enjoyed a Molière Festival, composed of a single acting company performing Molière's *The Misanthrope* and *Tartuffe* in repertory. The cast of eleven included eight actors of color. Produced at Court Theatre, the professional theater of the University of Chicago, this Festival served as the inaugural realization of Court Theatre's vision to create a Center for Classic Theatre at our host university. Working closely with Professor Larry Norman, a renowned Molière specialist in the Romance Languages Department, we produced not simply the stage productions, but also an international symposium, community discussions, and, most importantly, a public conversation around the question "Why Molière now?"

As director of the two plays, my starting place was how to create a sense of true necessity that would define each production. Court Theatre is located on the Southside of Chicago, specifically in the Hyde Park neighborhood. Our predominantly African-American community has been incredibly supportive of our productions celebrating the classic African-American canon. Led by our Resident Director, Ron OJ Parson, we have produced the works of Leslie Lee, Sam-Art Williams, Pearl Cleage, Nora Zeale Hurston, Katori Hall, and most especially August Wilson. A world premiere stage adaptation of Ralph Ellison's *Invisible Man* broke all previous box office records. More recently, Nambi Kelley's adaptation of Richard Wright's *Native Son*, directed by Seret Scott, broke more records, with new levels of community engagement. Our consistent and authentic commitment to producing works for our local community has been a singular achievement for Court Theatre; we are now a leading producer of African-American theater in Chicago.

With this success, we have developed a large, loyal group of artists of color who now think of Court Theatre as home. As Artistic Director, I am always looking for the next challenge we can tackle together. With the Molière Festival, it seemed obvious to me that there were many actors of color who were clearly suited for the roles. What an opportunity to cast a Molière play with actors who are rarely even seen for these parts. One actress told me, "Charlie, when you called me in to audition for the Molières, I assumed that you wanted me to read for Dorine, the maid in *Tartuffe*. When I arrived at the audition, I discovered that you wanted me to audition for Elmire, the female lead! On the ride home in my car, I wept with joy." (FYI, this actress, Patrese McClain, did play the parts of Elmire in *Tartuffe* and Eliante in *The Misanthrope* for the Molière Festival.)

So I knew that I could cast the hell out of the two plays with many actors of color. However, I wasn't interested in "color blind" casting; in fact, I don't think such a thing exists. How can an audience possibly disregard an actor's ethnicity? Rather, we should ask how might their race inform the audience's response? In other words, how might a company of actors of color approach the text in a way that would bring a sense of immediacy and connection to these great works of Molière?

I knew that the approach needed to be quite different for the two texts. After a brainstorming whirlwind with the team of designers, we arrived at the following: *The Misanthrope* would be set essentially in its French Baroque period, drawing parallels to the brutality of the contemporary Black music industry, especially toward women. And *Tartuffe* would be set in the present day, mirroring the highly successful community of African-Americans that live in the upscale Kenwood community just north of Court Theatre. (As many of you probably know, this is the neighborhood where the Obamas own a home.)

In *Tartuffe* we wrestled with the critical question of why the powerfully successful Orgon would come under the spell of the obvious impostor Tartuffe. To truly invest in his emotional journey, and therefore actually care what happens to him and his family during the onslaught of becoming "Tartuffed," we imagined a wildly prosperous family that had recently been splintered by the death of the mother, further fractured by the quick addition of a society woman as stepmother and second wife. We imagined the patriarch having been raised in poverty, in a devout religious tradition, now feeling adrift amid the extravagance of his newfound wealth and without real emotional connections to his family. So he seeks solace under the spell of a devout Christian evangelist. And what if the entire nuclear family were African-American? And with a Latina housemaid? Might such a family resonate with our core audience, especially given the density of such families living near our theater? Finally, might the stakes be raised to an uncomfortably provocative level if Tartuffe were played by a Caucasian actor? And in the famous table scene? What if the physical comedy begins as flirtatious entrapment by Elmire, only to devolve into brutalization approaching rape? And all the while, Orgon remains inert under that table? Imagine the destruction that this "comedy" might wreak upon this family.

One of the great lessons from Garland Wright was this simple notion: In a Molière play, with its highly stylized rhyming verse text, one must imagine a world in which the people *have to speak in such a heightened way* in order to survive. In other words, they don't talk this way simply because they are in a Molière play. Rather, their environment creates such high stakes that language becomes a weapon; the person with the most masterful use of rhyme, rhythm, and tempo wins the day. For actors and audience alike, this immediately sets up a dangerous world of verbal dueling, where words draw blood.

Thus it was in *The Misanthrope* that we decided to escalate some of the verbal jousting into actual physical violence. In Act III, Scene 1, when Acaste and Clitandre discuss their rivalry for the affections of Célimène, they draw blood. Similarly, the conflict between Oronte and Alceste in Act I, Scene 2, escalates from a philosophical discussion to an actual threat of physical violence. As we further explored this use of language in rehearsals, we were inspired by videos of contemporary rap battles (check them out online!). And at the denouement of our production (Act V, Scenes 4 and 5), we directed Célimène to receive the cascade of accusations from her many suitors without answering back. This most verbally astute and socially adept creature responds only with silence; she loses all her power by being speechless. Her destruction is complete, her isolation profound. And it breaks our hearts.

I hope this Afterword has been in some ways useful, if only to provoke both the reader's and the theater practitioner's imagination for what Molière's work can achieve today. I can only hope that these thoughts have propelled your own relationship with Molière forward. If we can find the deeply embedded necessity within Molière's text, and then bring that forward by any means necessary, then productions of his plays will resonate with a powerful need. Audiences will be grateful for their new understanding of Molière, and demand more such humorous *and* dangerous theater.

—Charles Newell

Selected
Bibliography

Plays by Molière

La Jalousie de Barbouillé, 1645–50
Le Médecin volant, 1645–50
L'Étourdi, 1655
Le Dépit amoureux, 1656
Les Précieuses ridicules, 1659
Sganarelle, 1660
Dom Garcie de Navarre, 1661
L'École des maris, 1661
Les Fâcheux, 1661
L'École des femmes, 1662
Critique de L'École des femmes, 1663
L'Impromptu de Versailles, 1664
Le Mariage forcé, 1664
La Princesse d'Élide, 1664
Tartuffe, 1664–69
Don Juan, 1665
L'Amour médecin, 1665
Le Misanthrope, 1664–66
Le Médecin malgré lui, 1666
Mélicerte, 1666
La Pastorale comique, 1667
Le Sicilien, 1667
Amphitryon, 1668
Georges Dandin, 1668
L'Avare, 1668
Monsieur de Pourceaugnac, 1669
Les Amants magnifiques, 1670
Le Bourgeois gentilhomme, 1670
Psyché, 1671
Les Fourberies de Scapin, 1671
La Comtesse d'Escarbagnas, 1671
Les Femmes savantes, 1672
Le Malade imaginaire, 1673

Selected Biography and Criticism

Bermel, Albert. *Molière's Theatrical Bounty: A New View of the Plays*. Carbondale: Southern Illinois University Press, 1990.

Calder, Andrew. *Molière: The Theory and Practice of Comedy*. London: Athlone, 1993.

Carmody, James. *Rereading Molière: Mise en scene from Antoine to Vitez*. Ann Arbor: University of Michigan Press, 1993.

Gaines, James F., ed. *A Molière Encyclopedia*. Westport, CT: Greenwood Press, 2002.

Gossman, Lionel. *Men and Masks: A Study of Molière*. Baltimore: The Johns Hopkins Press, 1963.

Guicharnaud, Jacques, ed. *Molière: A Collection of Critical Essays*. New York: Prentice-Hall, 1964.

Howarth, W. D., ed. *French Theatre in the Neo-Classical Era: 1550–1789*. Cambridge: Cambridge University Press, 1997.

Hubert, J. D. *Molière and the Comedy of Intellect*. Los Angeles: University of California Press, 1962.

Lawrenson, T. E. *The French Stage and Playhouse in the XVIIth Century: A Study in the Advent of the Italian Order*. 2nd ed. New York: AMS, 1986.

Leon, Mechele. *Molière, the French Revolution, and the Theatrical Afterlife*. Iowa City: University of Iowa Press, 2009.

———. "The Poet and the Prince: Revising Molière and *Tartuffe* in the French Revolution." *French Historical Studies*. Summer 2005. 28(3): 447–67.

Mander, Gertrud. *Molière*. Trans. Diana Stone Peters. New York: Frederick Ungar, 1973.

McBride, Robert. *The Sceptical Vision of Molière: A Study in Paradox*. London: Macmillan, 1977.

McCarthy, Gerry. *The Theatres of Molière*. London: Routledge, 2002.

Moore, W. G. *Molière: A New Criticism*. New York: Doubleday, 1962.

Norman, Larry F. *The Public Mirror: Molière and the Social Commerce of Depiction*. Chicago: University of Chicago Press, 1999.

Scott, Virginia. *Molière: A Theatrical Life*. Cambridge: Cambridge University Press, 2002.

Tobin, Ronald W. *Tarte a la crème: Comedy and Gastronomy in Molière's Theatre*. Columbus: Ohio State University Press, 1990.